MW00325192

China Intellectual Property — Challenges & Solutions

An Essential Business Guide

China Intellectual Property — Challenges & Solutions

An Essential Business Guide

Rebecca Ordish
Alan Adcock

WILEY

John Wiley & Sons (Asia) Pte Ltd

Copyright © 2008 John Wiley & Sons (Asia) Pte Ltd
Published in 2008 by John Wiley & Sons (Asia) Pte Ltd
2 Clementi Loop, #02-01 Singapore 129809

All right reserved.

No part of this publication may be reproduced; stored in a retrieval system, or transmitted in any form or by any means, electronic, mechanical, photocopying, recording, scanning, or otherwise, except as expressly permitted by law, without either the prior written permission of the Publisher, or authorization through payment of the appropriate photocopy fee to the Copyright Clearance Center. Requests for permission should be addressed to the Publisher, John Wiley & Sons (Asia) Pte Ltd, 2 Clementi Loop, #02-01, Singapore 129809, tel: 65-6463-4605, E-mail: enquiry@wiley.com.sg.

The publication is designed to provide accurate and authoritative information with regard to the subject matter covered. It is sold with the understanding that the Publisher is not engaged in rendering professional services. If professional advice or other expert assistance is required the services of a competent professional person should be sought.

Other Wiley Editorial Offices
John Wiley & Sons, Inc., 111 River Street, Hoboken, NJ 07030, USA
John Wiley & Sons Ltd, The Atrium, Southern Gate, Chichester PO19 BSQ, England
John Wiley & Sons (Canada) Ltd, 5353 Dundas Street West, Suite 400, Toronto, Ontariao M9B 6H8, Canada
John Wiley & Sons Australia Ltd, 42 McDougall Street, Milton, Queensland 4064, Australia
Wiley-VCH, Boschstrasse 12, D-69469 Weinheim, Germany

Library of Congress Cataloging-in-Publication Data:
ISBN-13 978-0-470-82275-3

Typeset in 10.5/13 points Palatino LT Std by Gantec

Printed in Singapore by Saik Wah Press Pte Ltd.
10 9 8 7 6 5 4 3 2 1

Contents

Preface

When asked recently what intellectual property is, a Chinese colleague responded: "I am not sure, but it's what China is always in trouble with the US for." He was partly joking (we hope), but his response reflects the current high level of awareness of intellectual property in China and the local mood surrounding it, in contrast to the international pressure and media hype about IP infringements there.

China is in the midst of a dynamic period of change and development. In a country where intellectual property has traditionally been considered more of a communal right than an individual one, it is not surprising that its IP regime has struggled to keep up with the pace of development. However, there is now an increasingly positive story around intellectual property in China. As the country starts to move from its status as the world's factory to a creator of its own technology and IP, and an exporter of Chinese brands, the impetus for a stronger system of implementation and enforcement of IP rights in practice will be inevitable. This is happening quickly, but will still take time.

This book sets out some strategies for companies wishing to navigate the minefield of conducting business in or with China while proactively taking steps to protect their intellectual property until the IP regime catches up with the rapid pace of change. It is based on our combined 17 years of experience in advising companies on IP protection and commercialization strategies throughout Asia and internationally, and on the ground in China.

But the book isn't intended to be legal advice. It simply shares some ideas and strategies. Each company's particular requirements will be different, and the facts of each infringement case will vary significantly. The book is also based on the laws and regulations at the time of writing. Given the rate at which changes occur in China, it is critical that companies obtain up-to-date and customized legal advice to ensure they are protecting their IP (and themselves) in the best possible way.

We could not have written this book without the generous support of the companies that shared their stories and experiences—both good and bad—with us. Special thanks go to the following: Rhonda Steele of Mars, Incorporated; Simon MacKinnon of Corning China; Sharmini Lohadhasan of BP; Linda Chang of Rouse & Co. International in Shanghai; Lisa Haselhorst of Bayer; and Alex Gerasimow of Rockwell. Thank you also to the *China Business Review* (in particular, Virginia Hulme) for permission to use parts of articles previously published in the Review in Chapters 2 (on franchising), 10 (on R&D centers), and 11 (on Olympics and sports in China). Chapter 4, on sourcing from China, draws largely on an article published in the *Journal of Intellectual Property Law & Practice* in January 2008.

Thank you also from Rebecca to the team at Diageo for their patience and support as she undertook this project and to her husband, Adam, without whom it would never have been written.

Best of luck with your business in China. Enjoy the challenges and opportunities in this exciting market, and we hope to add your positive experiences and ideas to future editions of this book.

Rebecca Ordish   *Alan Adcock*
Shanghai   Hong Kong

Part

I

Dispelling the myths

Chapter

1

Acknowledging China's IP challenge

Most people don't know that China's current intellectual property (IP) system is less than 30 years old. Better known are the images of IP infringements that occur in the People's Republic (PRC). Raids on markets selling fake DVDs, bulldozers destroying mountains of counterfeit shoes and handbags, patent owners complaining of invalidated patents, and joint venture partners stealing technology in order to set up unfairly competing businesses of their own are all common impressions of China. Consumer goods such as shampoo, toothbrushes, electronics, and clothes are widely counterfeited; even Viagra® and the flu medication Tamiflu®. Fake goods manufactured in China are exported to destinations thousands of miles away in both developed and developing countries. Rogue former employees have stolen confidential information and trade secrets vital to a company's competitive edge and have used these unfairly for their own commercial benefit, or have sold them to others who claim to have acquired the information in good faith and without knowledge of its belonging to another. Some unfair competitors are using China's IP system proactively and attacking patents granted in order to defeat them, so that they may enter the market unhindered by the property rights of others. Shadow companies holding themselves out to be branches of legitimate multinationals are being established by mainlanders in the separate legal jurisdictions of Hong Kong and Macau. Competitors try to register elements of foreign products as their own intellectual property. These things do happen. This is what is thought to be China's IP environment. It all provides great fodder to the Chinese spook mill as to why foreign investors should be wary, distrustful, and cautious in China. But there is another side.

There is no doubt that there are challenges to face when a company brings its intellectual property to China, as well as when local Chinese companies innovate and develop their own intellectual property. However, the reality is that the IP system in China is becoming increasingly sophisticated, that there are reasonably adequate laws in place to enforce IP rights, and that much can be achieved if a business gives sufficient and thoughtful priority to its IP preparation. With careful preparation, it is possible to maximize the commercial opportunities offered, while minimizing the IP risks. One need not be afraid of China.

1. CHINA'S IP LEGACY

To argue China's recognition of the concept of intellectual property by pointing to its first IP law is a mistake. That would be like playing the old parlor game where you compare the best that you have against the worst of your opponent so that, of course, you will always win. A better way to approach a discussion on China's IP legacy is to look back into its more than 4,000 years of history to search for precepts of our modern understanding of intellectual property.

From the first imperial dynasty, the Qin of 221–206 BC, to the last, the Qing of 1644–1911, there are acknowledgments of what we would today consider intellectual property, though these are predominantly related to copyright and more specifically to the protection of property owned by the imperial court. Little imperial recognition of trademark or patent rights existed in ancient China, except in certain situations involving goods or services associated with, or inventions used for, the emperors or the state.

Professor William Alford in his book, *To Steal a Book is an Elegant Offense, Intellectual Property Law in Chinese Civilization* points to Qin-era concern with the distribution of written materials and Han-era preclusion of the unauthorized reproduction of the Classics. By AD 835, during the Tang dynasty and with the growing popularity of printing, the emperor Wenzong had prohibited the unauthorized reproduction of items related to predictions made by observations of the heavens. Such items included almanacs, calendars, and other tools of divination. Far from being enacted for the purposes of protecting the intellectual labors of those who had originally created such items, control over the tools used to predict the future was central to the Tang emperors' control over their role as the link between heaven and earth. Following the Tang, the Song dynasty of 960–1279 is recognized for putting in place a system for state review of works prior to their being printed. The Song forbade the printing and dissemination of works considered to be within the ambit of the court's control, along with other works that could be classified as obscene or threatening to the social order. There were penalties for failing to abide by the prepublication review system.

Despite the lack of centralized and nationwide control over copyright, trademark, and patent, throughout ancient China's history there are examples of craftsman guilds who banded together to protect their particular wares by affixing marks or symbols to their goods and identifying these marks to local officials, who could then preclude others from using them on similar goods. But as Professor Alford points out, "Virtually all known examples of efforts by the state to provide protection for what we now term intellectual property in China prior to the twentieth century seem to have been directed overwhelmingly toward sustaining imperial power."

In Europe, in around the 17th and 18th centuries, the notion of intellectual property as a personal right, without any direct benefit owing to the state, began to emerge. This was the notion that when government recognized and enforced the IP rights of individuals, this would have a positive impact on society, which would benefit from the proliferation of new ideas and innovation. It would be a further 300 years or so before this same notion would be embraced in China.

With the expanding power of the foreign settlements in South China, particularly after China's humiliating defeat in the Opium Wars and the subsequent concessions made by the imperial court to appease the Western victors, and by the time of the fall of the Qing dynasty at the beginning of the 20th century, many foreign trademarks had begun to appear in China. Memorable even today are the famous "Shanghai girl" cigarette trademarks, and others for such things as soap and medicines. As these foreign products were introduced to China at the turn of the century and became popular among a growing bourgeois class, the inevitable copying of these marks ensued. At the time, because there was no real trademark law in China, the foreign concessions enacted a series of their own trademark recognition rules, though in no way can such enactments be considered as any sort of true trademark protection or enforcement system.

The Guomindang government enacted its Copyright Law in 1928, the Trademark Law in 1930, and the Measures to Encourage the Industrial Arts in 1932. Most accounts describe this body of legislation as relatively international in scope and measure, with considerable emphasis on German and Japanese law. As in the ancient times, there were also specific exceptions to the rules—such as use of images of the first president of China (in 1912), Dr Sun Yat-sen—so that they would not encroach upon the vestiges of the new government.

The Guomindang's approach to building an international-standard IP system, while impressive, was ill-timed. With the invasion of China by the Japanese in the 1930s and the ensuing civil war with the communists, there was little concern to protect the individual rights of inventors, authors, or tradesmen. Indeed, it would take a further 30 years after the founding of the People's Republic in 1949 for China's leadership to take up again the task of developing a modern system of IP recognition and protection.

The 1979 Sino-US Trade Agreement brought the People's Republic and the United States together to provide reciprocal IP protection even though, technically, the only IP law on China's books at the time was a provision in its Criminal Code criminalizing trademark infringement. In 1980, China joined the Convention for the Establishment of the World Intellectual Property Organization. Thereafter, it set out on an aggressive course to enact the legislation necessary to build a working IP system capable of encouraging innovation locally and foreign investment. As part of its open door policy announced during Deng Xiaoping's triumphant visit to Shenzhen, in Guangdong province, in 1992, China reiterated the importance of intellectual property during the course of early trade normalization negotiations with the United States.

The 1980s and 1990s saw an impressive State Council promulgation of the building blocks of IP legislation, including laws relating to patent, trademark, copyright, unfair competition, and technology contracts. Administrative agencies responsible for IP registration and enforcement followed suit, with regulatory guidelines addressing issues such as how administrative agencies were to enforce IP rights, how patent and trademark agents were to conduct their work, examination rules within the registries, and Customs procedures for export and import of products. As for the People's Courts, there were numerous judicial pronouncements regarding patent and trademark litigation, interlocutory injunctions in cases of IP infringement, and criminal sanctions for IP violations. All this can be viewed as a remarkable course for the recognition and enforcement of individual and private ownership rights in what remains today a communist nation.

Despite these and more recent developments in law and in practice, many of the IP problems in China arise from an immature system, rather than from the more colloquially bandied notion of an innate Chinese intention to commit IP wrongs. While China's Patent Law dates from 1984, the first patent law in the world was enacted in 1623, and the precursor to our current notion of copyright appeared in 1710 with the Statute of Anne. Most Western countries have a century or more of IP experience under their belts.

But how could a civilization in existence for over 4,000 years have entertained the idea of intellectual property only a few years ago, and how or from whom did it learn?

As mentioned above, in the early days of preparing and enacting modern IP legislation, China looked for direction not to the United States or the United Kingdom, but rather to Germany and Japan. This was especially true during the Guomindang period, but also after the communists had come to power in 1949. China's consideration of German IP steering is also seen when one considers the development of the Internet in China. In 1986, the first public data network was established at the Beijing Institute of Computing Applications, which had worked closely with Universität Karlsruhe in Germany and formed the China Academic Network (CANET). After the .cn domain was registered by China in October 1990, Universität Karlsruhe housed the domain until May 21, 1994, when China was able to relocate the root server from Germany to China.

Many believe that China preferred the civil law administrative tribunals and the courts to address IP concerns, rather than taking the common law route of judicial determination alone. Today, this is reflected in China's dual-track approach to protecting IP—administrative enforcement and civil/criminal litigation, which will be described in Chapter 8.

2. OVERVIEW OF CHINA'S IP LEGISLATION

China's modern IP history can be roughly divided into three major periods,

1. Early 1980s, promulgation of the Patent Law and the Trademark Law.

2. Early 1990s, promulgation of the Copyright Law, the Anti-Unfair Competition Law, and major overhauls to both the Patent Law and the Trademark Law.

3. Early 2000s, amendment of IP laws to reflect China's ascension to the World Trade Organization (WTO) and its Agreement on the Trade-Related Aspects of Intellectual Property Rights (TRIPS).

The Patent Law was first enacted in 1984 and was subsequently amended in 1992 and 2000. The amendments dealt mainly with providing expanded patent coverage for new inventions, including pharmaceuticals after the United States pressed heavily for this itself and successfully orchestrated a special Memorandum of Understanding with China in 1992 so that China would afford recognition of US pharmaceutical patents prior to amending its own legislation. Often in Chinese legislation, the main law will be accompanied by later enacted rules setting out in more detail how the main law is to be applied and interpreted. In the case of the Patent Law, this subsidiary legislation is called the Regulations for the Implementation of the Patent Law and was effected in 2001. Designs and utility models are dealt with under the Patent Law, unlike in the United States and the United Kingdom where they are dealt with in separate legislation.

In 1987, the General Principles of the Civil Law of the People's Republic of China set out a "right of authorship," which held that "Citizens and legal persons shall enjoy rights of authorship (copyright) and shall be entitled to sign their names as authors, disclose to the public and publish their works and obtain remuneration in accordance with law." The first Copyright Law of the People's Republic of China and its Implementing Regulations were enacted in 1991 and revised further in 1993 and 2001, mostly due to TRIPS compliance.

The Trademark Law was first enacted in 1982, and revised in 1993 and 2001. The concept of trademark has seen the longest history in China, having been recognized as long ago as in ancient times.

The IP laws passed in China since the early 1980s generally meet international standards, mostly due to the overhauls undertaken because of WTO and TRIPS requirements. Chapters 5 and 8 look more closely at China's IP laws, and discuss how best to understand and use these laws to devise and implement your IP strategy.

What Accounts for China's IP Problems?

Many find it easy to take the view that the rampant problem of IP infringement in China is China's own fault. However, the causes of China's IP problems lie not only in its own institutions, but also with domestic and foreign businesses, which, in their rush to enter the world's largest market, have failed or forgotten to include intellectual property in their entry strategies.

Even in cases where IP strategies may exist, often the support necessary to implement those systems is inadequate. Businesses fail to send technical or IP professionals to oversee their proprietary property. The notion that intellectual property cannot be protected results in decisions being made to forego the expense of even registering. The IP protection strategies used at headquarters are not transplanted to China for implementation. Reliance on contracts drafted under the principles of common law, without taking the time to seek localization advice, has resulted in difficulties in enforcing or interpreting them in China's civil law system.

There are numerous—and often-unreported—cases of investment in correct preventative strategies that have had tremendous success in China, both in terms of foreign introduction of intellectual property into the country and foreign and domestic creation of intellectual property in China. Many of these success stories have found that they may not necessarily need to invest heavily in corrective measures because they have successfully tackled the issues early on.

Smart IP owners will have gone to the same trouble in China as they would have in other countries to conduct the appropriate due diligence into Chinese (and, increasingly, foreign) partners to ensure that these partners have genuine aspirations to protect and enhance the value of the intellectual property being introduced (including their own). Site selection processes include geographical assessments of the levels of protection afforded by local authorities, allowing for effective risk assessment. Understanding industry attitudes in the proposed investment area in regard to molding, reformulating, sublicensing/contracting, research and development (R&D), employee sharing, and other local industry practices is emphasized. Strategic pre-establishment due diligence is undertaken on a proposed supply/distribution chain to ensure that areas of IP exposure are flagged early. Many foreign IP owners research, select, and implement the most appropriate strategies and mechanisms for building IP protection programs into their China business plans. These preventative measures are then practiced and followed up. IP registration and enforcement budgets are calculated, approved, and used.

Foreign participation in the Chinese economy is currently going through a second wave of "deal fever." Early joint ventures of the 1990s resulted in deals being pushed through without the wherewithal to acknowledge the importance of protecting the intellectual property and technology they brought with them. Naturally, as the country's nascent IP protection regime couldn't hold back the wave of IP infringement for which China is now known overseas, its reputation as a "pirate" country grew. While larger companies, having learned the navigation routes to protect their intellectual property and technology, are experiencing less infringement recently, smaller and more recently arrived companies may still need assistance with registration, investigation, enforcement, and commercialization.

But does the People's Republic actually provide and support a framework on which such preventative measures can be practiced and improved? It does.

While there are serious IP problems, there is also a huge range of solutions for dealing with them, with new options appearing as the system grows. Many foreign companies operate very successfully in China despite the IP problems so widely and anecdotally reported. Those companies with clearly established systems and procedures, the right people, and a commitment to proactivity are well set up to deal with the IP issues that they will invariably face.

China has come a long way in terms of developing its IP regime. However, there are—and will be for some time—numerous examples of where that regime has failed to address effectively the problems of infringement. Equally, it is important to understand the impact that corporate failure has had on the infringement problem, and to help ensure that rights owners learn from these lessons. All are critically important lessons to address before bringing intellectual property into China.

Disparate Treatment, Foreign versus Chinese

As in any homogeneous society, foreigners have always been treated differently in China. In terms of the law, however, is there any truth in the perception that foreigners are subject to different laws or are treated differently by the legal system? Yes; but interestingly, in many (though not all) cases, this is to the advantage of the foreigner.

Criminal law makes little distinction in its application to foreigners or Chinese. There have been several high-profile criminal convictions for IP infringement of foreigners in China, and these individuals would have faced the same criminal court procedures and evidentiary rules as Chinese infringers. For criminal cases in which the offenders are foreigners, however, one important distinction is that the Intermediate People's Courts have jurisdiction as courts of first instance; trials of Chinese offenders will usually start off in the lower courts. In civil cases, if foreign parties wish to commission a lawyer as their attorney, they can only choose a Chinese lawyer. A foreign lawyer can only be commissioned as a "citizen" in civil litigation (article 241 of the Civil Procedure Law).

Powers of attorney, and other foreign documents such as certificates of incorporation for civil litigation from foreign parties who have no domicile in China, should be notarized and legalized (article 242 of the Civil Procedure Law). This procedure is also required for documentation necessary to establish or change an existing corporate presence in China either by way of a representative office, joint venture, or wholly foreign-owned enterprise. The requirement has long been criticized by foreigners having to prove the authenticity of foreign documents, but the process is relatively straightforward. The foreign document is signed by the person authorized to do so, and this signature is notarized by a local notary public in the jurisdiction. The notarized document is then sent to the PRC embassy, or the nearest PRC consulate, in the country, as the case may be. At the embassy or consulate, a legalization officer will inspect the document and its notarization, and then affix a legalization notice to the document thereby rendering it prima facie authentic for China purposes. The problem lies in the amount of time necessary to finalize the legalization part of the process. Many times, the embassy or consular officer responsible for the task is away or simply backlogged with work. The entire notarization and legalization process can take as much as four weeks to complete. Evidence arising from foreign countries should be notarized and legalized (article 12 of the Regulations on Evidence for Civil Litigation). When providing foreign documentation as evidence, a Chinese translation must be included (article 13 of the Regulations on Evidence for Civil Litigation).

Some legal relationships are required to be adjudicated under PRC law, irrespective of any alternative jurisdiction in a contract governing that relationship. For example, actions brought for disputes arising from the performance of contracts for Chinese–foreign equity joint ventures, or Chinese–foreign contractual joint ventures, or Chinese–foreign cooperative exploration and development of natural resources in the PRC, are all required to be heard by the People's Courts (article 246 of the Civil Procedure Law).

In terms of procedure, while a Chinese defendant has 15 days to file a defense after service of a civil complaint, a foreign party has 30 days to do so (article 248 of the Civil Procedure Law). This benefits foreign parties by allowing them more time to prepare evidence. For civil hearings, the maximum duration before the court must issue a judgment is six months for ruling in the first instance of a domestic case, three months for appealing against a judgment, and 30 days for appealing against an order. However, there is no limit for ruling on foreign cases. This is seldom cause for complaint by foreign parties, who see the lack of a time limit as somewhat advantageous owing to the difficult task of collecting evidence in China, which has no discovery process (article 250 of the Civil Procedure Law).

A domestic party has 15 days to appeal a judgment from the day the judgment is served, and 10 days to appeal an order. However, a foreign party who has no domicile in China has 30 days to appeal a judgment or an order (article 249 of the Civil Procedure Law). Here, again, foreigners are given more time to prepare evidence.

IP administrative actions are a popular alternative to civil litigation for IP enforcement in China. When filing a complaint, the domestic party should submit their documents to the local administrative authority directly, while the foreign party should entrust a qualified trademark or patent agency in China to do so. Both the domestic and foreign parties' submissions are required to be in Chinese, and should include samples or photos of the suspected infringing products. While domestic parties are required to submit a copy of their business license stamped with their official company chop, or in the case of individual complainants their identity card, foreign parties need not submit such identification proof, though they are required to submit their notarized and legalized powers of attorney, as described above. If the administrative action is trademark based, then foreign parties are required to submit a copy of their trademark registration certificate. However, if the foreign party's trademark is an international registration and the territory designation includes China, the foreign party should first apply to the Trademark Office (TMO) to localize the international trademark registration. Copies of the international trademark registration certificate and the localization documents are required when filing the complaint.

3.   GOING FORWARD

While the Chinese government and the foreign community may continue to argue over how best to deal with IP violations in China, both sides admit that things are progressing. The disagreement lies more with the speed of progress, than with its direction. Both the government and the People's Courts have initiated specific IP reforms and initiatives that aim to further address infringement, unfair competition, and system misuse. In addition to establishing a National Working Group for IP Protection in 2004, the State Council now issues an annual IP Working Plan setting out the year's IP priority concern areas. At a grass-roots level, public advertisements regarding the importance of IP rights and IP protection are commonplace, and many even include local IP hotline numbers to call when citizens suspect IP infringements are occurring. Both the Patent Law and the Trademark Law are currently being revised, and an Anti-Monopoly Law came into effect in August 2008.

In addition to hearing an increasing number of IP cases and handing out harsher penalties against infringers of both domestic and foreign intellectual property, the People's Courts are stepping up to the IP challenge by maintaining existing and drafting additional judicial interpretations on the recognition, protection, and administrative handling of intellectual property. Their IP decisions are being published and shared more broadly than other court decisions. The courts are also weighing in on the importance of technology innovation, which is so vital to China's future as other markets begin to chip away at the country's manufacturing base. Beijing realizes that without fostering and supporting China's nascent technology sector, the economy may be unable to expand beyond manufacturing the lower product cycle products on which it now relies so heavily.

There is also an interesting argument that the foreign community, so vocal in its condemnation of China's attitude toward intellectual property, also has a role to play in China's IP development. There are many rights owners, both in China and abroad, who take the view that China is largely at fault for the rampant problem of IP infringement and that, because of the limited value of the law, there is little use in actually protecting intellectual property before bringing it to China. India—with its developed laws, and common law legacy and court system—is often considered a much safer destination for foreign intellectual property. Such conceptions are based on facts such as China's cheap labor supply, out of work factories willing to infringe, a huge market of brand-conscious consumers, local government protection of local industries, and a people who have only recently been introduced to the concept of private IP rights ownership; none of which a foreign rights owner can control or change.

What *can* be controlled, however, is the degree of security and protection placed around valuable property in order to decrease the chance that it will be copied or misappropriated. The following chapters in this book will identify likely mechanisms by which intellectual property can be stolen in China, and discuss measures that can be taken to help prevent this, or at least reduce the number of incidences.

We look at corporate entry strategies, and at the impact these strategies have had on IP rights protection. For example,

- Companies wishing to establish their business in China often choose to send operational staff who have little or no understanding of China, and of the need to invest in IP protection strategies.

- Foreign rights owners do little to properly protect their intellectual property when entering business relationships with Chinese parties, thinking that their partners will use and manage the intellectual property responsibly and not infringe it.

- Businesses transfer know-how, or trade secrets, despite being aware of the risks, but do nothing, practically or procedurally, to protect that intellectual property in the workplace. Protection of unregistered intellectual property is difficult in even the most sophisticated jurisdictions, but choosing to do nothing is the surest way to ensure theft and the loss of your trade secrets.

- Many business owners allow short-term commercial objectives to dictate strategy, such as allowing distribution, pricing, education, and marketing decisions to be driven independently of any discussion regarding IP.

- Many rights owners simply choose not to invest in IP protection. Instead, they focus on achieving rising market share value and volume, and on showing management that profitability is just around the corner.

- Too often, people simply rely on bad advice.

This book addresses these and other issues which, if recognized and addressed properly, may help to protect intellectual property introduced to or developed in China. Chapters 2, 3, and 5 (in Part 2) present the main issues companies face when entering the China market, such as how to establish your presence, how to select partners that will give your business the best chance of succeeding, and what types of intellectual property are generally shared with these establishments. Even if you don't set yourself up in China, but simply source your products from there, you may encounter IP risks through contract manufacturing. Chapter 4 provides direction on insulating yourself from problems arising from China-manufactured goods. Part 3 (Chapters 6–8) examines the various ways and means to protect your valuable intellectual property from being stolen or misused either by third parties or your own employees. In this part, we will also look at the more common types of IP infringement in China, and describe how you can prepare for and deal with infringement quickly and more effectively if it happens. Chapter 9, in Part 4, takes a look at further protecting your intellectual property by way of lobbying and training government officials and industry associations to assist you in your battle against infringement. Chapter 10 explores a new area of Chinese expansion and innovation—the R&D center—and explains why technology developed in China should be approached with as much caution as interest. Lastly, in Chapter 11 we look to the future, particularly 2008, when China will host the summer Olympic Games. If ever there was an opportunity for China to shake its IP pirate image, this is it.

Part

2

Entering the China market

Between 2001 and 2005, more than 57,000 foreign companies established some sort of presence in China. This represents a 28.5% increase over this five-year period, according to the National Bureau of Statistics in China (www.stats.gov.cn/tjsj/ndsj/2006/indexeh.htm). These types of establishments range from wholly owned foreign enterprises (WOFEs), to joint ventures (JVs) between a foreign and domestic partner, to representative offices. As China's economy matures and the laws and regulations on how such vehicles operate develop further, the number of new foreign-invested enterprises (FIEs) shows no sign of decreasing. Recent adjustments to earlier inducements and incentives for foreign investment to come to China have not had any substantial impact on the foreign investment decisions. As more and more overseas companies make the decision to set up operations in China, questions arise as to what intellectual property those operations need in order to conduct their business successfully, and what type of company affords the best protection for that IP. In Part 2 of the book, Chapter 2 looks at representative offices, WOFEs, and JVs—the foreign-invested enterprises most commonly established in China—and at how proper IP planning during the set-up phase can reduce the chances of infringement not only by your partners and employees, but also by the third parties your FIE will encounter during the course of your China business activities. It also looks briefly at franchising, which is a relatively new form of corporate vehicle in China.

Of course, there is no rule that says a presence in China is required in order to do business there. While the FIE often attracts more attention from the media and in shareholders' meetings, the fact is that the vast majority of foreign IP used in China is licensed in from offshore companies who are more comfortable operating in their own markets than in a market such as China. Chapter 3 explores how businesses can still participate in this dynamic economy by acquiring existing Chinese technology to give them a technological edge over their competitors. This method can be hugely beneficial, so long as you determine that the technology is suitable, that the owner actually owns it, and that it doesn't infringe the rights of others. Chapter 4 looks at businesses that source products from China, and at the steps they need to take to protect their IP along their supply chains. Chapter 5 describes the registered and unregistered IP rights that you may decide your China business needs in order to succeed, and offers practical registration and protection methods for fencing off as much property as possible. The strategies recommended in this book for protecting your intellectual property all aim to achieve the same thing: the opportunity to commercialize your IP in China while avoiding the risks inherent in participating in this developing IP arena.

Chapter
2

Contributing valuable IP to a suitable, newly set-up onshore company

In the earlier periods of China's opening up to foreign invest-ment, concerns over IP misuse or infringement were well documented. IP infringement that took place in the early days of foreign transfer of intellectual property to China may have been particularly rampant because of misunderstandings about how the IP shared with the Chinese FIE was to be treated. Many cases of trade secret infringement occurred in the early to mid-1990s as a result of failures of joint ventures set up in the late 1980s. For instance, an automobile manufacturer found that its designs for car interiors had been stolen, and a European train switch-ing company discovered that its technicians had copied propri-etary signaling technology and sold it to a competitor. Customer lists, pricing and forecasting software, and business and product development plans were stolen across industries. When JV com-panies were dissolved, former Chinese partners continued to use their ex-partner's trade secrets without recognizing that when the partnership ended, so too did their right to use this information.

Of course, many cases also involved rogue former employees of the FIE who would leave the company and set up a competing business utilizing the trade secrets from their former employer. Many of the trade secret cases we have dealt with over the years are difficult to establish because of the lack of good evidence that the plaintiff took steps to protect his or her property, as is required for a trade secret civil suit in any country. As such cases proliferated and were brought before the People's Courts or labor tribunals and then publicized, FIEs became more aware of the potential problems and overhauled their employment agreements and conducted employee exit interviews to address the issues of trade secret theft and unfair competition. With a better understanding of how to treat the intellectual property contributed by the foreign partner to the FIE, misuse and infringement from within the FIEs became less publicized. The focus then shifted to third party infringement, rather than infringement by partners or former partners/employees.

So, if lessons have been learned, if Chinese partners are now more reliable, and if laws and regulations protecting against infringement within the FIE are better understood and enforced, is there a preferred type of corporate vehicle that will provide greater IP advantages over another? In order to select the most suitable corporate vehicle, it is important first to understand the nature of the companies foreigners are permitted to set up, and transfer IP into, in China.

The expansive growth in China's economy since the early 1980s has had a lot to do with its ability to manufacture and sell abroad, but also of importance is the number of foreign companies that have come to China to do business there. The opening of this market of 1.3 billion people to foreign participation has attracted a huge number of multinationals from all over the world, who have to decide in which market sector to participate, in what location, and by way of which type of company. This chapter looks at the three most popular company vehicles foreigners are currently

Jargon buster

CJV: cooperative joint venture

EJV: equity joint venture

FIE: foreign-invested enterprise

JV: joint venture

MOFCOM: Ministry of Commerce

PSB: Public Security Bureau

Rep office: representative office

SAFE: State Administration of Foreign Exchange

SAIC: State Administration of Industry and Commerce

SETC: State Economic and Trade Commission

TSB: Technical Supervision Bureau

WOFE: wholly owned foreign enterprise

permitted to operate under in China. It also looks briefly at a new, and increasingly common, form of vehicle — franchising.

1. REPRESENTATIVE OFFICE

Representative offices were once a popular means of establishing a presence in China. They were easy to set up and required little direct investment. The application process from start to finish could be as little as one month. They can also be easily closed. However, offsetting the benefits were the legal and commercial realities of what a "rep office" could actually do.

Rep offices are just that—they represent their foreign parent. The head office is ultimately responsible for the activities of its China rep office. It is illegal for rep offices to engage in business themselves or on behalf of other businesses. This preclusion includes such activities as signing contracts in their own name or in the name of their parent. Sales are precluded, as is receiving payments for services rendered. Three years is the maximum term of a rep office, but this can be extended on successful application before the expiry of the initial term.

There are no restrictions on where a representative office may be set up, and there are no benefits to locating a rep office in a special economic zone. However, rep offices may only be located in buildings that are approved and licensed for foreign business tenancies. A common mistake in setting up a rep office occurs when leases are signed prior to official registration. If the leased premise is not licensed for foreign tenants, the lease won't be recognized by the government as an approved premise. This may lead to having to relocate and terminating the lease, in which case the return of a deposit is often troublesome.

Most rep offices are set up in order to test the waters prior to the creation of a more formal entity. The primary (and approved) role is to serve as the foreign parent's office in China in order to conduct such activities as market research and surveys, promotional activities, and liaising with local manufacturers, suppliers, distributors, the foreign office, and the like.

With minimal capital requirements and relative ease of application, the application process for a rep office requires the applicant to prove the true existence of the offshore parent in its home jurisdiction, including its name, address, and financial standing. Generally, the rep office naming protocol requires a clear association with the parent company by using the following form: (1) legal home jurisdiction; (2) name of the offshore parent company; (3) China location; and (4) the words "Representative Office" (for example: Germany Grandstoffe Consulting Limited Shanghai Representative Office). Some industries allow exceptions to this form.

Set-up procedures are relatively straightforward and begin with an application to the municipal-level Foreign Trade and Economic Commission where the rep office is to be located. Once approval is obtained, the Administration for Industry and Commerce (AIC) will issue the official registration certificate, which is a key document necessary to finalize establishment. After the business registration certificate is issued, various other procedures must be conducted, including:

- registration with the Administration of Foreign Exchange so that overseas funds can be received by the rep office;
- registration with national and local tax authorities; and
- opening of Renminbi (RMB) and foreign exchange (forex) bank accounts.

Because of the relative ease in setting up a rep office in China, there are many agencies that can assist with the process. They can be located through general business directories or foreign Chambers of Commerce operating in China. Many agencies also advertise their services online and provide services and support in English. Of course, local and foreign law firms can also assist with the setting up of a rep office.

Local staff are permitted to be hired, but only through designated government staffing agencies. An advantage of this requirement is that the agencies handle salary, pension, and insurance payments for local staff. However, up to 60% of the employee's salary may be deducted to cover these payments and service fees. Another disadvantage, particularly in light of the current heated job market in China, is that government agency recruits may be less skilled/qualified than recruits available on the open market. Foreigners are permitted to work in rep offices, and there is no limit on their numbers. Expatriate staff will, however, be subject to a health check regardless of what type of company they work with in China. A work permit must be issued by the State Administration of Industry and Commerce (SAIC). A local Alien Employment Permit from the Labor Bureau is also required, along with registration with the Public Security Bureau (PSB) in the municipal district where the lease is located.

Representative offices are not permitted to own intellectual property. Any intellectual property created by foreign or local staff of the rep office (even if simply copyright existing in marketing materials) will belong to headquarters.

Since rep offices are not permitted to conduct business in China, they are waning in popularity. The days when foreign businesses were unable to navigate the myriad of Chinese regulations and local practices are long gone, making the rep office less necessary than in the past.

2. FOREIGN-INVESTED ENTERPRISES

FIEs include both JVs and WOFEs. Both of these corporate vehicles are able to accept technology and intellectual property as part of the foreign investment, enter into IP license agreements, and develop and generate their own intellectual property, but each comes with different challenges and benefits.

Joint Ventures

Horror stories about JVs that have gone wrong are common in the media. In the early days of foreign investment in China, JVs were the only form of FIE available and thus were very popular by necessity more than choice. This has now changed, but there are still good reasons to enter into a JV and in some industries (such as media and education), it is still the only available option.

China recognizes two types of Sino-foreign JVs: the equity joint venture (EJV) and the cooperative joint venture (CJV). The EJV is the more popular of the two, as CJVs are more highly restricted and regulated and thus take longer to be approved by the government. The EJV acts as a limited liability company with a term as set out in the JV agreement. Parties to an EJV each receive a share of the company's equity equivalent to the percentage of the registered capital they have contributed; their liability is similarly limited based on their share in the registered capital. A CJV can be established as a limited liability company, like an EJV; or it can be a non-legal person, in which case its partners are subject to unlimited liability and thus are liable for all losses.

In order for a JV to be approved by the government as an FIE, and thus enjoy certain tax and other benefits, the foreign investor must invest at least 25% of the registered capital. This is true of both EJVs and CJVs. In reality, most Sino-foreign JVs in China see the foreign party holding a greater-than-majority shareholding. While there is generally no upper limit on the amount of contribution the foreign party can make, there are restrictions in certain industries that China considers should not be majority owned by foreigners, as is the case in most countries. Examples would include civil airlines, postal services, and industries utilizing technology that China already possesses and which thus don't need foreign participation.

Chapter 4 discusses the due diligence necessary prior to selecting any type of Chinese partner, but in terms of identifying potential JV partners, the following are some commonly used methods:

- obtaining lists, published by various Chinese organizations and distributed at "cooperation fairs," detailing the hundreds of "projects" proposed in various commercial sectors, and including brief information about the Chinese partner, the product, the anticipated sales volume, and the required investment;

- contacting the government departments responsible for the particular industry and requesting introductions;

- contacting your own government's trade development offices in China;

- attending trade fairs; and

- contacting key people and companies in the particular industry, building relationships, and requesting introductions.

Wholly Owned Foreign Enterprises

WOFEs have become the most popular vehicle for investment in China since the loosening of restrictions following China's joining of the WTO, mainly because they allow the investor to retain control over the enterprise. This greater degree of control enables WOFEs to prevent valuable or sensitive intellectual property and technology from falling into the wrong hands.

Like an EJV, the WOFE is a limited liability company, but with the difference that there is no local Chinese investment. Even if there are multiple foreign investors, the enterprise is still considered a WOFE.

Although a WOFE offers the freedom to operate without the participation of a local Chinese partner, this type of vehicle is only permitted to conduct the business that the government has agreed it can conduct. The business scope sets out the approved and legal business that a WOFE can undertake, so it is extremely important to get this right. It is not uncommon for a WOFE to prepare and submit for approval a business scope that the approval authorities will ultimately scale down or redefine.

WOFEs can be classified into three broad categories: (1) service WOFEs, (2) manufacturing WOFEs, and (3) trading and manufacturing WOFEs. As a WOFE grows and matures, normally there will be applications for changes to the business scope, but such amendments are sometimes met with even greater scrutiny. It is recommended in these cases to approach seasoned corporate lawyers for professional advice based not only on the law, but also on their recent experiences of what the authorities will allow.

3. THE PLANNING PAPER

Many China-bound companies will engage consultants, accountants, and/or lawyers to create a planning paper setting out the steps involved in establishing a corporate vehicle in China. Planning papers describe the practical and legal environments within which the business can be established and then sort through the possibilities to come up with the most practicable approaches that best meet the company's business requirements and which, at the same time, would be acceptable to the Chinese side.

Practical and legal issues are analyzed and described in terms of how they may represent either opportunities or issues to be resolved. Planning papers should address the near-term issues in the establishment phase of the project, as well as the longer-term considerations to be addressed to ensure, as far as possible, a stable and profitable operation.

In addition to addressing issues of type of corporate entity to establish and due diligence on prospective partners, planning papers should include explanations and advice on the FIE's name, location, capital contributions, technology and IP contributions, approval procedures and time frames, staffing, negotiations, and confidentiality. We look at each of these areas next.

FIE Business Names

Like a representative office, FIEs must have a Chinese name, which must not be identical, or even similar, to an existing name operating in the same industry in the same city. There are four requirements for an approved FIE name: (1) trade name, (2) city, (3) industry, and (4) "Company Limited" in Chinese. While the official legal name of the FIE will be its Chinese name, the FIE can operate using a foreign-language translation of the legal Chinese name—for example, Everstay Engineering Plastics (Shanghai) Co. Ltd.

Having the word "China" in a name, rather than the name of the city, is popular, particularly with shareholders back home. An enterprise wishing to use the word "China" in its name is required to have a registered capital of at least US$6.5 million (approximately). Choosing not to have an industry indication in the enterprise name requires a minimum registered capital of US$13 million (approximately).

The application process is relatively straightforward, requiring submission of the investor's registration certificate and the completion of various forms. Once accepted, registration of the business enterprise name can be reserved for up to six months. To prevent the investor from delaying the formal organization of the FIE, there are no procedures for this period of time to be extended.

Location

Finding the right location to establish your JV or WOFE has important implications not only in terms of achieving your commercial goals, but also for positioning your intellectual property in a locale that has a developed judiciary and capable local administrative officials on whom you can rely if your IP is ever endangered. While there are now many special development zones in China that have preferential policies to encourage investors, we are seeing an increasing number of establishment deals that include local consideration and special treatment for technology and IP protection. It is not recommended to consider setting up your FIE in a municipality or province that isn't interested in developing special working groups of officials who might be called on for special IP assistance. Just as requirements relating to minimum capital investment, approval procedures and time frames, tax treatment, fiscal support measures, and other matters vary significantly in different locations around China, so too does understanding of the importance of protecting the intellectual property that foreigners bring to their China companies.

If your China company will be invested with or be licensed to use technology or IP, then it is wise to know the authorities who may have some say over that property. These officials will likely not only have authority over your intellectual property and its registration and protection (for example, the Administration for Industry and Commerce, Technical Supervision Bureau (TSB), Copyright Administration, or Patent Bureau), but also will be responsible for approving your employee agreements and the restrictive covenants and confidentiality terms that you include. You should also have knowledge of the local or state authorities who assess the value of the technology and intellectual property that you contribute to the FIE, in case you ever want to take it out. It is also important to be familiar with the workings of enforcement authorities such as the People's Courts and Customs authorities in your area.

Capital Contributions

There are generally no restrictions on the form capital contributions can take; for example, cash, land, equipment, intellectual property, technology, sales contracts, and other forms of capital contribution are all permitted in China. Some of these do come with additional requirements.

You will need to provide a value for non-cash tangible property contributions. International-standard valuation methods recognized by the Administration of State Asset Valuation include:

- current market value;
- present value of earnings;
- replacement cost; and
- liquidation price.

Technology and IP Contributions

The valuation of intangible assets such as technology and IP is normally worked out between the parties in the case of a joint venture, but any agreed value must be accepted by the relevant approval authorities. If the Chinese JV partner is contributing state-owned assets (either tangible or intangible), the valuation exercise can become more complex. At the end of the day, valuation of IP and technology is difficult anywhere. The key difference in China is the involvement of the authorities in many cases in assessing the reasonableness of the valuation.

For contributions to registered capital in the form of intangible assets such as technology and intellectual property rights, the ratio of technology and IP should not be more than 20% of the total registered capital. For new and high-technology enterprises, the ratio should not exceed 35%. If technology and IP are used as capital contribution for setting up an FIE, the transfer documentation and approval formalities for evidencing assign-ment of the rights (such as the assignment agreement, license agreement, or services agreement) must be completed before the contribution can be recognized.

Of course, the decision to use intellectual property or technology as a part of your capital contribution may be risky if the proper degree of control isn't exercised. As part of the capital contribution, this property becomes the property of the FIE. If, after establishment, you assign additional IP to the joint venture, be aware that you may not be able to reassert ownership over that IP if, for example, a dispute leads to a judgment against you or a liquidator sells the JV's IP assets to satisfy creditors.

Approval Procedures and Time Frames

Approval of the provincial foreign trade authority, and registration with the provincial AIC, is required in order to set up an FIE. This normally takes two to three months. In certain special trade zones, such as those in Beijing or Shanghai, registration and approval procedures are fast-tracked and can take as little as two to three weeks to complete. In reality, however, it is difficult to predict exactly how long establishment will take, especially if there are prolonged negotiations with a Chinese partner to a JV, or if a WOFE is considered a large-scale investment, in which case national authorities will be involved rather than local provincial or municipal officials. The two basic approvals that are required are (1) project approval, and then (2) establishment approval. Additional time is also needed for the numerous post-registration procedures, such as those described above for the representative office. Things take time in China, but you should always take the time to prepare the necessary documentation in order to best protect your technology and IP.

Establishment of a JV or WOFE is usually handled by a local law firm, or by a foreign law firm that may have to obtain local legal opinion on tricky legal or regulatory issues. By law, foreign law firms are not permitted to advise on PRC law, but rather on the "general environment" of local laws and rules.

Staffing

JVs and WOFEs may hire as many employees as necessary. If technology has been contributed to the investment and its operation must be taught to local staff, or if the overseas investor performs an ongoing service, overseas staff may need to visit China. It is important to choose staff who are experienced in handling IP and to train them carefully. It is also good advice to confirm that local staff employment agreements contain the necessary restrictive covenants and confidentiality terms to prevent staff from taking the training and then leaving the employ of the FIE. One useful tip is to give your staff certificates of completion after they have received specialized training. The certificate is proof that they partook of your knowledge, in the event that they leave your company and breach the terms of their employment agreement by sharing that knowledge with others. We discuss employees and IP protection in more detail in Chapter 6.

Foreign staff of FIEs must obtain the same permits and approvals as outlined above for representative office employees.

Negotiations and Confidentiality

Setting up a business in China requires a considerable amount of negotiation time, not only with your prospective Chinese partners, but also with the various government officials whose approval you will need in order to get your business up and running. In terms of meetings and negotiations with your prospective Chinese partner, we advise preparing a letter of intent early on for both parties to sign. The letter should set out the non-disclosure and confidentiality terms. For meetings with approval authorities, where you may be asked to disclose confidential information about your proposed deal such as trade secrets, new product ideas, and financial and accounting information, ensure that your representatives don't disclose anything that hasn't been pre-determined and pre-approved. We will discuss confidentiality in more detail in Chapter 4.

4. TO JV OR NOT TO JV?

A question often asked by potential investors in China is: "Which type of company—JV or WOFE—will afford better protection for my IP?" There is no easy answer to this question, as each vehicle has advantages and disadvantages. The best choice will depend on a number of factors, including:

- the location of your business in China;
- whether you already have potential partners or contacts in China;
- the type of intellectual property involved in your business, which will dictate the preventative measures you will need to take to safeguard against theft;
- the type of previous intellectual property infringement you have experienced and from whom (that is, partners/employees or third parties);
- how tightly regulated your industry is in China; and
- your company's size, experience in the business, business model, and so on.

JVs are often more attractive to small to medium-sized foreign companies who are interested in establishing a business with a Chinese partner who already has an established business reputation or brand, as this will make the JV's products more quickly accepted in the marketplace. If your selected location is outside the more established eastern or southern investment corridors, then a local partner may have valuable local knowledge and contacts, including existing distribution networks, technology, or capabilities in areas that can enhance your current product line.

WOFEs are a "go it alone" type of vehicle, but therein lies their greatest advantage: the foreign investor has full control over the company. This is an especially attractive characteristic for foreign investors who are transferring cutting-edge proprietary technology to China, which, if it were to fall into the wrong hands, could have a devastating effect on a business.

As with any partnership, business or otherwise, communication is the key. Running a JV means that you will need to listen to, and take into account, the views of your Chinese or other foreign partners. Consensus needs to be reached before actions can be taken. Your partners will enjoy certain veto rights regardless of the percentage of your majority shareholding. If your partner conducts some of the JV's business in its own factory (that is, not in your shared JV factory), then you will need a clear understanding of what this means so as to avoid commingling of JV information with the other company's information, as well as diversion of products. Discourage your partner from maintaining some separate production within the JV unless this is clearly demarked as separate from the business of the JV and is treated separately by way of an independent written agreement. Underreporting and diversion of production is a common complaint from partners to a JV (as will be discussed below). Control of intellectual property is sometimes unclear, particularly in regards to improvements to technology you may have contributed. We will discuss improvements further in Chapter 10.

A JV takes longer to set up than a WOFE, because of the amount of documentation required to prove your existence and worthiness to establish a Sino-foreign JV. Often, the type of corporate documentation that PRC corporate law requires has no foreign equivalent. This results in the foreign party having to go back and forth to the approval authority to see if they will accept alternative documentation. Initial direct investment costs for a JV are high. JVs are also difficult to dissolve, requiring approvals from authorities such as banks, the Public Security Bureau, Immigration, and a host of other government agencies.

The primary legal relationship between the parties to a Sino-foreign joint venture is set out in the JV Agreement. This critically important document must set out in detail what each party will contribute to the company in terms of skills, cash, technology, and IP, how the company will be allowed to use that valuable property, and the penalties if that property is ever misused. While the law requires certain provisions to be included in the JV Agreement, the parties are relatively free to include their own deal-specific terms as well. Of course, these will need ultimately to be accepted by the relevant approval authorities.

The JV Agreement

There are several ways to ensure that the technology, IP, or confidential consultancy/training services you will provide are protected in the JV Agreement. The following review of the relevant parts of the JV Agreement is not exhaustive, as each deal will be different, but it aims to provoke ideas:

1. *Establishment of the joint venture company:* If technology/IP are going to be important for the success of the JV's business, then describe that intent here in order to confirm that this is a critically important part of the whole deal.

2. *Purpose, scope, and scale of production and business:* Refer to your contribution of the technology/IP as being integral to the success of the JV and its ability to perform its business scope and to produce quantities of quality product in order to generate profits.

3. *Total amount of investment and registered capital:* Ensure that the technology/IP/services contribution you make is valued to your satisfaction (though noting that the parties' valuation is subject to government approval, as described above) and set out accordingly. Also, leave room for revaluation in the future if its value appreciates. Does your technology/IP/services contribution need to be made all at once, or can it be staggered into the JV at later dates? You don't need to contribute your most valuable property first (unless this is integral to early production targets, etc.), though your partner will likely ask for this. Set out here your contribution timetables, verifications, and any overpayments. You should also deal here with the possibility of you or your partner wanting to transfer interest in the JV, setting out how this will be dealt with. While you won't want to keep a partner locked into the JV, you will want to have some say in who he transfers his interest to, especially if it might be a competitor! We are aware of a French light industrial manufacturer whose Chinese partner in Ningbo sold its interest in the JV to a German competitor of the French partner's EU business. Not surprisingly, the JV relationship soured quickly and the company was eventually terminated.

4. *Responsibilities of each party:* Representations and warranties from both sides should be expressly set out. Don't warrant any of your untested technology/IP/services contribution,

and limit your warranties only so far as you can control how your partner uses your contribution. You shouldn't suggest in the agreement that you are responsible for the effectiveness of the operations manual if your partner is responsible for training employees. Neither should you be responsible for patented machinery that doesn't integrate successfully into your partner's Chinese factory.

5. *Technological services:* Services, including training and upkeep visits, can be contributed to the JV as part of your investment, or they may be charged separately under separate agreements. (The latter is more common, owing to difficulties in getting services valued, agreed, and approved by the authorities.) Regardless of whether they are contributed or charged separately, they should be identified in the JV Agreement because this is very likely to be considered know-how or confidential information, or even a process patent, all of which need to be recognized accordingly and specifically set out as deserving due consideration and protection by your partner.

6. *Selling and exporting products:* As your technology/IP will go into the JV's products, you will need to identify how it will be used not only in China during distribution, but for exported products as well. You may also want to consider adding a non-competition clause to protect against your partner's cannibalizing a part of your market where the JV's products weren't intended to be sold.

7. *The board:* In Sino-foreign JVs, a majority foreign shareholder will usually retain the right to appoint the majority of the board members. Chinese law requires that all companies have a "legal representative," who needs to be appointed by the board and whose name must be recorded with the local AIC when the company is set up. The legal representative is recognized as having full legal power to represent the company in signing agreements with third parties. Appointment of the legal representative is also a right that is normally held by the majority shareholder. Control of the board and of the legal representative will afford greater protection for your technology/IP. Given the power that the legal representative has to bind a company in China, it is important to appoint someone you know and trust.

8. *Purchase of equipment and materials:* The attractions of establishing a business in China include not only the potential huge market for goods the JV may produce and sell in China, but also the ability to source component materials at prices often more competitive than in other countries, and the ease of distribution within the Chinese market. However, bringing in materials from third parties runs the risk of taking on any IP infringement problems these component materials may harbor. Distribution channels may often commingle your non-infringing products with those that do infringe, or, even worse, are of poor quality. This can be addressed in the JV Agreement by controlling how third-party component material parts are sourced, assessed, and used. How the JV distributes its products can be controlled as well.

9. *Labor management:* Chinese law is quite regulated when it comes to the protection it gives to local staff, but the JV Agreement may set out provisions for holding technical staff to higher degrees of responsibility when they use JV technology/IP. It is also a good idea to check not only national labor regulations, but local regulations as well, in order to know how far you can go in controlling JV employee use of technology/IP/confidential information, and so on. The issue of employee control should be fully set out in individual labor contracts, but a general mention can be made in the JV Agreement. We discuss employees further in Chapter 6.

10. *Taxes, finance, and audit:* Currently, FIEs are required to withhold taxes assessable to technology/IP royalties at a rate of 14.5%. This means that if you don't contribute the technology/IP to the JV, but rather license it to the JV for its use and charge a royalty for such use, the JV must withhold the assessable tax that it pays to the state. This 14.5% is actually comprised of two taxes: the foreign enterprise income tax and the business tax. The income tax is 10% for royalties paid offshore and is assessed first. The business tax is 5% and is assessed after the income tax. For example, if you charge the JV a US$10,000 royalty for the use of your technology or IP, the JV will be required to withhold US$1,000 for income tax, leaving US$9,000 to be assessed against the

business tax. The business tax will be US$450, which must also be withheld. The combined US$1,000 and US$450 is equal to the 14.5% withholding tax. If the JV agrees for this to be offset and the overall royalty to be paid to you to be net of this tax, you may provide for this in the JV Agreement. You should note, however, that a new PRC Enterprise Income Tax Law, approved by the National People's Congress on March 16, 2007, and taking effect on January 1, 2008, will change this withholding tax rule. The new law will subject both domestic and foreign enterprises to the same tax treatment. The new withholding tax rate on IP royalties paid out of China will increase to 20%.

11. *Termination:* The JV Agreement should be clear on what happens with the technology/IP when the JV ends. Will it be sold off along with the JV's other assets? Will the contributing party keep it? Or will the parties enter into a new, separate agreement if they want to share it? Purchase options are a useful means by which one party can take over the interest of a party who wants to exit. While many JV horror stories involve continued use of technology/IP after the JV terminates, such incidences are becoming less frequent.

12. *Confidentiality:* Obligations of confidentiality are important not only for technology/IP and trade secret matters, but also for business strategies, new product ideas, and financial and accounting information.

13. *Dispute resolution and governing law:* Contracts for the establishment of FIEs in China must be subject to PRC law, rather than foreign law. JV Agreements will typically take a dual arbitration and litigation approach to addressing disputes. Arbitration is the most common dispute resolution procedure, but this should be triggered only after good faith negotiations toward an amicable resolution have first been exhausted. The China International Economic and Trade Arbitration Commission (CIETAC) is today regarded as a reputable arbitral body whose panel of arbitrators include both Chinese and foreigners. CIETAC rules can be followed in venues both within and outside of China.

    Consider reserving the right to make applications to the People's Court for injunctions, irrespective of the binding arbitration provision. This is a practical way of intervening quickly in stopping the unauthorized use of IP or trade secrets, rather than waiting until a decision is made by an arbitration panel.

It is crucial that any existing agreements that you wish to use in your China deals be localized for use in China. Local parties will expect an agreement to be translated into Chinese. Additionally, some terms that are common in US or UK agreements are unfamiliar to local companies. In our experience, if these agreements are localized to reflect the terminology that local companies expect, the negotiation process becomes a lot less cumbersome. This will be discussed further in Chapter 4.

Is Your Chinese Partner/Licensee Authorized?

In China, an entity is permitted to operate only within its approved business scope. Often companies have a very limited business scope, for which it is easier to obtain approval. Their business may then have expanded without them having obtained the required additional approvals. It is important to check that the parties you are dealing with have the approved business scope to offer the services they are providing for you.

If you enter into supply or manufacture relationships with Chinese companies, you need to check whether they have the right to engage directly in import and export. Otherwise, you may request that the Chinese party cover the costs charged by a third party that has the relevant license. Alternatively, you can require the Chinese party to obtain the import and export right from the relevant government agency as a condition for entering into any agreement.

Approvals are particularly important if your business is in a regulated area such as food and drink, pharmaceuticals, cosmetics, and so on. Product registration certificates are required by most countries for the manufacture and sale of these types of products. If your China JV or WOFE is manufacturing and selling these, then applications should be made in the name of the JV or WOFE. However, if you are simply distributing such products in China and they were made elsewhere, it is normally your China distributor who applies for the product registration certificates. You should always keep copies of these for your own records even though, technically, they belong to the Chinese distributor. We would advise that, in the distribution agreement, you require the distributor, upon termination of the distribution arrangement, to destroy these certificates or to surrender them either to you or to the relevant issuing agency. Failure to do so may result in delays in the issuance of new product registration certificates when a new distributor is appointed. Consider adding some reasonableness to this requirement by paying for the testing/analysis required as a part of the product registration process yourself, rather than relying on your distributor to do so.

Despite Your Best Efforts...

Sometimes, despite all the efforts of both parties, a JV just doesn't work out. A recent high-profile case of partners in a Sino-foreign JV falling out is Groupe Danone SA and Hangzhou Wahaha Group Co., Ltd., China's leading domestic beverage producer. The two companies joined in 1996 to form five new subsidiaries, of which Danone owns 51% and Wahaha the remainder. Thanks to Danone's money and the corporate gymnastics of Wahaha's chairman Zong Qinghou, Wahaha's production doubled in the first year alone. Unfortunately, relations became estranged over the next 10 years, and Danone announced in June 2007 that it was suing two companies closely related to its Chinese partner and some of Zong's relatives in Los Angeles, whom it accused of selling products that competed unfairly with the JV's products and of diverting JV revenues to other companies. The lawsuit is seeking damages to the tune of over US$100 million. Zong resigned and began a public relations war, accusing Danone of trying to quash a famous Chinese brand (not an uncommon strategy in China for elevating foreign brands over local ones) and of setting up similar businesses in competition with the JV.

The parties are also in dispute over who owns the trademark "Wahaha," which mimics the sound of a laughing baby and was thought to be highly attractive to China's single-child households. Danone is arguing that in an agreement with Wahaha, the trademark was assigned to the JV. Wahaha is arguing that this agreement was never recorded with the PRC Trademark Office and therefore is invalid. While most observers consider the case a classic illustration of a Sino-foreign JV gone bad, and perhaps as sounding the death knell for such ventures, it could simply be the expected outcome of any deal where the foreign investor rushed in without proper preparation. Chapter 10 explains this phenomenon in more detail.

5. FRANCHISING IN CHINA: A NEW BUSINESS MODEL

China has been described as "the mother of all franchise markets," inspiring international franchisors such as Burger King Corp., Super 8 Motels, Inc., and Uniglobe Travel International LP, among many others, to launch their franchising plans in China in recent years.

Franchising is a relatively new business model in China, having appeared for the first time in the 1990s. In fact, until a couple of years ago, there was no word for "franchise" in Chinese. The model is based on a business relationship in which the franchisor (the owner of the business providing the product or service) assigns to the franchisee (independent parties) the right to market and distribute the franchisor's goods or services and to use its associated business name for a fixed period of time. After more than a decade of rapid development and growth, the franchise model has been adopted in a variety of industries across China and the continued growth of China's consumer base provides a potentially lucrative opportunity for foreign franchisors. It is estimated that, in 2006, there were more than 2,600 franchise operations in China (ranking number one in the world) involving more than 168,000 franchise outlets in more than 60 industries. In many ways, franchising is the perfect fit for China, which has many budding and ambitious entrepreneurs eager to acquire business know-how, management experience, and a brand name.

Many of the familiar foreign franchise giants are visible in China. Yum! Brands, Inc., which operates the KFC, Pizza Hut, and Taco Bell franchises, has had a presence in the country since 1987 and has gained substantial experience in navigating China's regulatory minefield. Until recently, however, all of its stores were company-owned chain stores rather than traditional franchises, because it was concerned about IP protection and an inadequate legal framework. Yum! now opens company-owned stores and operates them directly for 12 months or until they become profitable, after which it trains franchisees in the stores before delegating to them full responsibility for the business. This process allows franchisees to avoid struggling with the initial set-up of the store—they are simply given a store that is already profitable, while learning valuable business operation skills along the way. Yum! has also reduced its franchising fee, to as low as

RMB2 million (US$250,000) for its KFC franchises in second-tier cities, to encourage rapid growth outside the major cities. McDonald's Corp. has adopted a similar, albeit slower, approach to franchising in China: all of its company-owned stores operate with a local partner. Peter Tan, president of the China branch of the McDonald Development Co., claimed in 2002 that "McDonald's will begin franchising only after relevant regulations and laws are defined in China." True to Tan's word, McDonald's started to consider franchising only after new franchise regulations were introduced in 2005.

As franchising is a new business model in China, it requires a great deal of education at all levels of involvement—from the authorities who enforce the regulations to the franchisees, managers, employees, suppliers, and consumers. The Chinese parties are usually confused about the difference between chain stores and franchises, a confusion compounded by the fact that the same quasi-government body, the China Chain Store and Franchise Association (CCFA), is responsible for both industries. Also, Chinese franchisees often don't understand the significance of the "system" they are acquiring, and often question why they need to pay such high fees up front to obtain access to the system and the brand name. It is thus important for companies to localize a franchising model in China to ensure success. Eastman Kodak Co., with more than 5,500 photo printing stores in China, has led the way by teaming up with local banks to allow prospective franchisees to pre-qualify for business loans.

In China, a business activity that is not expressly allowed by a regulation is generally considered prohibited. As recently as the end of 2004, China lacked formal regulations that allowed foreign companies to franchise in China, and foreign franchisors could not engage directly in commercial franchising. For foreign franchisors that wanted to target the Chinese market, the only option available was to partner with a local franchisee that had import and export licenses. This approach generally left foreign franchisors in China with a lack of control over their brands and limited profit because they had to share it with the Chinese partner.

All of this changed, however, on February 1, 2005, when the PRC Ministry of Commerce's (MOFCOM) Administrative Measures on Commercial Franchising took effect and replaced the 1997 Interim Measures for Regulating Commercial Franchise Operations, which didn't explicitly allow foreign entities to franchise in China. The new measures, which were issued on December 31, 2004, were part of China's WTO commitments to open up its franchising sector to foreign-invested enterprises. The rules clearly allow FIEs to compete in the Chinese market. Since most of the measures apply to all Chinese legal entities, they ostensibly create a more level playing field for domestic and foreign franchisors, although there are a few important exceptions.

Then in February 2007, the new Regulations on the Administration of Commercial Franchise Operations were passed. The regulations, which came into effect on May 1, 2007, clarified some of the issues in the interim measures but raised more questions in relation to others. Although the 2005 Administrative Measures on Commercial Franchising have cleared the way for FIEs registered in China to engage in franchising, they fell short on one key issue that wasn't clarified by the regulations: whether a foreign company can directly engage in cross border franchising agreements with Chinese franchises without establishing a wholly foreign-owned enterprise in China first. Indeed, the measures include a unique provision, not used anywhere else in the world, that requires all franchisors to operate at least two stores in China for a minimum of one year before starting franchising operations. Although the provision is intended to protect Chinese franchisees from the unfamiliar waters of franchising, many companies consider it an overly burdensome requirement that essentially prohibits foreign companies from operating franchises without first either opening two stores in China and running them for a year or entering into a joint venture with a local partner. This provision remains under the regulations, although the requirement that these stores be run in China has been removed; this raises the possibility of stores being run elsewhere to satisfy the rules.

The measures and the regulations set out a detailed disclosure regime aimed at protecting potential and current franchisees. In addition to a broad list of information that the franchisor must provide to the franchisee at least 20 days before the execution of the franchise agreement, the measures contain a "catch-all" provision that allows the franchisee to request the franchisor to disclose "other information," a term that is left undefined. The right to information appears not to be restricted to information required to make a decision on franchising, but rather is an open-ended right reserved for the duration of the agreement. Failure to comply with the disclosure provision could prove costly—the measures stipulate fines of up to RMB30,000 (approximately US$3,774) and possible cancellation of the franchisor's business license. The measures also state that the franchisor must compensate the franchisee for any losses caused by inadequate disclosure and misrepresentation of information, although the types of information are not defined.

Foreign franchisors should carefully select their franchisees and conduct appropriate due diligence on all potential partners. This procedure should not only cover the usual financial and business experience checks, but also attempt to identify whether the potential franchisee has a solid track record on IP management, which could include testing its awareness of the value of intellectual property. Franchisors must also carefully train their franchisees on the importance of IP protection and maintaining uniform standards. For example, Super 8 opted to set up special schools to help train staff in China, an unnecessary step in other countries in which it operates. Subway realized the importance of finding the right franchisees when, after training one of their early franchisees in China, the franchisee changed the name and appearance of the restaurant when he opened!

Franchising is an exciting potential business model, but companies need to go into it with their eyes open. The regulations and their implementation remain vague and, in an environment in which the market is still coming to terms with the concept, franchising can be a risky industry in China. But it can also be a very rewarding industry if managed carefully with the right partners.

CHECKPOINT

In order to select the best corporate vehicle for your business in China, particularly if you plan on contributing your intellectual property to it, you will need to ask yourself:

- Do you need a partner in China? Do you need connections? Local market experience?
- What industry are you operating in?
- Are you bringing technology to China?
- Will your entity need to be conducting business in China, or is it acting more as a representative office for market research and establishment?

- Have you prepared a planning paper?
- How much control do you want to have over the business?
- Have you conducted due diligence on any potential partners?
- Are you confident that your partners will respect your IP and are appropriately licensed and experienced?
- If your business fails or you have a dispute with your partners, what will become of your IP?

RESOURCES

- http://english.ccpit.org: China Council for the Promotion of International Trade
- www.customs.gov.cn: General Administration of Customs
- www.aqsiq.gov.cn: General Administration of Quality Supervision
- www.mof.gov.cn: Ministry of Finance
- www.fmprc.gov.cn: Ministry of Foreign Affairs
- www.mofcom.gov.cn: Ministry of Commerce
- www.ndrc.gov.cn: National Development and Reform Commission
- www.pbc.gov.cn: People's Bank of China
- www.saic.gov.cn: State Administration for Industry and Commerce
- www.safe.gov.cn: State Administration of Foreign Exchange
- www.chinatax.gov.cn: State Administration of Taxation

- www.ccfa.org.cn: The China Chain Store and Franchising Association is the quasi-government organization responsible for assisting franchisees and franchisors in China.

Chapter

3

Acquiring Chinese technology

1. INTRODUCTION

Who said you have to be in China in order to take advantage of what it has to offer? Many companies are investing in China by way of acquiring Chinese technology and then commercializing that technology elsewhere, or by licensing it or assigning it to companies based in China.

IP acquisitions are becoming commonplace in China and other Asian countries as these economies move to become more knowledge-based. Agricultural and manufacturing economies may not have been prolific creators of intellectual property, but these are often key territories for global or regional deals. In many cases, the acquiring companies are not Western, but Asian, looking to fast-track the design/invention/branding process and acquire IP as future assets. Even domestic Chinese companies are showing huge increases in their acquisition consumption. PricewaterhouseCoopers reports that domestic deal volumes in China increased by 20%—to 808 inbound deals—in the first six months of 2007, up from 674 in the same period the previous year.

IP, in legal terms, is the classic intangible asset. IP can create value, including cash, in a number of ways. It can be sold. It can be licensed in or out. It can be contributed as capital into a joint venture. It can be offered to enter into strategic alliances. It can be integrated with a current business or used to create a new business. It can also be used as collateral when it is pledged, mortgaged, or charged.

The value of intangible IP assets is a changing paradigm. IP is fast becoming a focus for capital markets and the investment community. It is a "tradable" commodity in its own right and serves as a vital tool for a company's ability to sustain its competitive advantage. IP value has seen a dramatic increase in recognition in recent years. Today, IP is less a defensive tool and more a layer of additional value on products and services, and in some cases a pure asset in its own right. For this reason, Chinese companies are now waking up to the value of Intellectual Asset Management (IAM), a business process in which IP experts review a company's IP assets and align them to the business's corporate strategy, realizing cost savings and creating new revenue streams, as well as increasing the overall value of the business.

When purchasing or obtaining a license for Chinese technology, or when Chinese technology is contributed as part of a joint venture's capital, companies should conduct due diligence on that technology to verify three key elements:

1. Identify the technology to a degree sufficient to confirm that it fits the needs of the company or of the joint venture.
2. Confirm that the seller or the partner owns the technology and whether any state funds were used in its development.
3. Ensure that the technology doesn't infringe upon any third party's IP rights.

The process of acquiring IP in China is much the same as anywhere else. However, there are several areas of concern, which, if left unsettled, may cause difficulties in the future. This isn't a job that should be left entirely to your corporate mergers and acquisitions (M&A) lawyers at head office.

Identifying the Technology

A Chinese seller should be able to describe the technology in sufficient detail for a buyer to understand it fully. This can be a simple step if the target technology is a product, but if it is a process for formulating something or for effecting some desired result, then the description may be more complicated, especially if the process is a trade secret kept in the heads of a small reference group of employees or inventors, or in an operator's manual that the seller may not want to share until the deal is completed. The parties to a transaction can address this problem by entering into a non-disclosure agreement, but the buyer or JV partner should understand that even this is sometimes insufficient to convince the seller to make full disclosure of the technology. We have seen many cases where it takes a considerable amount of time to convince a Chinese seller that the only way for the buyer to assess the viability of a technology is for it to be revealed. As will be discussed in Chapter 4, when a seller refuses to enter a non-disclosure agreement, you may have to consider whether he truly does possess what he is hoping to sell.

Identification of the exact technology to be acquired is also critical in order to confirm whether it falls within certain categories of "prohibited," "restricted," or "free" technologies as set out in the 2002 Regulations for the Administration of Technology Import and Export, which serves as the principal guide for foreign acquisition, use, and export of Chinese technology. If the technology to be acquired belongs to the prohibited or restricted category, then it may not be transferable at all, or it may be transferable only with government approval. Technology transfer will be discussed in detail in Chapter 10.

If your acquisition includes trademarks, you will need to determine whether they are in the appropriate classes for the goods/ services you will use them with. Full searches are ideal, but are not always practical in the time available or if the budget is limited, in which case prioritization is crucial.

Confirming Ownership

Determining whether the seller actually owns the technology under consideration normally requires several meetings between the parties, including with relevant technicians, to understand how the technology was developed step by step. It is also crucial for a prospective buyer to know who developed the technology, when, and with whose funds (state or otherwise). If the seller no longer employs the technicians who were involved, the prospective acquirer should attempt to determine their present whereabouts. If external subcontracted testing and development was involved, a buyer should ascertain to what degree that input might give rise to third-party inventorship rights to the technology in question.

In addition to understanding the history of the technology, a prospective buyer should thoroughly review the employment agreements of the seller's employees who assisted in the development, to confirm that the seller owns the employees' contributions and has imposed confidentiality restrictions on its employees—and, if so, whether these have been enforced. As will be discussed in Chapter 6, certain statutory provisions preclude employees who contributed to the development of the technology, but who subsequently left the seller's employment, from claiming inventorship rights within 12 months after their departure. As long as the seller can prove that the departed employees made the contribution during the course of their employment in relation to their normal duties, the seller will be able effectively to refute the employees' subsequent claim of inventorship after the statutory time limit expires.

Potential buyers should also confirm whether the employees have been properly rewarded for their contribution to the technology in question. Article 16 of the PRC Patent Law requires that an employer "reasonably" remunerate employees for the inventions made while performing their duties once the resulting patents are commercialized. The law and its implementing regulations don't stipulate the amount of remuneration for foreign enterprises. (Foreign R&D centers in China generally adopt the employee reward schemes of their home offices, which would most likely meet the reasonableness test.) For state-owned enterprises (SOEs), the Implementing Regulations of the Patent Law require a minimum of 2% of after-tax profit derived from the use of the invention and at least 10% of any after-tax license fees. University and research institutes may adopt their own rules and may have even higher requirements for employee rewards. Buyers should also be aware that local regulations may encourage higher levels of remuneration. For example, Shanghai regulations mandate that employee inventors in private enterprises receive as much as 30% of after-tax profits resulting from the use of a patent, including its acquisition or license to a third party. A seller's failure to adequately reward the employees responsible for the development of the technology in question could give rise to future claims against the buyer.

Finally, apart from reviewing relevant employee agreements, prospective buyers should ensure that additional legal research includes a complete review of all licenses, authorizations, consents, options or rights to acquire, charges, pledges, and liens or other forms of security over or affecting the technology.

In particular, prospective buyers of Chinese technology should investigate whether the technology's licensees have been involved in counterfeiting or in civil or criminal litigation for counterfeiting or breach of agreement, have procedures in place to protect IP licensed to them, produce for competing brands, or outsource production to third parties. In addition, buyers should find out details concerning licensees' subcontractors and sub-subcontractors involved in the licensing arrangements and their current and planned distributors, marketing agents, and component suppliers.

Buyers should also perform a "brand hygiene check" to ensure the licensees' ethical, regulatory, and environmental compliance. This is normally done through specialist agencies or law firms familiar with the process and who know what to look for. So often in China, what you see on your first few visits may be very far from what the situation actually is once you leave.

Finally, buyers should investigate what kind of tooling and equipment the licensee has used in manufacturing for the licensor, and whether tooling and equipment have also been licensed under the licensing agreement. We have had experiences where the tooling was later discovered to be an integral part of the technology, though at the time of the acquisition the buyer didn't fully understand this. Buyers should also review copies of any executed powers of attorney into which the seller has entered, because they too may affect the seller's right to assign the technology.

Assuring Non-infringement

To address the possibility of infringement, a buyer should normally begin with a "novelty search" at the State Intellectual Property Office (SIPO) to obtain an authoritative opinion on whether the technology is new and inventive, two of the three criteria for patentability. This search could be beneficial to a buyer if the seller hasn't made the technology public and it is still suitable for patenting. The novelty search also identifies patents, patent applications, and publications, which can help the buyer determine whether a seller may have infringed upon third-party IP rights. China's Patent Office is generally thought to conduct in-depth and relatively complete novelty searches. Of course, such searches can be enhanced with searches in other patent offices around the world, particularly the US Patent Office or the European Patent Office.

2. STARTING THE IP ACQUISITION PROCESS

An IP buyer's first step in deciding whether Chinese IP is worth buying is to conduct the basic preliminary due diligence necessary for a non-binding bid or offer letter to be made. This may involve review of licenses and agreements, financial and manufacturing data, customer lists, and, most importantly, IP registration details. Most often this is done by the buyer's lawyers, who compare what the buyer wants with what the seller has to sell. Preliminary due diligence will usually not include everything in the subsequent disclosure information, which the seller will be asked to provide as the deal progresses.

A seller must determine what information can be disclosed at this early stage. When the seller is offering the IP out to tender, he may have to set up a data room where, after the necessary non-disclosure agreement is signed, potential purchasers can review relevant information. In our China fieldwork experiences, we have learned that the more you prepare in advance of any trip to the seller's office to conduct the preliminary assessment, the more likely it is you will have something to work with once you arrive. It is also very important to ask for particular individuals to be present at the site during your visit, so that you don't waste time dealing with people who are either unable to answer your questions or are not authorized to provide you with the information you require. Planning and preparation are the key to successful preliminary fieldwork.

3. NEGOTIATION

Once the preliminary due diligence for bidding purposes is completed, the parties are in a better position to begin hammering out a deal. At this point, heads of terms may be drawn up and could culminate in a binding letter of intent or a binding offer bid if the buyer's valuation is completed. A formal offer is made (which may be binding), but the offer and acceptance will be subject to a formal written contract.

4. VALUATION

How can IP be valued in order to come up with an offer? IP valuation has always been somewhat of a black art, with various valuation models available. Two common factors do, however, seem to be included in most of these—namely, marketability of the IP and revenue generation potential. This is a highly specialized area for experienced accountants only.

A market approach to IP valuation asks whether IP purchased will be used in an existing and growing market or a new market. IP will be more highly valued where the market is already clearly identified and there is more certainty that the goods/services will sell. An obvious example would be a patented product for increasing the shelf life of fresh foods, where the market is clear and sales predictable enough to project forwards. This is less true of new market sectors (such as a unique new design for a beverage container) where uncertainty as to success and market acceptance creates more risk.

Measuring revenue generation is referred to as the income approach to valuation. A buyer would look to existing licenses or other agreements the seller enjoys to determine the value of the IP to be acquired. From this review, royalties/license fees can be anticipated, future licensing possibilities can be explored, and use of the acquired IP for other purposes/applications can be considered. In terms of patent/technology acquisition, valuation based on bringing such assets into your business, particularly in regards to improving your existing technology, is called the cost approach.

Once marketability and/or revenue generation is ascertained, any discounts for risk are considered. Here, due diligence (described below) will lead the buyer to an assessment of third-party rights that may conflict with those being purchased, potential litigation, or defective IP. Territories where the IP will be used need to be especially scrutinized for known revenue-generating value, IP defects, potential disputes, or other problems. Value should be recalculated to reflect the risk. All this can drive down the purchase price.

5. DISCLOSURE

Preliminary due diligence in order to offer a bid is normally controlled by the seller. After bids are accepted and the parties exhibit genuine deal-making sentiment, the buyer begins a much more detailed request and scrutinization of more of the seller's information. Due diligence will cover both commercial/financial disclosures, as well as legal disclosures (see the appendix to this chapter).

The core IP due diligence information will begin with the registration details of the various IP rights, including the territory where registered, registration number (or application number if the registration is pending), goods/services covered (for trademarks), renewal/annuity details, registered proprietor's name, and so on. After this should follow details of licenses or other encumbrances, including copies of any such agreements (though sometimes these will be provided only under terms of confidentiality). Patent disclosure will relate to the identities of the relevant inventors and whether they have assigned the inventions to the vendor, laboratory notebooks and other records of the date of the invention, and any details of claims for remuneration by inventor employees together with details of all licenses entered into relating to the patented technology. These licenses may include licenses-in of third-party technology necessary to make full use of the invention, and licenses-out to third parties which may be on terms that could affect the commercial attractiveness of the deal. Copyright information should include creation history and author details, including copy agreements relating to commissioning works. Other IP rights may exist of which the seller may be unaware. A savvy buyer will request information on domain names, common law unregistered passing off and unfair competition rights, confidential information/trade secrets, foreign language marks, all lapsed and abandoned IP rights, and brand descriptors/brand extensions. These should all be added to the overall property being acquired and be specifically set out in the sale and purchase agreement. However, in practice, even at the documentation stage, the parties are likely still to be arguing over what is included and what is not. This is especially likely when the seller is retaining some segment of the market for himself.

6. DUE DILIGENCE

According to the Chinese, "sharpening the axe before chopping the tree is not a waste of time." In the context of intellectual property, due diligence is critical. This should include not only review of the status of registered rights, but also an analysis of previous transactions and other relevant agreements that may affect what can be done with the IP.

Due diligence must consider all disputes and litigation related to the IP, including IP registry actions by trademark, patent, copyright, and industrial design offices in each jurisdiction where the IP is registered. Contested IP may come at a lower price, but a buyer may be precluded from using that IP or may be sued for using it upon acquisition. This needs to be addressed and settled long before the signing of any acquisition agreement, and it is unwise to rely solely on indemnifications.

Additionally, the IP itself may not be completely sufficient on its own to market goods/services in a particular territory. For example, there may be necessary regulatory permits or product certifications or accreditations that should flow with the IP from the seller to the buyer. This is normally true for IP covering food, beverage, pharmaceutical, nutritional, and personal care items. There may also be valuable know-how, associated materials, or technical knowledge related to the IP for use in manufacturing products or dealing with customers. This needs to be identified, verified, and included in the acquisition. If such know-how, etc., is transferred only by way of license, it is best to understand who else will be allowed to use it, where, and under what terms.

Patents will require an assessment of the technology in question by the buyer's patent attorneys and an analysis of the strength of the patents to be acquired. Patent mapping can identify related technologies and current competitors, as well as key inventors in the field (buyers may want to recruit them) and, through forward citation mapping, who will be a future competitor.

The amount of time required to complete the due diligence depends on the amount of disclosure and the depth of investigation the buyer thinks necessary and the seller thinks reasonable. The exercise itself culminates in the production of two very important documents. First is the Due Diligence Report prepared by the buyer's counsel, which sets out in condensed format a complete picture of all the relevant information disclosed by the seller and obtained by the buyer's counsel. The Due Diligence Report will assess legal risks and liabilities so that a decision can be made whether or not to proceed. The second document is the Disclosure Letter, which is prepared by the seller's counsel and identifies the IP, defects in the IP, and any other risks. The Disclosure Letter often serves to limit the warranties set out in the sale and purchase agreement so that the buyer will be precluded (save for fraudulent misrepresentation) from taking action against the seller after the deal is completed.

7. DETERMINING THE TYPE OF IP TO ACQUIRE

Many times the type of IP that you want to acquire is a mixed bag of properties. It may be a registered right, such as a patent or trademark, which can be easily identified and verified by checking with the particular country registers where the IP is located. Or it may be an unregistered right, such as copyright, know-how, or common law rights to various enforcement options such as passing off. Determining the type of IP rights will assist in drafting the acquisition agreement, particularly in terms of the types of warranties you will demand from the seller. Specialist IP lawyers are often instructed in IP acquisition deals in China, because they are best placed to determine how far to investigate what the seller claims is valid and belongs to him. Chinese patent attorneys are best brought in to assess the claims of Chinese patents, which can be quite different from any English-language corresponding patents that were the likely basis of their Chinese counterparts.

8. OBTAINING FURTHER ASSURANCES

If, after the due diligence is completed, the buyer isn't fully satisfied with the due diligence disclosure, or if questions remain unanswered, a buyer may want to obtain statements from the seller and, if necessary, from the relevant technicians. Such statements would confirm that all disclosures made during the course of the due diligence are true and would indemnify the buyer against liability for infringement of IP rights if such an infringement stems from something that wasn't disclosed or was disclosed incorrectly.

After obtaining these statements, the parties can draft an acquisition agreement to keep the deal alive. In the case of restricted technology, however, such an agreement doesn't take effect until the government approves it. This isn't the case for free technology: the acquisition agreement can be drafted and executed and will serve as the basis for the government review required as part of the process to register the agreement. Technology classifications are further discussed in Chapter 10.

9. THE AGREEMENT

Agreements usually used when IP rights are acquired are either the sale and purchase agreement (sometimes called the asset purchase agreement) or the share purchase agreement. Such agreements are normally divided between the terms and the schedules. Usually the seller pushes out the first draft agreement for the buyer's counsel to consider. Boilerplate terms would include definitions, completion details, consideration, seller's and purchaser's warranties, non-compete clauses (if certain territories/markets are retained), liability, confidentiality, and further assurance. In an IP acquisition, the further assurance clause is often a key clause because it serves as the post-completion confirmation that the seller will continue to assist the buyer to achieve the terms of the agreement. This is normally called upon when IP registries may call for additional documentation, rather than just the assignment form, in order to accept the record of the assignment. Further assurance is also helpful when the buyer seeks to gather from a seller, or a seller's brand manager, more information regarding past use of the IP, which may be useful in proving reputation in any later passing off/unfair competition action.

The schedules to an IP acquisition agreement can be tricky. If the acquisition includes a number of IP rights (trademarks, patents, designs, copyright), then a schedule needs to be prepared for each type of asset. In terms of unregistered IP, schedules are of little help; counsel will have to re-enter the agreement, sharpen his or her pencil, and begin the arduous task of defining know-how or trade secrets to a degree sufficient that it may be recognized.

Transitional arrangements may be a necessary interim measure whereby a buyer can easily move into the seller's business. These arrangements are best decided at the time of negotiating the acquisition agreement, rather than later on, as often a seller will be less amenable to making a buyer's life easy after an agreement has been signed and the check cashed. Transitional arrangements also are likely to involve parties other than the buyer and seller, so be vigilant as to who else should be brought in for discussion/agreement on what is decided.

The warranties, though normally boilerplate, may be an area where certain loose ends can be tidied up. Internal/external license termination letters, novations, extensions, and so on, can be dealt with later, but they should be specifically mentioned in the agreement and guaranteed to be actioned in whatever way has been agreed in the warranties section. The same is true for employee confidentiality obligations or restrictive covenants in employee contracts. If the acquisition involves the taking on of existing staff who are under confidentiality obligations from the seller, carrying these on through to the benefit of the buyer should be specifically addressed in the warranties section of the agreement.

10. POST-COMPLETION ISSUES

After the acquisition agreement is signed, there is still a considerable amount of work to do. The IP that has now been assigned must be communicated to the TMO and Patent Office so that these authorities can update their records to show the details of the new owner. In China, it is important to do this quickly in case the new owner needs to enforce his or her rights against infringers. Until the new owner is identified in the TMO and Patent Office records as the owner, fast and effective enforcement won't be possible.

There may also be conditions subsequent to the deal that need to be taken care of. For example, if a condition subsequent to the signing of the acquisition agreement is that the seller will terminate all existing license agreements he or she has in place in China, then this needs to be prioritized and dealt with quickly so that the seller's licensees will be stopped from using the IP now belonging to the buyer. We have seen a post-completion undertaking from the seller to withdraw a trademark application uncovered during the course of the due diligence. After the deal was completed, the buyer didn't follow up on forcing the seller to comply with his promise and the trademark subsequently was registered. That trademark proved to be a blocking mark for a trademark the buyer was hoping to gain in China as he expanded the line of his goods. The situation was ultimately taken to the People's Courts and was eventually settled, but only after considerable time and legal expense.

After the dust settles, the buyer should conduct a full IP audit to confirm whether it may be necessary to expand coverage, especially of trademarks. If the acquisition included the right to take over ongoing disputes with infringers in China or abroad, then these need to be dealt with as soon as possible. There may be pending deadlines to respond to court or administrative actions, which the seller may not have disclosed to the buyer.

11. JUDICIAL SCRUTINY OF TECHNOLOGY ACQUISITION DEALS

Although China encourages Sino-foreign collaborations in technology creation and use, the PRC government has acted to tackle concerns about foreign misuse of Chinese technology. In December 2004, the PRC Supreme People's Court released an Interpretation on Certain Issues Regarding Laws Applicable to Trying Cases Concerning Disputes Involving Technology Contracts. The Interpretation seeks, in part, to help prevent the misuse of Chinese intellectual property by clarifying article 329 of the PRC Contract Law, which stipulates that a technology contract is ineffective if it illegally monopolizes the technology, impedes technological advances, or hampers other parties' technological creation. The Interpretation sets out specifically precluded provisions, such as anti-improvement clauses or tying terms in technology-related contracts, and obtaining other technologies competitive to that in the contract as well as other situations that, before the Interpretation, were never clear.

Improvements are an interesting issue and one that you should be aware of if yours is a technological business in China. Article 27 of the Technology Import and Export Regulations holds that improvements made by the Chinese party are owned by the Chinese party. This means that if your foreign-invested enterprise developed an improvement on a patent, then the FIE owns it. Is this what you want? If you want to obtain the ownership of IP in any improvements that your Chinese licensee/partner may develop, then this needs to be specifically dealt with in the relevant agreement. For example, you might agree to pay the Chinese improver some reimbursement for acquiring such ownership.

While there are creative ways around this (for example, by carving out "improvements" from a distribution agreement that concerns money remittances and setting this out in a separate agreement, or by providing for royalty-free license grant backs to you of the improvement), it is best to avoid it all together. You should be considering the likelihood of improvements that may occur during the course of your China deal.

A contractual party to a technology acquisition that finds itself unsatisfied with the deal may reasonably seek to challenge the contract based on the Interpretation. PRC courts will scrutinize these deals more closely now that more specific rules are available. Although how judges interpret the Interpretation itself may vary, it is important to note the growing policy emphasis on local innovation. Over the past few years, senior PRC leaders have sent clear messages that there must be more PRC innovations independent of foreign ownership. Moreover, judicial committees appointed by local officials still advise judges on important policy decisions, and it is likely that such committees are scrutinizing judges in cases involving technology acquisitions, particularly those in which the technology has strategic importance. As a result, prospective buyers should exercise extreme caution when considering this issue, and be aware that any assignment-back provisions normally acceptable in the West, whereby local innovations are assigned back to the licensor of the original technology, bear risks. How courts interpret such an assignment clause depends on the technology itself, the venue, and the extent to which the assignment clause meets the basic requirement of reciprocity and reasonableness between the licensor and the licensee.

One sign of the growing emphasis on local technological innovations is the anticipated toughening of China's "first filing" rule. Currently, article 20 of the PRC Patent Law states that inventions "made" in China by a PRC entity or individual should be "first filed in China." Currently, there is no penalty for failing to comply with article 20 (although there have always been concerns that this loophole would one day be closed or that such inventions may not be certified for transfer back to China). A draft amendment to the Patent Law made in July 2006 would subject the inventions of all entities and individuals in China to this requirement, including those developed by Sino-foreign joint ventures and wholly foreign-owned enterprises. The draft law would also direct the State Intellectual Property Office to reject patent applications that don't meet this "first filing" requirement, as well as expose for invalidation those patents that may later be discovered to have been developed in China, but were first filed overseas. If adopted, these proposed changes would have a significant impact on foreign companies that develop IP in China. Foreign companies interested in acquiring Chinese technology would have to ensure that the technology is filed first for patent protection in China so that it can receive protection if it is ever used again in China.

12. PROSPECTS

According to the Organization for Economic Co-operation and Development (OECD), China spent an estimated US$136 billion on R&D in 2006, more than Japan and second only to the United States. This reflects China's desire to enter the realm of innovative economies and, for foreign companies, presents opportunities to acquire new technologies for commercialization in China and abroad.

A savvy buyer knows that technology acquisitions in China must be approached with the same care and due diligence one would require of similar deals in other countries. This is particularly true now that the PRC government is seeking to address what it calls the "misuse" of Chinese innovations by plugging holes in the relevant legal framework. Barring any surprises, however, changes to rules on the acquisition of Chinese technology shouldn't discourage foreign buyers. The government's expanded support for technological development should lead to a wealth of choices for those hoping to acquire technologies in China.

CHECKPOINT

- If you are acquiring Chinese IP, have you conducted the necessary due diligence?
- Does the IP you are acquiring really contribute substantially to your business?
- Can the seller or licensor of the IP you want to acquire prove that they have the rights they say they do?
- Does your license agreement or acquisition agreement contain the necessary warranties and undertakings to protect you if something goes wrong?

RESOURCES

- http://english.ccpit.com: China Council for the Promotion of International Trade

- www.customs.gov.cn: General Administration of Customs
- www.aqsiq.gov.cn: General Administration of Quality Supervision
- www.mof.gov.cn: Ministry of Finance
- www.fmprc.gov.cn: Ministry of Foreign Affairs
- www.mofcom.gov.cn: Ministry of Commerce
- www.ndrc.gov.cn: National Development and Reform Commission
- www.pbc.gov.cn: People's Bank of China
- www.saic.gov.cn: State Administration for Industry and Commerce
- www.safe.gov.cn: State Administration of Foreign Exchange
- www.chinatax.gov.cn: State Administration of Taxation

APPENDIX: ESSENTIAL DUE DILIGENCE FOR THE ACQUISITION/LICENSING OF IP AND OTHER PROPERTY IN CHINA

1. Trademarks

The following is required in relation to trademarks:

1.1 A complete and accurate schedule of all the trademarks to be acquired under the agreement, noting:

   (a) jurisdiction (and in respect to International Registrations, each country)

   (b) trademark (including precise wording of full slogans and representations/images of device marks, non-alphabetic marks such as Chinese characters, Arabic, etc., as applicable)

   (c) class(es)

   (d) application number

   (e) registration number

   (f) status

   (g) last renewal date (with renewal confirmation)

   (h) next renewal date

   (i) registered proprietor (with confirmation that said proprietor is/is not a member of the seller/licensor and, if not, full details of said proprietor)

(j) license, assignment, or encumbrance status (with details as to parties, dates, territory, etc.)

1.2 Confirmations of any pending applications and supporting documentation.

1.3 Copies of all registration certificates.

1.4 Summary of the history of each country requested or each country.

1.5 Details of all lapsed/expired marks in the last five years.

1.6 Copies of any searches conducted for or on behalf of the seller/licensor that may impact the trademarks under consideration.

1.7 Copies of written or description of unwritten brand developments plans of the seller/licensor in regard to the trademarks.

2. Copyright

Copyright may subsist in any number of container/packaging/marketing materials/logos/trademarks/recipe compilations and books, etc. In regard to copyright, the following is required:

2.1 A full list of the copyright works, noting full details of:

(a) date of creation

(b) place of creation

(c) full name, citizenship, and contact details of author(s)/creator(s)

(d) current ownership of the copyright, identifying the full name and contact details of each owner

(e) the date of copyright acquisition

(f) the mode of acquisition of copyright (employment agreement, assignment agreement, copyright waiver, license, etc.)

(g) license, assignment, or encumbrance status (with details as to parties, dates, territory, etc.)

3. Designs

Designs (registered or unregistered) may subsist in packaging material elements, containers, etc. In regard to designs, the following is required:

3.1 A full list of designs, noting full details of:

(a) jurisdiction (and in respect to Hague Registrations, each country)

(b) design and image thereof

(c) Locarno class(es)

(d) application number

(e) registration number

(f) status

(g) last annuity/extension date (with payment confirmation)

(h) next annuity/extension date

(i) registered proprietor (with confirmation that said proprietor is/is not a member of the seller and, if not, full details of said proprietor)

(j) license, assignment, or encumbrance status (with details as to the parties, dates, territory, etc.)

3.2 Details of all expired/invalidated designs in the past 10 years.

4. Patents

With regard to patents, the following is required:

4.1 A full list of patents/patent applications, noting full details of:

(a) jurisdiction (and in respect to international registrations, each country)

(b) application number

(c) registration number

(d) status

(e) registered proprietor (with confirmation that said proprietor is/is not a member of the seller/licensor and, if not, full details of said proprietor)

(f) license, assignment, or encumbrance status (with details as to parties, dates, territory, etc.)

4.2 Copies of all patentability opinions rendered to the seller/licensor.

4.3 Copies of any searches to locate any patents of others with one or more claims that might impact the seller/licensor's products, services, or patent portfolio.

4.4 Copies of patent plans for or by the seller/licensor.

4.5 Copy of the seller/licensor's patent portfolio with the description of its products and services.

4.6 Copies of descriptions of current or past "design around" efforts by the seller/licensor in light of any patent rights of another entity or person.

4.7 Copies of any infringement assessments, freedom to operate (FTO) opinions, clearance opinions, or validity assessments regarding the patents.

5. Other intellectual property rights

5.1 In regard to other intellectual property or other rights, identification of the following is required:

   (a) Domain names—a list of all domain names owned, used, previously used, reserved, or previously reserved by the seller/licensor and the status of each. (Note: A domain name could incorporate a trademark, especially if there is a split brand.) Copyright in the content?

   (b) Common law, unregistered and unfair competition rights relating to the trademark(s). Rights in common law goodwill may need to be transferred.

   (c) Unregistered trademarks, logos, and/or business names relevant to the acquisition, including those in foreign languages.

   (d) Brand descriptors or brand extensions, or any other tag lines, sub-brands, and slogans that have been used with the trademarks.

6. Security over intellectual property

Are there any security interests, charges, mortgages, lieu, pledge, right of set off, or other encumbrances over any intellectual property to be transferred?

7. Other encumbrances

Are there any assignments, licenses (internal and/or third party) options, charges of any encumbrances, licenses, or other rights affecting the intellectual property? If so, full details and copies of any documents are required.

8. Third-party rights

8.1 If any third-party rights related to the intellectual property or any other property to be assigned are to be retained by any third party, then a detailed description of those rights, including identification of the relevant jurisdiction those rights relate to, is required. Copies of any and all relevant agreements regarding such third-party rights to the intellectual property or other property being assigned are required to the extent they are not confidential. If any such information is confidential in nature, then the sellers are required to disclose as much information as possible.

8.2 A complete and accurate list of all third parties with any interest in the intellectual property or other property being assigned globally is required, which should include, but not be limited to, all relevant seller companies, the manufacturers, and any others. Please supply details of which rights they have and the source of those rights, and provide any relevant documentation relating thereto, including any agreements that will be terminated prior to completion and any that will be terminated after completion.

9. Assignment forms

Forms of draft assignments to be used on completion for the intellectual property and other property to be transferred are required.

10. Trading names

Are there any companies in the seller's group incorporating the mark in their trading name? If so, full details are required.

11. Litigation and disputes

In regard to litigation and/or disputes relating to the intellectual property or any other property to be assigned, the following information is required:

11.1 Complete and accurate details of any actual, pending, or threatened litigation and/or disputes including, but not limited to, information as to parties, nature of dispute, jurisdiction, cause(s) of action, status, etc.

11.2 Complete and accurate details of any trademark opposition, invalidation, cancellation, or other proceedings filed or pending.

11.3 Complete and accurate details of any agreements or settlements affecting right to use the intellectual property or other property to be assigned, including copies of any such agreements/settlements to the extent that these are not confidential.

11.4 Complete and accurate details of any court, administrative, or other judgments, including copies of any such agreements/settlements to the extent that these are not confidential.

11.5 Details regarding the well-known or famous status of any of the trademarks to be assigned, including identification of jurisdiction and a copy of such status designation.

11.6 Complete and accurate details of any domain name dispute(s).

12. Regulatory issues

Food, beverage, pharmaceutical, nutritional, and personal care items require regulatory approvals/product registration/product accreditation certificates in most countries. A list of all countries for which regulatory approval has been obtained or applied for, but not yet obtained for each of the products, along with a copy of such approval (with English translation as appropriate) is required.

13. Know-how, associated materials, technical knowledge, etc.

Know-how, associated materials, technical knowledge, or other additional information relating to the use of the intellectual property, manufacturing of the products, customers, etc., may be assigned or made available to the purchaser. In regards to such information, the following is required:

13.1 A complete and accurate list of all items to be assigned/made available and, subject to any seller's requirements on confidentiality, a full copy of each of these sufficient for the purchaser to assess/verify.

13.2 Assignment/license form or other instrument by which such information will be transferred to the purchaser.

13.3 If copyright subsists in any of the information to be assigned/made available to the purchaser, full copyright details (see Section 2 above).

13.4 If the seller will retain current usage rights, or if future usage rights are reserved, please identify in full detail the nature and extent of such current and/or planned use.

13.5 If any third party will retain current usage rights, or if future usage rights are reserved for any third parties, please identify in full detail the nature and extent of such current and/or planned use. Identification here must include identification of any non-authorized disclosure to third parties.

13.6 Confirmation as to whether any software or computer programs are included in the information.

13.7 To the extent that any of the information to be transferred is confidential in nature and must be maintained as confidential in order to enjoy confidential information/trade secret protection, exact identification of such type of information is required.

14. Employees

Employees of the seller/licensor may have some impact on the intellectual property to be acquired and, in this regard, the following information should be requested:

14.1 Lists and full details of technical and R&D personnel among the employees.

14.2 Copies of any employment agreements of the seller/licensor for individuals having access to the IP.

14.3 Copies of any (including settled, ongoing, pending, and threatened) disputes, settlements, claims demands, civil actions, arbitration, and administrative proceedings in relation to IP issues (such as ownership, attribution, reward of invention regarding company's equipment, products, technology and other IP, confidentiality obligation, training and non-compete obligation) between the seller/licensor and any employee, with a detailed explanation of the situation.

15. Seller/Licensor structure and its competitors

In regard to the seller/licensor's structure, the following information is required:

15.1 A description of the seller/licensor's business, including its products and/or services.

15.2 A description of the seller/licensor's planned future products and/or services.

15.3 An internal organizational chart of the seller/licensor along with (1) a description of the respective internal organization's responsibilities, and (2) a description of the main products and business activities of the seller/licensor.

15.4 A schedule of all connected/associated and subsidiary company-related companies, including (1) a description of the main scope of business of each, and (2) identification of each common company shareholder along with that common shareholder's relevant contribution and shareholding proportion.

15.5 Identify all significant competitors for each of the seller/licensor's products and services, whether current or anticipated.

15.6 Regarding the seller/licensor's competitors, obtain descriptions of any significant IP-related litigation or other IP-related dispute in the seller/licensor's area or involving a significant competitor of the seller/licensor's and of which it is aware even if the litigation or other dispute does not involve the seller/licensor directly.

16. Trade secrets and security measures

In regard to trade secrets, the following information is required:

16.1 Identification of all relevant trade secrets of the seller/licensor and sufficient description of each (can be disclosed by way of a non-disclosure undertaking).

16.2 A description of any and all specific measures the company has taken for the purpose of protecting and maintaining confidentiality in its trade secrets, including manuals or other written guidelines.

16.3 Copies of any confidentiality agreements, non-disclosure agreements, and any other agreements by which the company has agreed to maintain certain information secret and/or binds another entity or person to maintain certain information in secrecy.

17. Product formulations

17.1 Are there any specific product formulations related to the branded products? If so, how does the seller plan to make the product formulation available to the purchaser (that is, by way of assignment, license, included in know-how, associated materials, technical knowledge, or otherwise)?

17.2 A copy of the formulation for each of the products is required.

17.3 If the seller retains rights to allow others to use any product formulation, full details of the nature of such use including, but not limited to, user identification, jurisdiction, and product identification is required.

18. Manufacturing

In regard to manufacturing of the products, the following information is required:

18.1 A list of all current and past manufacturers of the products.

18.2 Copies of the current manufacturing contracts.

18.3 A list of all current and past label and packaging printers, including printing plate and mold ownership details.

19. Customer lists

Identification of customers/shops/outlets/wholesalers, etc., is often a part of the commercial due diligence.

20. Territory

Territory identification is critical if the acquisition is non-global.

21. Other owners of the intellectual property

When the acquisition is non-global, identification of others' retaining rights to the intellectual property is important.

22. Transitional arrangements agreement

If any transitional arrangements are necessary, full details are required.

23. Agent details

Full contact details of each of the seller's agents in each relevant jurisdiction are required. This is critically important if assignment forms (see Section 8 above) are to be delivered post-completion.

24. Government funding

24.1 Obtain description of any projects financed or otherwise supported by any government (including any past, current, and potential ones), including any commitments, liabilities, and copies of all the relevant agreements or documents. A description of any projects cooperated on with any other third parties (including any past, current, and potential projects), including any commitments, liabilities, and restrictions undertaken by the seller/licensor under these projects, and copies of all the relevant agreements or documents.

The world's factory: Sourcing from China

1. SETTING THE SCENE

We live in an age where many companies don't know where their products are actually manufactured, as a result of the use of sourcing agents, licensees, and distributors with manufacturing rights. We have come across many examples of companies that have suffered damage due to loss of their valuable intellectual assets in China, losses which could have been prevented had they taken simple steps to protect their investment. As the US Chamber of Commerce's "No Trade in Fakes Supply Chain Tool Kit" comments, "Counterfeiters prey on weaknesses in the legitimate supply chain." Companies that fail to take steps to protect their supply chain in China run a much higher risk of infringement of their IP.

A few typical scenarios will set the scene.

A branded licensee's products were found in the market in Guangzhou, despite the fact that the licensee's rights covered only North America. The licensee, citing the different item codes, denied ownership of the products. On further investigation, it was found that the products were in fact the licensee's, but the labels were from an earlier range, both sourced from the same supplier in China. The supplier was contacted and initially claimed that the products hadn't come from its factory. On seeing the evidence, however, it admitted that the products did appear to have come from its factory, but claimed that employees had been taking the waste products from the factory in parts, finishing the products at home, and then selling them into the market. Although skeptical that this was the case, the brand owner worked with the licensee and the factory to put processes in place to ensure that it wouldn't happen in the future. Six months later, more of the licensee's products were found in the market, and in greater quantities. Rather than approaching the licensee immediately, the brand owner conducted a covert investigation into the supplier and found that the factory was selling all the waste, sub-quality products as well as overruns to a door-to-door trader who would go around to all the factories collecting these types of products, which he would then sell into the wholesale markets. In fact, because this was an easy way for the factory managers to supplement their income, the factory was manufacturing up to the maximum waste allowed under its agreement and selling this to the trader. The factory denied the sales, despite the evidence, and the brand owner rejected the factory as an authorized supplier for the licensee, leading the licensee to have to identify an alternate factory and the initial factory to lose the licensee's business.

In a second example, a European company sourced branded lighting from China, but hadn't registered its trademark there. A Chinese company registered the trademark and threatened to take action against the European company for trademark infringement, which could have prevented the European company from sourcing its product in China. A solution was negotiated, but it cost the European company a substantial amount of money and time.

Finally, a law firm was instructed to raid a suspected counterfeit factory in Nantong. A large quantity of counterfeit product was seized, but during the raid the factory showed officials a purchase order from a Nantong trading company. It turned out that the client was sourcing product from this trading company. However, eventually (after a lot of red faces), the client confirmed that these products weren't authorized. The factory had been producing extra quantities and selling them out the back door.

The good news is that China is now predictable enough that companies can, and should, plan to avoid these scenarios by taking control of their supply chain. The damage suffered by these companies could have been prevented with some forward planning and closer management of their supply chains in China.

2. KEY RISK AREAS

In the past, companies weren't so concerned about "midnight runs" of their products being sold into the Chinese market by their own suppliers, or about whether their trademarks were registered in China, because they weren't conducting business there. China was seen as a sourcing center, rather than as a business opportunity. This meant that many companies didn't want to spend the money required to take precautionary steps to protect their IP in China, and didn't see keeping the market clean of fakes as a high priority. As one IP counsel joked, "One upside of the widespread infringements we faced in China was that we had quite a high brand awareness before we even launched here! Not for the right reasons, though." However, as companies are now seeing China as a huge business opportunity, and as Chinese companies are stretching their wings and becoming more global and using more technology, foreign companies are struggling to recover trademarks and rights they failed to protect in the past.

There has also been a move by counterfeiters toward selling to the buyers of unauthorized products sold out the back door of factories. In this way, counterfeit products are mingled with unauthorized genuine products, making them more difficult to detect and easier to get to market. If companies can control their supply chain, they reduce the demand for unauthorized products and therefore possibly counterfeits as well.

The following are some of the common issues to watch out for:

- *Factories subcontracting production to a smaller, less reliable factory with lower awareness of IP issues:* When factories are busy, they may subcontract their smaller orders to another factory. Many manufacturers have a "showcase" factory, which they show potential customers when they visit, but in reality the products may be manufactured in a smaller factory nearby with few facilities and often terrible labor standards for workers. In one extreme example, the factory visited appeared to be new, with none of the usual signs one would expect to see in a factory in operation, such as scraps, photos of workers' families, and waste products. The actual production site turned out to be a prison nearby. The "factory" had been set up for the inspection.

- *Outsourcing production of designs, labels, molds, and other supplementary elements of manufacturing to third parties without confidentiality agreements or IP assignment agreements in place:* This is one of the key risks of infringements, as there is no control over the use of the IP or the systems in place to protect it.

- *Factories supplementing income by selling excess products out their back door, whether it is waste product, sub-quality products, overruns, or midnight production runs:* Apart from the obvious quality risk of sub-standard products being sold into the market, companies lose control of the channels through which their products are sold (which may be in breach of their agreements to distributors and also risks misalignment with their brand strategy).

- *"Me tooing" of products (that is, copying of another product or design with minimal changes):* This is a particular risk when using a sourcing agent, but it applies equally to companies that select products from a supplier's catalogue or at a trade fair. The risk is that your sourcing agents or suppliers will take a product they have seen in the market or produced for another customer and copy it with your branding, which may infringe that customer's IP rights. Companies need to take steps to ensure that the products they source from China are free from infringements of a third party's rights. A number of companies mentioned during discussions that they have had to turn down opportunities in China involving products designed by local companies, due to the fear that the products had been copied and potentially infringed a third party's rights.

3. THE SOLUTION

A comprehensive supply chain strategy for protection of IP in China involves three key stages, similar to those required for any IP management strategy in China.

1. *Pre-sourcing:* Before selecting any sourcing company in China, it is important to conduct appropriate due diligence into its operations to ensure that it is a good fit with your company's expectations on IP protection. You also need to ensure that you get your own IP in order by registering it, conducting an IP audit of your complete supply chain, working out how much IP you need to send to China, and putting systems in place to protect it.

2. *Building a relationship and negotiating strong contracts with suppliers:* It is important to have strong IP protection

terms built into your standard terms and conditions of supply, as well as clear expectations of agreements with all levels of the supply chain.

3. *Managing the relationship with your supply chain in China:* There is a Chinese saying: "The mountains are high and the emperor is far away." Having some mechanisms in place to ensure that your suppliers respect your IP is critical when sourcing from China.

Many companies are strong on building relationships and negotiating strong contracts with clients, with some due diligence undertaken. Once the agreement is signed, however, they assume they can trust their supplier and that all is on track. This is often not the case. All three stages of protection are critical.

Pre-sourcing: What Due Diligence Should Companies Conduct?

Before trusting any company in China to manufacture or source products, it is important to conduct appropriate checks to ensure that the supplier can meet the customer's expectations.

Are You Looking for a Supplier or an Agent?

Prior to deciding on the best way to source products, it is critical to be clear about the role of the company you are looking for: are you looking for a factory or an agent? There are benefits of each, and your choice will depend on the nature of your business, your structure, your product, and your objectives.

One foreign company asked a Chinese firm for a report on the risks in their supply chain for their merchandising program. They were asked to provide a list of their factories in China so that visits could be arranged to conduct an audit of their processes. The Chinese firm named about 35 companies, the majority of which turned out to be agents based in Hong Kong. When this was pointed out, the firm was insistent that those named were in fact its factories. After six months of investigating and then conducting an audit of the entire supply chain, it was found that nearly 400 factories in China were involved in manufacturing the foreign company's products! This example highlights the risks of appointing a "factory" from a distance without further investigation and management of the relationship.

What Extra Precautions Should You Take When Coming to China on Trade Missions?

Many companies identify their trading partners in China by attending a trade mission organized by their home government's trade authority or other organizations associated with China. Trade missions can be an effective way to meet potential partners, and there are many examples of successful relationships with Chinese companies that started this way. However, it is important to be aware of the risks. It is not unusual for a foreign company, after having entered into a business arrangement with a Chinese company introduced in this way, to find that the local company is unable to deliver the products or services it has been contracted to provide. If a foreign company is introduced to a prospective Chinese partner by a government authority, extra due diligence is necessary. Often these introduced companies are years behind in their technology and are still at least partly state-owned, creating a conflict for government agencies who may be trying to bring in business to keep the company going.

How Can You Conduct Due Diligence into Potential Suppliers?

There are a number of ways to obtain information on potential suppliers; some overt, others more covert. Obviously, one of the best ways is to visit the potential supplier and ask them some questions. This will enable you to get a sense of their reliability, as well as to begin to build a relationship with them.

As with any business relationship in China, the key is the quality of the relationship that can be built with your supplier. Spending time discussing with them their views on IP and the risks associated with exploiting it in China will not only assist the relationship, but will also give you an idea of your potential partner's depth of understanding of the issues surrounding IP. Universal Pathways, a small Australian company that supplies horse transportation, decided to source horse trailers from China and immediately set up visits to potential suppliers. In this way, they began developing a relationship with their suppliers straight away, while also learning about the associated risks.

It is also possible to instruct a consulting company in China to conduct an investigation for you. There are some excellent consultancies in China who are able to prepare professional reports for a reasonable fee. The best way to select a consulting company is to approach your country's embassy in China, your government trade authority, or another China business council for a recommendation. Always ask for a reference from the consulting company first, to ensure they are reputable. There are many examples of foreign companies relying on a local consulting company that proved to be unaware of the IP issues that were of concern to the foreign party, and of how to investigate, legally and ethically, a local supplier. If you have been introduced to a supplier through a third party, be aware that the introducer may be taking a cut for the introduction, or may have a relationship or connection with the supplier; thus you won't get an accurate picture from them of the supplier's capabilities and any associated risks. It is preferable to use an independent company to conduct your due diligence.

Some companies opt for a covert investigation as well, to obtain further information about their potential partners. This may include sending an investigator, posing as a buyer, to visit the company. The investigator's intention may be to see if the company is willing to accept an order to supply a product that infringes the potential customer's IP, or to get more information on the labor conditions in the factory.

What Questions Should You Ask During the Due Diligence Process?

The following questions will provide valuable information about a potential partner:

- *Is the company properly set up? Is it solvent? What is its business scope?* In China, companies are only permitted to conduct business within the limited scope of their business license. It is critical to ensure that your potential partner has the authority to conduct the business for which you are contracting with it. Some information can be obtained by reviewing documentation provided by the company—for example, its financial information and business registration certificate. While it can be quite difficult to obtain public information about companies in China, as there are no central authorities and information is often incomplete, this is changing and information is becoming more readily available. Business license information can usually be obtained from the local company registry office (the Administration for Industry and Commerce, or AIC). The amount of information available on the file will depend on the AIC's willingness to release it and the location of the supplier.

- *Is the company reliable? What references can they give you? What other international companies have they worked with?* This information can be very telling. A number of companies have commented that if a potential supplier works with Disney, for example, they are much more likely to want to work with that company as Disney's standards are known to be high and their factories are generally well-respected and trustworthy.

- *What is the supplier's awareness of and track record with managing intellectual property rights? Do they own their own brand or other IP?* Registered IP can be confirmed with the relevant authorities. In one IP audit, the factory was asked what systems were in place to protect their customers' IP. Their response was: "Oh, the Chinese government does everything to protect it. We don't need to do anything." Another factory, when asked if they knew what IP was, commented that it wasn't relevant to them because they didn't manufacture DVDs or Louis Vuitton® products. Needless to say, neither of those companies received orders from the company involved!

- *How many subcontractors will they need to use? Do they have contracts with their subcontractors that contain IP provisions?* Often suppliers don't think of using outside mold developers, labels and packaging suppliers, and designers as subcontracting. But if they need to use third parties, they will be sharing the customer's IP and therefore steps need to be taken by the customer to ensure the supplier is aware of their expectations. During the due diligence, it is advisable to get a sense of the factory's capabilities and of how many third parties will be required. It is also important to identify with the supplier their capacity for production, and to ensure that they understand the customer's expectations in regard to using subcontractor factories for production of the orders.

- *Where is the factory located? Is it in a known counterfeiting "hotspot"* (that is, an area known for protectionism and/or where there are significant numbers of small factories benefiting from "economies of scale" allowing raided factories to rely on neighboring factories to fulfill orders)? *Is it an area where the authorities are alert and active in protecting IP? Is it an area with a high awareness of IP?*

- *What are the factory's processes and procedures for managing IP? How much quality control monitoring do they have? Do they have waste management processes in place?*

The extent of the customer's investigations and due diligence will depend on the type of product being manufactured, as well as the industry, the ongoing scope of the relationship (is it a one-off order or an ongoing supply?), and the type of IP involved. Obviously, more intensive due diligence is recommended if technical IP or confidential information is necessary to manufacture the products.

How Can You Protect IP during Discussions with Potential Suppliers?

When talking to any potential supplier, one of the first steps is to ensure that they sign a confidentiality agreement before any information is disclosed to them. Some companies raise concerns about asking a potential partner to sign a legal document before they have built up a level of trust, believing that this may have a negative impact on the potential for the relationship. In our experience, having a short letter form agreement in English and Chinese that simply sets out the expectations and obligations of both parties in relation to each other's confidential information can have a positive impact on the discussions. The scene is set for productive and frank discussions if the parties have a mutual agreement that places the same obligations on them both, and which clearly expresses their desire to work together and to respect the information being shared, while also highlighting the importance the foreign party places on protection of its IP. If the Chinese party refuses to sign such an agreement, claiming that it indicates a level of distrust, we would question their motives and whether they are the type of company you would want to be working with in China.

One common risk is when companies send specifications to potential agents or factories in order to obtain quotations. Often these are sent electronically, and there may be no follow-up with the Chinese company. There have been a number of examples, usually in the clothing industry but not exclusively so, of suppliers manufacturing designs, despite not having been selected to do so by the brand owner, and releasing them into the market before the genuine range reaches the shelves. Unfortunately, unless you have people on the ground in China who personally visit potential Chinese suppliers with specifications to obtain quotations and don't leave copies of any confidential information with them, this risk cannot be eliminated. However, there are a number of steps that can be taken to minimize the risks:

- Reduce the number of potential companies to whom specifications and designs are sent. Carefully select potential suppliers before sending them any information, and make sure they have signed a confidentiality agreement.

- Don't send the entire specifications to potential suppliers. Assess the information that is critical for them to have in order to provide an accurate cost estimate, and limit what you send them accordingly. This is always a matter of finding a balance. As one person commented, "If I don't give them all the information, they can't give me an accurate estimate and I end up paying for it later." It is important to find an appropriate level of disclosure at this stage of the relationship.

- It is essential to follow up with any potential suppliers who aren't used, to request that they delete all copies of the specifications and designs from their systems (with confirmation that they have done so in writing) and reminding them of their obligations not to infringe the brand owner's IP. Putting them on clear notice of your company's rights, and indicating that action will be taken against them if they infringe those rights, ensures that you have a strong basis on which to take action if necessary.

At the end of the day, selecting a supplier in China is no different from selecting one anywhere else—common sense and a gut feel for the IP risks, as well as taking into account the IP environment in China, should help you to avoid issues arising later.

Is it Safer to Have a Number of Smaller Suppliers or One Major Supplier?

Each option has advantages and risks. The best option will depend on your products and industry. Having one major supplier enables you to build a strong relationship with them, to invest in the relationship, and to use the importance of your business to your supplier as leverage to incentivize them to comply with your IP expectations. However, it can also be a risky approach. For example, if your supplier is found to be infringing your IP, it will be more difficult and costly to move to another supplier. If you work with a number of smaller suppliers, more management time will be required to create the relationships with and to monitor all the suppliers. However, it can be an effective way to create competition between suppliers, and IP protection can be one of your key decision-making criteria.

Does OEM Manufacturing in China Infringe Local Trademark Rights?

OEM (or "original equipment manufacturing") refers to products manufactured in China purely for export. There has been a long-unsettled question as to whether this manufacture of products simply for export infringes a registered trademark in China if it is owned by a different company from the foreign customer of the OEM order. To infringe a registered trademark, a company must use the mark "as a trademark." If it is simply applying a trademark to a product to be exported and sold in a country where the foreign customer owns the mark, as in OEM manufacture, there is a very strong argument that this isn't trademark use. However, different courts in China have come to contradictory conclusions on this. If a foreign company hasn't registered its trademarks in China and finds its marks have been registered by a local Chinese party, it may find (as did the company in the example at the beginning of this chapter) that it is unable to source its products from China unless it is able to reach an agreement with the local Chinese party. There are numerous examples of companies that failed to register their trademarks in China, only to find that their OEM manufacturers then registered the marks and held the foreign companies to ransom by putting up the prices and threatening to sue the customer and their new supplier if they tried to source the products from a third party. Trying to recover trademarks is expensive and time consuming; and in the meantime, companies may be prevented from sourcing from any other factory in China.

While this issue remains unresolved, companies need to ensure they apply to register their trademarks in China before sourcing from there, regardless of whether they are simply sourcing products from an OEM manufacturer. If your trademark has already been registered in China by a third party and you wish to source from China, you will need either to get permission from the trademark owner through a license agreement or to start an action in the Trademark Office to cancel the existing registration.

Building a Relationship and Negotiating Strong Agreements with Suppliers

Are Face-to-face Meetings Valuable?

It is commonly commented, in relation to conducting business in China, that building a strong relationship with your suppliers is critical. This is very difficult to do without visiting China and meeting the suppliers face-to-face. Although this isn't always feasible, companies that don't make this investment upfront are more likely to face issues later. Universal Pathways, the Australian horse trailer supplier mentioned earlier, made a number of trips to China during the course of negotiations to meet with potential suppliers and to build up a relationship with the chosen supplier. As a small company, it saw this initial investment as critical to the success of its business in Australia.

Are Contracts in China Worth the Paper They Are Written on?

A strong contract forms the basis of any legal relationship anywhere in the world. In China, from an IP perspective, the contract is even more critical. It is the "relationship bible" and must set out very clearly the obligations and expectations of both parties. Although the legal system in China is still catching up with the pace of development, and Chinese parties are still coming to terms with the legal obligations associated with signing a contract, the situation is improving. Chinese parties see a contract as a reflection of the relationship today, which will change and grow in the future. They will understand the express obligations they are agreeing to in the agreement. However, anything omitted is "fair game," so be sure to cover every matter of importance expressly and clearly.

Chinese or English Agreements?

We strongly recommend having a Chinese-language version of all agreements. Although you can provide for the English-language version to prevail in case of inconsistency, the Chinese version will give both parties comfort. Foreign companies can be more confident that the Chinese party understands its obligations, and the Chinese party will be more comfortable with what it is agreeing to. Have an independent person review the Chinese version of the agreement—don't just rely on a translation provided by your supplier or agent.

Can You Use Your Standard International Agreement?

We are often asked whether companies should use their standard international agreements or create China-specific contracts. We have seen companies ask their Chinese partners to sign their standard 60-page, English-language agreement, which is subject to English law and hasn't been customized for use in China. We have also seen companies throw their standard agreements out the window and accept their local supplier's assurances that contracts aren't required in China, or they accept their agent's advice on a "standard Chinese version of the contract" which they never review. Both approaches come with a number of risks.

A standard international agreement is unlikely to be enforceable in China, as Chinese courts will rarely, if ever, agree to apply foreign law and it is close to impossible to enforce a foreign judgment in China. However, China has recently entered into a reciprocal enforcement of judgments treaty with Hong Kong, which will hopefully open the way for similar treaties with other countries in the future.

The Chinese party, keen to get the business, may sign the agreement without understanding it—and so won't comply with its obligations. Foreign agreements tend to have a lot of implied terms, which are commonly understood in common law jurisdictions. One of the challenges with China's young legal system is that much of the legislation adopts language from foreign jurisdictions, but doesn't yet have a business or legal culture underpinning it. For example, the meaning of the term "best endeavors" is highly debated and litigated in the UK and Europe, but there is as yet no equivalent case law or business meaning attached to the term in China. This leaves a key term open to interpretation by the parties, who come from very different cultural and business backgrounds. The common law term "hold harmless" also effectively has no meaning in Chinese. Rather than including vague terms that are open to interpretation, expressly include the actions you expect the Chinese party to undertake. A good example of this is sports sponsorship (which is discussed in more detail in Chapter 11). A clause in a Chinese sponsorship agreement that grants the sponsor the right to include logos in the stadium may mean that the sponsor ends up with logos behind the doors in the stadium toilets. There are examples of where this has happened, and the government authority involved has claimed, quite rightly, that the agreement didn't specify *where in the stadium* the logos would be displayed! The sponsorship industry in China is very new, and the authorities' understanding of sponsors' expectations can still be quite different to the sponsors' position on their rights.

There are obvious risks associated with accepting a Chinese agreement provided by the supplier or agent without obtaining local advice, or falling prey to the Chinese partner's assurances that there is no need for a contract and that the relationship is sufficient in itself.

The best approach is a combination of the two: start with an international-standard agreement—whether it be terms and conditions of supply, a manufacturing agreement, or an OEM agreement—and adapt it for use in China. It is critical to get local advice to ensure that the agreement is enforceable, and so that it provides a strong basis for your relationship with your supplier.

The following key IP provisions will need to be provided in the agreement.

Ownership of IP, use of IP, and protection of IP and confidential information

All of the usual IP protection clauses should be included in the terms of supply. If the products have been designed by your supplier, or bought from their catalogue, or sourced through a sourcing agent, make sure you obtain warranties as to ownership of the IP rights in the product and that the product doesn't infringe the IP rights of any third party, as well as an indemnity covering the costs of any losses the customer suffers globally as a result of an infringement claim.

Promotional use of customer's brands or company names by suppliers

Many Chinese manufacturers want to be able to include some of the products they have manufactured in their catalogues, in their sample rooms, on their Web sites, and in their booths at trade fairs. In some cases, this may be acceptable; in most situations, though, it should be avoided. Many suppliers will then accept orders for the products if requested to do so by a third party, regardless of the fact that they have no right to do so as the products contain a customer's IP. The agreement should always prohibit the use of your products or company name in promotional materials without prior written consent.

Subcontracting

If you allow a supplier to subcontract elements of production (for example, molds, labels, design, packaging, etc.), ensure that the agreement requires them to obtain approval for all subcontractors prior to providing them with any information.

It is also important that you require your suppliers to provide you with copies of agreements with each of their approved subcontractors that provide for assignment of any IP created by the subcontractors (for example, for molds, packaging, etc.), as well as including all necessary IP protection clauses.

Ownership of tooling

This is a critical issue that many companies overlook. There are two different types of tooling: (1) tools that are generally required for the products being manufactured and which don't contain any of the brand owner or customer's IP; and (2) tools that are specifically created for a particular customer's order and which contain the customer's IP (for example, silk-screens that contain the customer's brand, or molds that are specific to the customer's designs). A mold for an M&M's® Character dispenser, for example, will contain IP of Mars, Incorporated, owner of the M&M's® brand, because of the distinctive shape and design of the M&M's® Characters. However, the specifications of an umbrella won't contain IP owned by Mars, but the screen with the images of the M&M's® Characters will. Another example is the Happy Meal figurines at McDonald's—usually there will be IP in the figurines owned by the relevant brand owners.

Many companies neglect to provide for ownership of molds and designs in their agreement, and so the IP in these materials may in fact be owned by their supplier, allowing them to continue to use the molds or to lease them out to other suppliers. If tooling does contain the brand or IP owned by the customer, there are actions the customer can take to recover the molds. However, it is safer and easier to provide for ownership in the agreement. Usually, the more generic tooling (the first category above) will be owned by the factory.

For category (2) tooling, companies may need to pay for creation of the specific molds up front to ensure they own them outright. Other companies amortize the cost of the molds over the full value of the order, so that after an agreed number of products have been ordered, the customer will own the tooling. An alternative method, which is what most factories will do regardless of whether there is provision for ownership of molds in the agreement, is for the cost of the mold to be built into the cost of the products themselves. If this is the case, the factories are effectively charging the customer for creation of the mold, so the customer should ensure they obtain ownership of the molds. The value of these molds is significant. In some cases, molds have been leased out by factories for over US$10,000 per day to allow other factories to produce the relevant products and sell them without authorization. Companies need to provide expressly for ownership, control, and collection of molds in their agreements. Collection of molds is discussed further below.

Destruction of waste or substandard products

It is very common for factories to sell their waste products or overruns to discount traders, or to give them to staff in lieu of overtime. There are two schools of thought on the sale of these products into the market. Obviously, substandard or waste product runs the risk of poor-quality products being associated with the customer. However, in the case of overruns, some companies argue that they act as free marketing and promotion. In one respect, this may be true. On the other hand, the customer loses control over the distribution channels, and the way in which the products are sold and advertised. They may also be in breach of their agreements with distributors or partners in China by allowing these products into the market. In our experience, many agreements allow for a certain percentage of waste product or overruns and Chinese suppliers tend to produce right to this limit and then sell these products out the back door of the factory. As stated earlier, there are salesmen who trawl the factories buying these products.

The agreement with any supplier needs to provide expressly for the customer's expectations in relation to management of waste, overruns, seconds, and excess inventory. All waste should be destroyed. If it is possible for the trademark and any other IP to be removed from the products, some companies allow for it to be recycled. For example, plastic figurines may be melted and reformed into a different product. All overruns should either be destroyed or offered to the customer to purchase. Alternatively, some companies allow for the supplier to store these products for their next order, but if you allow this, you need to be sure that an additional order will be placed soon with this supplier for the same product or the supplier may, to save on storage, sell the products, assuming that the customer has forgotten about them.

Insurance

Product liability insurance is available in China and, given the recent issues on product liability discussed later in this chapter, is critical to obtain. Although your Chinese partner is likely to argue that it isn't available, this is because it tends to be quite expensive for Chinese companies. Ensure you include it in your agreement and review a copy of the policy, with your company named as a third party, before accepting products.

Audit rights

All standard manufacturing agreements provide for a right to audit the factory to confirm that it is complying with the terms of its agreement. It is important to provide a right for the customer's authorized representative to visit the factory, particularly during production of your order, to ensure that all the necessary steps for protection of your IP are being complied with.

Non-competition clauses

Non-competition clauses are generally valid under PRC law if they are considered fair and reasonable. If the products being sourced embody any technology supplied or licensed by you, then to a reasonable extent you may request a supplier or manufacturer not to divert, knowingly or directly, any of the products under your agreement to others without your consent.

If no technology is involved in the supply (technical contribution, know-how, patents, trademark license, etc.), then it would be unlikely that such restrictive covenants would be held valid by the People's Courts, due to the common public policy principle that every commercial entity should be allowed and given the opportunity to compete fairly with others. It is important to word your restraints very carefully so as to link them back to something of value you are contributing, to ensure you can enforce the clause later.

Indemnification

Indemnities for compensation from Chinese partners are generally valid under Chinese law if:

- the agreement is valid and enforceable under PRC law, meaning that the terms of the agreement are not in breach of any PRC law; and

- the indemnification compensation requested is not more than the actual damage caused to you. If it is, the Chinese party may ask the court to readjust or reduce the amount of such compensation requested. This is common in China.

In terms of liquidated damages, the People's Courts tend to like reasonable liquidated damages clauses because they help them assess value for damages payments. The PRC Contract Law has provisions for reducing liquidated damages if actual damages are "lower," as well as provisions for increasing liquidated damages if actual damages are "significantly higher."

Product recalls

Given the recent product liability issues (discussed later), it is important to set out the parties' responsibilities and the process in the event of a product recall, including who has the right to call a recall and who covers the costs.

What Type of Agreement Do You Need?

Whether you rely on terms and conditions attached to each purchase order, or whether you need a head manufacturing agreement, will depend on your relationship with the supplier. You may also need an OEM agreement or a separate design agreement. There are some key questions to ask:

- *Is this an ongoing relationship or a one-off sourcing order?* Some companies use an umbrella agreement to cover all future orders where they are working with a supplier for the longer term. If it is a one-off order, many companies use their standard terms. If you use standard terms, it is important to ensure they are reasonable or a court in China may not enforce them.

- *Is the supplier conducting any additional services—design, packaging, mold production—or is it simply manufacturing products?* If there are additional services being provided, or if subcontracting is required, a more comprehensive agreement is usually necessary.

- *What is the product? What types of IP are involved in its manufacture?* If the products are simple "off-the-shelf" products with brands applied, terms and conditions may be sufficient. If they are highly technical, obviously a much more comprehensive agreement is recommended.

- *How long have you worked with this supplier?* Some companies have used suppliers over a long period and are comfortable relying on short terms attached to each purchase order, as well as on the history of the relationship between the parties.

At the end of the day, what you call the agreement isn't critical, as long as you are comfortable that you have covered all your legal rights and that your IP is going to be sufficiently protected.

Managing Your Suppliers

Ongoing Relationship Building

The companies with the strongest supply chain management systems continue to build their relationships with their suppliers throughout the manufacturing process. If you have a committed, mutual relationship with your suppliers, they are less likely to exploit your IP without authorization. Ford, for example, spends a lot of energy on developing strong relationships with its suppliers. Joe Wiegand, global brand protection manager of Ford, comments in the *No Trade in Fakes* publication: "Our principal advantage is that Ford's relationship with suppliers is usually more important than anything they could establish on the side. So once we find inappropriate activity, the threat of losing Ford's business is usually enough to make a supplier reconsider its actions." They also put systems in place to ensure they are able to monitor, from a distance, the production of their order. There are a number of ways to achieve this: appoint a local agent to oversee the production process, or send representatives from your overseas office to monitor the manufacturing process, for example. However, these alternatives obviously add costs and are not always viable options. Another option is to require the factory to submit a series of reports that can be cross-checked to ensure the factory is respecting the customer's IP—for example, reports as to quantities manufactured, confirmation of destruction of waste, and so on. Although there are ways around these reports, they provide evidence if required against the factory and will put the factory on notice that you are watching them. If factories continuously produce surplus or seem to have unreasonable waste figures, this is cause for concern and companies should consider whether to continue using this supplier.

Create a "Win–Win" IP Relationship with Your Supplier

Investing in the relationship creates loyalty with suppliers, too. In our experience, Chinese suppliers are keen to find a competitive edge and many of the companies we have worked with pitch the IP protection mechanisms they expect their suppliers to implement as a competitive advantage. If suppliers have strong IP protection mechanisms, they are able to use this in their proposals to future customers—to explain the steps they have taken to ensure their customers' IP is respected. This can be a very powerful tool.

Something that has worked for some companies is providing an IP training pack for suppliers, which they can use with their employees. The pack includes a brief training presentation on "What is IP, and why is it important?", posters for display in the key areas of the factory reminding employees about IP requirements, and checklists of steps required to protect their customers' IP. We are occasionally asked, "But if we train the suppliers and their employees to recognize the value of IP, aren't we just encouraging them even more to steal it?" In our view, it depends on your commitment to the long-term resolution of this issue. If you put the systems in place to protect your IP and engage in education of your suppliers at the same time, the overall awareness of IP will increase, creating a more stable IP environment in which to conduct business.

Implementing some of these IP protection systems costs money for suppliers as well. If you are constantly driving down the price with your suppliers, they will look for other ways to supplement their income and this is often through midnight runs or selling overruns. It may also be the case if you force suppliers to purchase large quantities of component materials in anticipation of orders that you never send. And naturally, they will choose the products of those customers who have loose controls over their IP protection processes and toward whom they feel no or little loyalty. Of course you want to get the best price possible for your business, but keep in mind these possible consequences of paying your suppliers as little as possible while at the same time expecting them to implement systems to protect your IP.

Managing Raw Materials and Components

A key way of managing suppliers is to control the raw materials, component parts or labels, and packaging. A number of companies source labels separately and deliver a limited quantity to the manufacturer to be affixed to the products. For example, adidas provides its suppliers with just enough authentic trim to produce the order required. This way, it is able to monitor the quantities of products being manufactured by the supplier. New Balance, another global athletic products company, also supplies its manufacturers with labels that have an embedded code, making them difficult to copy. Through limiting the quantities of labels given to the manufacturer, it is able effectively to control the quantities produced and minimize unauthorized overruns or counterfeits. This also helps with producing accurate figures in audit reports. Be aware that factories may claim that additional labels were never received, or were destroyed or stolen, and be prepared to follow through on threats if they continue to be unable to account for excess labels.

Managing How Much Information You Give Your Supplier

As we explore in our next chapter, it is important to assess carefully just how much of your IP you need to provide to your suppliers in China. Many companies will choose to manufacture overseas components that require a lot of confidential information to produce internally; shipping them to, say, China to be assembled with the Chinese-made elements of the product. If the processes required are a part of your company's core competencies or embody critical confidential information, outsourcing production to China can be very risky. For example, many companies only outsource production of their older ranges of products. Their new and innovative products are manufactured internally to avoid infringement risks. If you do outsource production that requires sharing of confidential know-how with your suppliers, have systems in place (such as those outlined in Chapter 4) to minimize the risk that this information will be disclosed to third parties.

Anti-counterfeiting Devices

The use of technology to ensure product security is an increasingly viable option, with simple, low-cost solutions now available to help differentiate genuine products from counterfeits. For example, many companies are now using covert markings on packaging, or deliberate misspellings, to identify genuine products. There are also new, more complex technological solutions such as Radio Frequency Identification tags (RFID), which are attached to products to allow them to be traced and monitored, and fakes eliminated from the supply chain. RFID technology is being used in the pharmaceutical industry by Pfizer to trace and eliminate counterfeits of its often-copied Viagra® product, and by Purdue Pharma to protect its popular painkiller, Oxycontin®. Although this is an expensive option, it can be viable for products with high consumer safety risks, such as pharmaceuticals, or for high-end products such as watches. (Rolex has also trialed the technology.)

Other methods include holograms, watermarks, covert marks, micro-taggants, and anti-counterfeiting ink technology. Often a combination of these solutions is used. For example, one of the major sporting brands uses eight different solutions on its products and labels to assist with identifying counterfeits; some are open marks, while others are covert marks that are not made public and are known only to a handful of people within the company.

Even within one device—such as a hologram—there will be layers of anti-counterfeiting protection. For example, Nokia's holograms on its phone batteries have four layers: (1) the Nokia name; (2) the Nokia logo; (3) dot markings that vary when viewed from different angles; and (4) a unique 20-digit number that can be authenticated through Nokia's Web site. Provided access to the labels is carefully controlled, such a system provides a much stronger protection against counterfeits.

Activating Audit Rights

It is critical that companies activate the audit right in their terms and conditions, and yet only a very small percentage of companies actually visit the factories they use. We recall one visit to a factory for a pre-approval inspection for a client. We sat in the boardroom with eight senior management representatives of the factory. They gave a very impressive two-hour presentation on the steps they had implemented to improve their protection mechanisms for their customers' IP and tried to convince us of their understanding of the importance of IP to their customers. On the surface, they appeared to be a great factory. When we asked for a tour, however, they were initially reluctant. Eventually they agreed and our entourage headed off to the factory floor. As we wandered through the factory, we were dismayed to see old molds from previous orders thrown haphazardly in corners, and confidential specifications from previous customers stuck up on the walls. But the biggest concern was that there were workers in a small room out the back packing what appeared to be sub-quality products into boxes neatly lined up in batches of 100, with different brands in the same box. We asked the managing director what these products were being used for and, after a long, animated discussion with his staff in Cantonese, he tried to tell us that they were being taken to the recycling center to be recycled. Unlikely! Needless to say, the client didn't go on to work with this factory.

This example highlights the fact that it is important actually to visit the factories and not just listen to their standard spiel. Another one of our favorite stories was from a multinational company that was looking for a supplier of promotional items. The procurement director insisted on visiting a potential supplier. After a very impressive presentation and viewing of their sample room, he was convinced of the quality and experience of this company, which had worked with some major brand owners and produced some innovative promotional items. As the members of the party walked through the factory, a senior manager rushed up to the customer with a collection of samples and specifications in his hand. "Look, sir, we have just designed and made these for your competitor. This is their next six months of promotional items, which we will be manufacturing. You could copy these designs because they have paid for them already, and we can just put your brands on them. We can give you a better price," he announced with a very satisfied smile. "Ah, no. Thank you. I think I'll be leaving now," the customer replied.

Another company was sent a sample by its Chinese supplier of tin moneyboxes for approval prior to going to final production. The quality of the sample was excellent and the customer approved it. However, when the order arrived, the products varied substantially in quality; some could be used, while others were so badly made they had to be written off. In addition to not having sufficient quantity to fulfill its needs, the customer had additional costs associated with separating out those products that were usable from those that weren't. The customer had selected the factory using the internet and hadn't conducted any due diligence into the supplier, nor had it entered into any agreement with them. This meant that, at the end of the day, it had no recourse against the supplier other than to take its business elsewhere. Had the company sent a representative to visit the factory during production, or taken various other steps, the quality variance issues could have been avoided.

Whether you choose to audit prior to or during production of your order, or as a follow-up, will depend on your budget, the types of products involved, and how easy it is to organize someone to visit the factory.

There are a number of ways to manage these audits. If your company has a presence on the ground in China, it is relatively straightforward to send someone to the factory during production to oversee the quality and the processes. If you don't have a team on the ground, you could consider sending a representative from overseas. Many companies do this, seeing it as a relationship-building opportunity. Alternatively, if you have used an agent to identify the supplier initially, the agent will be able to follow up during production for you. Alternatively, there are agencies in China and in Hong Kong who will visit factories on behalf of clients. Before using one of these agencies, check their references and experience, and brief them on your expectations of the factory and their report. Your local trade associations should be able to recommend some Chinese agents to assist. Some companies simply ask a friend or contact who is living in China to assist, which is often a very cost-effective way of carrying out an audit!

Of course, as mentioned above, an audit is only useful if the figures are accurate. Injecting a control mechanism into the process (providing limited quantities of labels, for example) is thus recommended. Any discrepancies uncovered by your audit should trigger a penalty against the supplier, who should also have to pay your audit costs. These provisions should be expressly set out in your agreement.

Product Liability

In the summer of 2007, the image of China as the world's factory—able to produce just about anything quickly, cheaply, and to a high standard—came to a screeching halt. Spurred by the US media, revelations of countless examples of poor-quality or faulty products coming out of China's factories made the world stop and ask itself whether China's low prices were really worth being fobbed off with potentially harmful products. The number and types of shoddy products recalled in the US alone were astounding:

- faulty blade guards on electric saws that injure users;
- electric heaters filled with oil that sell for under US$50, but which catch fire;

- oscillating fans with faulty wiring that cause fires, burns, and smoke inhalation injuries;
- exploding air pumps;
- portable notebook computer batteries that burn users and destroy computers;
- baby carriers and baby swings that injure children;
- children's party hats and jewelry that pose choking hazards;
- toys containing high levels of lead paint, dangerous magnets, and parts that pose choking hazards;
- children's shoes and clothing with components that can detach, posing a choking hazard;
- Chinese fireworks that travel uncontrollably and in dangerous directions;
- toothpaste that contains diethylene glycol, an antifreeze agent (cough syrup containing this agent has resulted in the deaths of at least 96 Panamanians since 2006);
- cosmetics containing various toxins;
- fake pharmaceutical products;
- tainted pet food; and
- pesticide-laden food products, including farm-raised catfish.

Investigations by US media confirmed that, at least in regard to food and drug imports, China is considered a regular source of products containing carcinogens, illegal pesticides and additives, and other banned antibiotics and preservatives. The US Consumer Product Safety Commission has reported that as much as 60% of recalled goods in the US are Chinese-made. The usual course of action is for governments to return such products to their country of origin, but the same goods are often re-shipped or are sent to other countries with less onerous inspections.

Most experts believe that China's weak domestic system of inspection and product quality regulations, combined with the astronomic increase in production to feed the world's hunger for cheap goods, has resulted in a toxic brew of unsafe goods. The fact that Western consumers demand rock-bottom prices, which the multinationals then drive down to the Chinese manufacturers, certainly plays a role as well. In the EU, stringent product quality guidelines and zealous government product testing help to keep harmful goods off the shelves. In the US, which has less strict product quality guidelines and less government testing, it is the court system and the ability of injured consumers to sue for damages that helps keep manufacturers in check. China has a weak inspection regime and an even weaker tort system for suing manufacturers/distributors of harmful goods, and most industry analysts believe that the problem with unsafe Chinese-made products will get worse before it gets better.

Perhaps a positive outcome of 2007's product quality scandals in China is the fact that Chinese consumers are becoming increasingly aware of quality issues, which naturally leads to a greater understanding and appreciation of IP rights. Faulty products affect the Chinese, too. In 2004, at least 50 infants died when they were fed unsafe and fake infant formula; another 200 or so were left severely malnourished. In 2007, Zheng Xiaoyu, the former head of the State Food and Drug Administration, was sentenced to death after antibiotics approved on his watch were found to have been responsible for the deaths of 10 people before they were recalled from the market. Zheng was found to have accepted over US$800,000 in bribes and gifts from various drug manufacturers to fast track approval of the poisonous drugs. The court held that Zheng had failed in his duty to "make careful arrangements for the supervision of medicine production, which is of critical importance to people's lives."

As mentioned above, sourcing relationships work best when they are mutually beneficial. Choosing the right supplier, and communicating with them often and directly on quality assurance, will help to decrease the chances of being supplied with unsafe products.

What, then, are the issues with your selling goods in China? Are there product quality regulations of which you should be aware? How might your products be recalled in China? Given China's recent experiences with goods being rejected overseas, will awareness of product quality, and of consumers' rights against suppliers of harmful products, develop in China to a degree that will affect your business? Answers to these common questions about product liability are provided below.

Product recall

While there is currently no special product recall law in China, following 2007's product quality meltdown, the government quickly enacted a system to deal with food and toy recalls. There is talk among regulators of other goods to be added soon.

On August 31, 2007, the General Administration of Quality Supervision, Inspection, and Quarantine (AQSIQ) set up a system for tracking and recalling unsafe food and toys in the domestic Chinese market, as well as food and toy products for export. It followed an earlier system set up for defective cars on October 1, 2005. The recall system provided by the Regulations for the Administration of the Recall of Defective Automobile Products was planned to serve as a test bed for other sectors. Before automobiles, defective drug products were subject to recall under article 14 of the Rules regarding the Implementation of "Some Regulations on the State Supervision and Testing of the Quality of Products" of February 2, 1987.

The new mechanism means AQSIQ can force a food product recall for dangerous and unapproved foods, and issue a consumer alert if producers are negligent or if a food safety incident occurs. Toy manufacturers must stop making and selling toys that are unsafe by other countries' standards, even if they abide by Chinese laws and regulations. The recall systems are some of the most concrete steps Beijing has taken so far to address the ongoing product safety crisis. Some provincial regulations require the recalling of defective products upon the request of authorities in charge. For example, article 309 of the Regulations of the City of Shanghai regarding the Supervision and Control of Product Quality, dated August 26, 1994, holds that the authority in charge can order to "recover" a product that doesn't comply with state standards, industry standards, and local standards for the protection of life, health, and property.

Product liability

In addition to the recent recall systems for food, toys, and autos in China, there are important regulations covering product liability:

- General Principles of Civil Law of the PRC, effective since January 1, 1987 (the "General Principles");
- Product Quality Law of the PRC of February 22, 1992 (the "Product Quality Law"); and
- Law of the PRC on the Protection of the Rights and Interests of Consumers, dated October 31, 1993 (the "Consumer Protection Law").

None of these laws, however, provide specific procedures for product recall.

Some laws and regulations in China that address questions of product liability in general require sellers and/or manufacturers of defective products to minimize the damage potentially caused by such products. As the case may be, such obligations can also include the duty to recall defective products. In this context, in particular, the following regulations are particularly relevant:

1. The General Principles contain general provisions governing tortious liability. Article 122 of the General Principles states:

   > If substandard product causes property damage or physical injury to others, the manufacturer or seller shall bear civil liability according to law. If a transporter or shopkeeper is responsible for the matter, the manufacturer or seller shall have the right to demand compensation for its losses.

According to article 134 of the General Principles, the methods of bearing civil liability also include, among others, the "elimination of dangers." This phrase could be interpreted so that in a particular case the obligation exists to recall defective products if such a reaction is necessary in order to avoid any personal injury or damages.

2. Further, article 18, paragraph 2 of the Consumer Protection Law states:

   > A business operator which finds a commodity or service provided by it to have a serious defect which may cause harm to the safety of persons or the property of a consumer, even if such commodity or its service is used correctly, must immediately make a report to the relevant authorities, inform consumers and adopt preventative measures against such occurrence.

"Preventative measures" may also include the obligation to recall defective products if such recalling is necessary in order to prevent any harm to the safety of a person or to the property of a consumer.

Determination of whether or not a product is defective

Neither the General Principles nor the Consumer Protection Law contain a definition of "defect." However, article 34 of the Product Quality Law defines a defect as follows:

> For the purpose of this Law, the term "defect" shall refer to the unreasonable danger in the products where such danger threatens personal

safety or another's property. Where a product is governed by national or industry standards for protection of health or personal safety or the safety of property, the term "defect" shall refer to non-compliance of the product with the standards.

The "standards" referred to in the Product Quality Law are those that are found in the Standardization Law of the PRC, dated December 29, 1988, and its Implementing Rules dated April 6, 1990. The standards are set by the PRC central government, by provincial, autonomous, and municipal government authorities, and by industry authorities.

Specific recall action that must be taken

Pursuant to article 18, paragraph 2 of the Consumer Protection Law, action to be taken in case of the "provision" of defective products includes the making of a report to the "relevant authorities," information to be provided to the purchasers, and the adoption of additional preventative measures against any harm to the safety of a person or the property of any person that may be caused by the defect of the related product.

Further, the obligations to "eliminate dangers," as mentioned in article 134 of the General Principles, and to take "preventative measures," as mentioned in article 18 of the Consumer Protection Law, are meant to prevent any losses caused by defective products. Therefore, according to those provisions, everything has to be done that may, in a particular case, be necessary to prevent any harm to the health of a person or to his or her property. Such measures could include (as the case may be) provision of special instructions and advertisements—for example, in newspapers—if those endangered by the defective goods cannot be identified. Again, due to the lack of specific regulations, we advise that this be decided on a case-by-case basis depending on which specific measures are required.

Time period within which action must be taken

No specific regulation exists with regard to the time period within which recall action must be taken. However, taking into account the above, we normally advise that action be taken as soon as possible in order to avoid any damages or personal injuries.

According to article 33 of the Product Quality Law, the statute of limitations for product liability cases is two years calculated from the date on which the claimant knew or ought to have known that his or her right had been infringed.

Impact of product recall on potential liability

We are not aware of any statutory provision that may mitigate liability for personal injury or damage to property in the event that defective products are recalled. Action taken in this regard could, however, be taken into account by the courts or administrative authorities dealing with such matters. If in a particular case it would be necessary to recall a defective product in order to prevent any damages or personal injuries, and if damages or personal injuries are caused because the defective product wasn't recalled, then this could consequently lead to a liability for such damages or personal injuries.

Scope of liability

Liability for the manufacturing or sale of products that are substandard or defective isn't limited to personal injury or damage to property caused by such product. To the contrary, product quality liability appears also to include damage to the product itself (and damage caused by the product failing to obtain the required standard). For example, liability for a paint product wouldn't necessarily be limited to damage or injury caused where the paint was poisonous. It may extend to situations where, because of a defect or substance of quality, it peeled off and had to be removed and re-applied. The course of removing and re-applying the paint in that later situation would be recoverable by a third party without a need for a contract with the manufacturer.

Who is liable?

Product liability primarily falls on producers and sellers. Where sellers are sued, they are entitled to seek indemnity from producers. Where transportation or warehousing of the products leads to a product being substandard or ineffective, the party responsible for transportation or warehousing can also be held liable.

Contractual exclusion of liability

It is not clear to what extent it is possible to limit or exclude by contract the liability for bringing into circulation a defective product that causes damage or personal injuries. However, article 53 of the Contract Law of the PRC, promulgated October 1, 1999, stipulates that clauses which purport to exempt one party from liability for causing to the counterpart personal injury or property damage by intentional action or gross fault or negligence are null and void. In addition, the Consumer Protection Law, in article 24, provides that contractual terms, circulars, announcements, and shop notices used by business operators in order to unreasonably reduce or avoid civil liability to consumers shall be null and void.

On the other hand, under article 28, paragraph 4 of the Product Quality Law, if product purchase and sale contracts, as well as product processing contracts, concluded between producers, between sellers, or between producers and sellers, exclude the possibility of recourse, the parties to such contracts shall proceed in accordance with their contractual agreement. This seems to indicate that in contracts where neither of the parties is a consumer, the liability for defective or substandard products can be excluded *except* for personal injuries or property damage caused by gross fault or negligence or intentional action. However, the legal situation remains unclear.

The number of product liability cases could increase in the future as the market for industrial and consumer products grows and propaganda of PRC government authorities is enlarged in order to prevent damage and personal injuries caused by defective goods. Foreign companies, or Chinese companies with foreign investment, are regarded as being rich. Therefore, it is very likely that such companies may become the main targets of product liability suits. Companies need to cover these issues clearly in their agreements with their Chinese suppliers, as well as ensure they take active steps to monitor the quality of products sourced from China.

Ending Relationships with Suppliers

Whether terminating a long-term relationship with a supplier in China, or concluding the relationship after having placed a single order with them, following through to prevent any future IP risks with the supplier is critical. This is one of the key risk areas, as suppliers no longer have the incentive of future work to stop them infringing the customer's IP rights.

You need to take at least the following steps:

- Send the supplier a letter reminding them of their obligations in the terms and conditions relating to confidentiality, use of IP, use of brands in promotional materials, etc.

- Obtain confirmation in writing from the supplier that they have destroyed or returned to your company (at your company's discretion) all confidential information, samples, molds, etc.
- Obtain confirmation in writing from the supplier that they have collected all similar materials from their subcontractors.
- Agree with the supplier what happens to any remaining inventory they may be holding, and ensure it is either purchased by your company or destroyed.
- Preferably, visit the supplier's factory to ensure that they have complied with their obligations.

We also recommend having someone on the ground in China conduct checks in the market for the products over the next couple of months to ensure that the factory isn't continuing to manufacture your products.

4. CONCLUSION

There are many companies that have a very strong handle on their supply chain in China; as such, they have been able to take advantage of the efficiencies of manufacturing there without suffering damage to their brands through IP infringements. The best examples are those companies that invest in their relationships with their suppliers and see their suppliers as "partners" in the fight against counterfeits and poor-quality products.

One of our favorite examples is Universal Pathways, the Australian company we have mentioned previously in this chapter. They have invested in a number of the recommendations in this section, including:

- investing time in traveling to China to meet with their potential suppliers;
- signing confidentiality agreements with both of the potential suppliers, to ensure that they protected the company's IP, prior to entering into an agreement with their chosen supplier;
- obtaining local advice, both on the contract (to ensure that it was enforceable in China and that it contained all the relevant IP protection clauses) and on practical measures the company could take to protect its IP;
- signing English and Chinese versions of the agreement to ensure the supplier understood its obligations; and

- sending a representative to China to monitor production while also continuing to build the company's relationship with the supplier.

Despite its small size, Universal Pathways provides an excellent example of a company that is taking simple but effective steps to protect its supply chain from IP issues in China.

CHECKPOINT

- Have you taken steps to protect your IP before sending your specifications to potential suppliers?
- Have you collected all the specifications from suppliers you chose not to use?
- Have you conducted appropriate due diligence into the chosen supplier?
- Are you comfortable that the supplier understands IP and your expectations of them to protect it?
- Have you ensured that you have the best IP protection provisions in your terms and conditions with the supplier?
- Have you reviewed your IP to ensure you are only sending the supplier what is necessary to manufacture the products?
- Have you taken steps to minimize sale of seconds/overruns by your supplier?
- Are you managing the ongoing relationship with the supplier in order to protect your IP?
- Have you sent a representative to audit the factory during production?
- Once you have ended a relationship with a supplier, have you collected all the IP and taken steps to ensure the supplier doesn't infringe your IP?

RESOURCES

See the 'Resources' section in Chapter 9 for a list of some of the main business councils in China.

The following resources can also provide some useful advice:

- www.chinabusinessreview.com: *China Business Review*, the magazine of the US–China Business Council, contains very practical and useful articles on trade and investment in China, including the IP regime. You need to subscribe to view some of the articles.

- PricewaterhouseCoopers, "Redefining Intellectual Property Value—The Case of China," www.pwc.com/techforecast/pdfs/IPR-web_x.pdf, accessed on July 22, 2007. An interesting report that explores some ways in which companies need to shift their focus in order for IP management to minimize IP challenges in China.

- US Chamber of Commerce Coalition Against Anti-counterfeiting and Piracy, "No Trade in Fakes—Supply Chain Tool Kit," www.thetruecosts.org/NR/rdonlyres/ekj5ugvm77u346ckglt-wkgehlhsbdxloq3cix25ayxvsu7ydraxj3jgdoqp2nifjhev3qza-pqgwgpqduepeeymgxn4h/FinalSupplyChainToolKit1.5.07.pdf, accessed July 22, 2007. A very practical report of options to help minimize the risks in the supply chain of IP infringements, with some interesting case studies.

Identifying IP for registration and use in China

1. INTRODUCTION

No doubt you already have a view on what "intellectual property" means. Who would buy this book if they did not? You probably consider that intellectual property is made up of things such as patents, trademarks, and copyright. You have probably seen the word defined in license agreements, normally to the effect of something like this:

> Intellectual Property shall mean, by whatever name or term known or designated, any and all intellectual and industrial property rights, tangible or intangible, now in existence or hereafter coming into existence relating to the [products, services, etc.] as well as the relevant designs, prototypes, and samples, excluding [the other side's] trademarks and intellectual and industrial property rights. Intellectual Property shall encompass any invention, patents, patentable rights, copyright, design rights, utility models, trademarks (whether or not any of the foregoing are registered) and including the licensed trademarks, trade names, service marks, brands and distinctive signs, labels, commercial or confidential information, rights in inventions, rights in data, database rights, rights in know-how and all other intellectual and industrial property and similar or analogous rights existing under the laws of any country and all pending applications for and right to apply for or register the same (present, future, and contingent, and including all renewals, extensions, revivals, and all accrued rights of action) belonging to the Licensor.

As "IP lawyers," however, we take the view that by using the term "intellectual property," clients often will make the mistaken assumption that what we are talking about is really just patents, trademarks, and copyright. To prevent this misunderstanding, we prefer the terms "intellectual assets" or "intellectual capital." The process of developing, capturing, and managing knowledge and then fully exploiting it for commercial gain is commonly referred to as "Intellectual Asset Management." This knowledge can manifest itself in both registered and unregistered ways (see Figure 5.1).

For several important reasons, the intellectual assets of any organization need to be managed. While intellectual assets are intangible and don't have any visual dimension, they do have value. Getting your IP house in order will enhance your business plans and help to pinpoint key areas of expertise within your company. It also demonstrates an understanding of where the value lies in your organization. Protecting your IP drives innovation and new product development, because your business will look for ways to improve your products so that patents can be granted and trademarks registered. New business models may even emerge.

Regardless of what type of IP you possess (confidential information/trade secrets, patents, designs, or copyright works material), it can be traded. Routes for commercial exploitation include licensing and co-branding, assignment (selling), franchising, mortgaging, and so on.

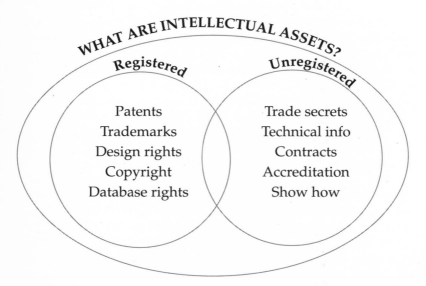

Figure 5.1 What are intellectual assets?
Source: Intellectual Assets Centre of Scotland (www.ia-centre.org.uk).

As the market value of a business can be a significant multiple of the "book value" or physical assets, managers are increasingly looking at how they develop, manage, and exploit their intellectual assets. Intangible asset budget spent now increases the "book value" of your company, which investors and strategic partners find very attractive.

Doing business in China is even more reason to look at your intellectual capital and decide how to protect it. In developing countries, the enforcement of registered IP rights is much easier than the enforcement of unregistered IP rights. The cost of registering your IP so that your rights are more easily identified and enforced is much less than the cost of litigating in local courts on principles of unfair competition or breach of contract, where a defendant will be able to present any number of defenses for the court to consider.

Another good reason to look at IP in as broad and all-encompassing a manner as possible is so that you get buy-in from all the people in your business who deal with it and need to know how to use it every day. These include your salespeople, business development people, lawyers, IT team, public affairs/government relations team, lenders, licensees, and so on. The more they understand what you consider to be valuable intellectual assets or intellectual capital, the better protected—and commercially more lucrative—those assets or capital will be. Having your entire business address your intellectual property in this way will serve your company well in presenting it to the Chinese, including government officials. It will help define your strategy, as discussed in Part 3 of this book.

Let's now take a look at some of the more traditional and well-known types of IP.

2. PATENTS

There have been many periods in China's history where what can be recognized in today's context as patents can be seen. Early emperors would sometimes reward their supporters with monopoly rights to control aspects of trade, including trade in commodities such as salt. Limitations on such granted monopolies would be marked by time or geography, or the continuation of fees paid to the emperors to maintain the right to exclude others from the trade. These are all characteristics of what we today call patent rights. Western principles of a patent system arose significantly during the 19th century as Western-educated bureaucrats gained power and influence in the courts of the various emperors. During China's last dynasty, the Qing, limited monopoly rights were granted to inventors of new technologies, marking a turning point from the ancient custom of rewarding merit with commodity trading rights to the modern sensibilities of encouraging creation and innovation in technologies. This drew to an unfortunate close by the end of the 19th century as China underwent a chaotic transformation from an ancient civilization ruled by imperial authority to a society ruled by warlords, which saw the demise of old China and the onslaught of modern war. Vestiges of patent rights were either abolished, or were not carried forward from one government to its successor.

After the founding of the People's Republic in 1949, the nation's focus was on socialist societal building; there was no place in such a society for the encouragement of individual IP rights. This changed on April 1, 1985, when the first PRC Patent Law came into force. The new law was influenced by the German patent laws. There have been two subsequent overhauls of the PRC Patent Law, in 1992 and 2000. Some of the more significant amendments made in 2000 included the adding of an "offer for" to be considered an infringing act for invention and utility model patents, and the provision of court review of validity decisions made by the Patent Review and Adjudication Board for utility models and designs. Preliminary injunctions and property preservation orders were made available to patent owners and their licensees, and statutory damages for patent infringement were increased to RMB500,000.

There is currently a draft amendment to the Patent Law, which has been sent to the State Council, as well as an amendment to the Examination Guidelines, which dictate how patent examiners conduct their duties within the Patent Office.

What is a Patent?

In China, a patent can be obtained for a new product or process, or for an improvement to an existing product or process. Like other types of property, a patent right can be bought, sold, mortgaged, licensed, or charged. Patents are territorial, which means that a patent registered in China will only give the

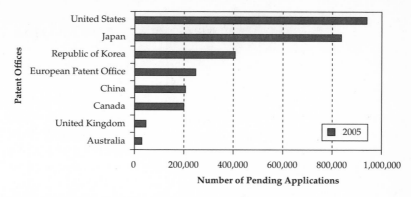

Figure 5.2 Number of pending patent applications, 2005
Source: WIPO Statistics Database.

patentee rights in China and not elsewhere unless the patentee registers elsewhere. If you are considering doing business in China or sourcing products from China, it is critical to register your key patents there. China operates a first-to-file, not first-to-invent, patent protection regime. Chinese companies will often go through the patent registers overseas, select patents that they think may be valuable, and then, if they are not registered in China, make slight changes to them before proceeding to register them there. Although there are often ways to invalidate these patents, it can be expensive and time consuming and may prevent you from conducting business in China in the meantime.

According to the 2007 edition of the WIPO [World Intellectual Property Organization] Patent Report (www.wipo.int/ipstats/en/statistics/patents/patent_report_2007.html), the PRC Patent Office became the fifth-largest recipient of patent applications in 2005, with an increase of almost 33% over 2004 (see Figure 5.2). In terms of granted patents, China ranks fourth in the world (see Figure 5.3).

Types of Patents

China recognizes three types of patents:

- *Invention patents:* inventions, including products and processes, that are "novel" and not obvious and which have been developed to the point where they can be utilized in industry.
- *Utility model patents:* creations or improvements relating to the form, construction, or fitting of a product (but not a process).

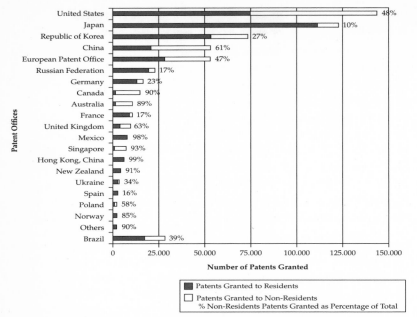

Figure 5.3 Number of patents granted, 2005
Source: WIPO Statistics Database.

In general, the technical requirements are not as high as for an invention patent.

- *Design patents:* Original designs relating to the shape or pattern of an object, or to a combination of shape and pattern, or a combination of color and shape or pattern.

Invention Patents

The workhorse of a patent stable, the invention patent encompasses all the traditional notions of what a patent is. As set out in article 2 of the Implementing Regulations for the PRC Patent Law, an invention patent is a new technical solution relating to a product or process, or an improvement for a product or a process. Technical solutions, while not defined in the Patent Law or its Implementing Regulations, can be considered as the answer to a technical challenge. PRC law precludes the patenting of several things that may be patentable in other countries. Examples of non-patentable subject matter include business methods, methods of diagnosis and treatment of diseases, and animals and plants, including transgenic varieties such as the famous Onco cancer mouse from the US (although products derived from such animals can be patented by process patents).

Utility Model Patents

A utility model is defined in article 2(2) of the Implementing Regulations as a new technical solution relating to the shape or structure, or their combination, of a product fit for practical use. Utility models must provide solutions to technical problems; so, in this sense, they are similar to invention patents. Utility models are limited to solutions to products of certain shapes, while invention patents provide solutions for products and processes. Processes of manufacturing, testing, and applications, as well as products without a definite shape (such as pharmaceutical active ingredients, compounds, and cement), are out of the scope of patentable utilities. Abstract concepts or theories are excluded from being patentable for utility patents.

Design Patents

Design patents relate to functional elements in manufactured products and are recognized by way of their being considered commercially useful articles by virtue of the features of shape or ornamentation applied to such commercially useful articles. Unlike copyright, which focuses on the aesthetic characteristics of a work, design focuses on the functional elements and often the two rights are argued collectively. China, like many countries, recognizes (though only recently) the separability test to distinguish copyright from design (the separation of the aesthetic from the functional).

Protection in China

Inventors or designers (or their assignees or successors in title) can apply for registration of the above three types of patents in China. Inventors may claim priority (12 months for invention or utility model patents, and six months for design patents) in accordance with the Paris Convention to which China has acceded. Some foreign inventors can also designate China when they file a Patent Cooperation Treaty (PCT) application. The effect of this is to enable filing in China to be delayed for up to 30 months from the priority filing date, thus affording the applicant more time. Additional time is helpful in terms of deferring or spreading filing costs around until more money is available. Also, when the first examiner's search report comes back for the applicant to review, this additional time may be useful in helping the applicant decide whether, based on the preliminary feedback, it is worthwhile to continue to pursue the patent in other countries.

How Long Does Registration Take?

How long it will take you to register a patent in China will depend on the type of patent you wish to acquire. Designs can take a mere six to eight months. Utility models can take up to a year. Invention patents are more likely to take two to four years from filing in China, or four to six years from the priority date (if requested). Often, it can be a good idea to register for utility model and design patents to plug loopholes in your portfolio while your invention patent is pending, to prevent Chinese parties from registering around your patent and to give you rights to enforce if necessary. Equally, if your invention patent cannot be registered in China now, consider applying for some design and utility model patents around the process to give you at least some protection.

Design and utility model patent applications are not examined for substance by the State Intellectual Property Office. They are merely checked to ensure the formalities are met, and then, in due course, the grant is officially published in SIPO's journal. Invention patents, by contrast, are substantially examined. This takes time.

An invention patent application must be filed with SIPO. If all the appropriate application materials are in place, and other formalities have been met, SIPO will publish a preliminary approval of the application within 18 months, or earlier if a request is made. The next step involves the substantive examination. There is no set time within which the examiners at SIPO must reach their decision. They will conduct research, both in China and abroad, to see whether the invention satisfies the three basic tests of patentability. These tests are:

- Is the invention new, meaning is there any prior art that defeats it?
- Is the invention non-obvious, meaning would the people most familiar with inventions of that type consider it inventive?
- Is the invention useful, meaning is it useful for society?

What Will be the Duration of Protection?

A patentee's right to exclude others commences from the date that the grant of patent right is officially published in SIPO's journal and lasts as follows:

- Invention patent: 20 years from the filing date in China.
- Utility model patent: 10 years from the filing date in China.
- Design patent: 10 years from the filing date in China.

Can Patentability be Denied?

If any of the following conditions apply, a patent registration will be denied:

1. For invention and utility model patents:
   - Before filing or the date of priority claimed, the same invention or utility model was published anywhere in the world or was put to public use or made available to the public in the PRC.
   - A patent has already been granted for the same invention or utility model, and that application was filed earlier than the current application.
   - The invention or utility model uses conventional techniques and knowledge available before the application was filed and is thus obvious.

2. For design patents:
   - Before your PRC filing, the same or a similar design was published anywhere in the world or was publicly put to use in the PRC.
   - A registration has been previously granted for the same or a similar new design that was filed earlier than the current application.
   - The design conflicts with the prior rights of others.

What about Invalidation?

In relation to invalidation proceedings, the position in China is similar to that in the United States. The patent is assumed to be valid, and the party claiming its invalidation must provide evidence proving that the issued patent doesn't meet the relevant requirements of patentability. Even though the issued patent passed through substantive examination prior to registration, prior art will be considered by the court in an invalidation hearing (if such evidence is put before the judge by the claimant), even if this evidence was considered during examination of the patent application. A decision on the registrability of a patent application will be made by an individual examiner, whose views may differ from other examiners'.

During the course of both administrative proceedings and civil litigation proceedings, the defendant usually files a request for patent invalidation with the SIPO. Retaliatory invalidation is a common response in most countries. In practice, the Patent Review and Adjudication Board and the court will suspend the case during patent invalidation proceedings, which will take about six to 12 months. If one party isn't satisfied with the decision of the invalidation, he or she may raise another patent administrative litigation against the SIPO, which will obviously draw out the proceedings.

When May Compulsory Licensing be Granted?

The Patent Law allows a compulsory license for "invention and utility model" patents to be granted in a number of circumstances, including in the case of a national emergency or if the license was in the public interest. In practice, however, these provisions haven't been exploited since they were introduced in 1985.

The Patent Law was amended in 2001 to comply with the Agreement on the Trade-Related Aspects of Intellectual Property Rights (TRIPs) requirements relating to compulsory licenses for commercial needs. Under the old provisions, a compulsory license could be granted if a later patent involved a "technical advance." Under the amended law, this has been changed to require "an important technical advance of considerable economic significance," which is in compliance with article 31(L) of the TRIPs Agreement. It is possible to appeal the decision to grant a compulsory license.

3. TRADEMARKS

As with patents, trademarks were recognized in China prior to the founding of the People's Republic in 1949. Trademarks were used mainly by Chinese manufacturers of goods who wished to brand their products to denote some sort of government approval, or by Western companies—mostly in Shanghai—advertising foreign goods (most famously depicted by the "Shanghai girl" cigarette poster ads so popular with historians and antique buffs today). In 1950, China's first modern law to recognize and protect trademarks was the Interim Regulations on Registration of Trade Marks, promulgated on August 28, 1950, by the Government Administrative Council (later to become the State Council). These Interim Regulations set out the basic framework of the registration process of marks, and identified the rights they could enjoy after successful registration. These Interim Regulations were replaced in 1963 by the State Council's Regulations on the Administration of Trade Marks, which lasted until March 1, 1983, when the Trademark Law came into effect. On March 10, 1983, the Implementing Regulations of the Trademark Law were passed.

The Trademark Law was subsequently amended in 1993 and, most recently, in 2001, just after China's ascension to the WTO, in order to harmonize the law with international standards. The 2001 amendments provided protection for marks of geographical indications. A geographical indication would protect things such as "Parma" for ham or "Napa Valley" for wine. Other new types of trademarks included color combination marks and three-dimensional marks. The former requirement that foreigners use a designated trademark agent for the trademark applications was abolished. Preliminary injunctions and property preservation relief was made available to trademark owners and their licensees. Statutory damages for trademark infringement were also raised to RMB500,000.

In 2003, the concept of well-known marks and the process for application for well-known status were clarified by the Regulations for the Recognition and Protection of Well Known Marks under the Paris Convention. Well-known trademark status is very useful, because it provides protection in all classes of goods and services regardless of whether or not it is actually registered in those classes. However, it is unwise to rely on this protection alone and we still recommend filing applications in the key classes. The People's Courts, the PRC Trademark Office, and the Trademark Review and Adjudication Board are authorized to grant well-known status to a trademark, but there must be a contentious platform from which to raise an application (that is, an opposition or infringement). This used to be the responsibility of the Administration for Industry and Commerce and was criticized as being not much more than a creative finance scheme for that agency. Putting the power into the hands of the courts and the Trademark Office follows international standards. As of 2006, over 500 trademarks have been confirmed as well-known, including 180 in 2006 alone. In 2007, an additional 197 well-known trademarks were recognized, including the Chinese trademarks Neiliansheng (for shoes) and Xinhua Bookstore. Of these, 183 were for goods, with the remainder for services. These are comprised of 182 owned by Chinese registrants, one by a Hong Kong registrant, two by Taiwan registrants, and 12 by foreign companies. It is very difficult to obtain well-known status, and a strong case with significant evidence showing how famous the brand is in its country of origin as well as globally, together with substantial use in China, is required.

While China's Trademark Law is widely considered to be compliant with international standards, there remain some distinctions particularly in terms of subclassifications, which differ somewhat from the International Classification of Goods and Services (Nice). It is always wise, therefore, to refer to specific subclassifications when applying for trademark protection in China in order to ensure that the specific goods or services you wish the mark to cover are recognized that way by China's subclassifications. Getting your subclass right is also important when you need to enforce or license your rights.

What is a Trademark?

A trademark is any word, phrase, symbol, design or combination of colors, product configuration, group of letters or colors, or combination of these used by a company to identify its products or services and distinguish them from the products or services of others. The primary purpose of marks is to prevent consumers from becoming confused about the source or origin of a product or service. Marks help consumers answer the questions, "Who makes this product?" or "Who provides this service?" This is a sometimes less recognized role of trademarks in China, where many consumers feel that a trademark serves as a sort of badge of government approval of quality rather than an indication of origin.

Non-traditional trademarks—such as three-dimensional shape marks, colors, sounds, and smells—are relatively new indicators of origin with which the global IP community is coming to terms. In China, sounds and smells cannot currently be registered as trademarks, although under the current draft of the third amended Trademark Law, these will be allowed. Combinations of colors can be registered as a trademark in China, but single colors cannot. Whether single colors can function as a trademark is a hotly debated topic in IP circles around world, so it will be interesting to see where China falls on this issue. With combination marks, technically two or more colors could be registered; in practice, the vast majority of applications are rejected at the application stage without evidence of use of the marks. Duracell has registered its gold and black color combination used on batteries; however, a company that tried to register its use of gray and orange on welding rods was rejected by the TMO and the Trademark Review and Adjudication Board (TRAB), and then on appeal by the Intermediate Court. In order to register color combination marks, you need to be prepared to provide evidence of your use of the combination and its reputation. However, the prize of registration for a color combination is a very powerful right against infringers.

As competition becomes fiercer, marketers become more creative in finding ways to make their products stand out. Three-dimensional trademarks are an increasingly popular way of doing this. As with color combinations, the TMO will usually reject the initial applications for 3-D marks. Applicants will need to appeal to the TRAB and provide evidence of use and reputation

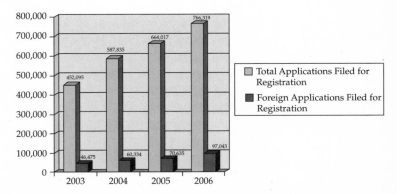

Figure 5.4 Total applications, including foreign applications, filed for trademark registration, 2003–2006
Source: Annual Report on China's Trademarks 2006 (Trademark Office/Trademark Review and Adjudication Board and the State Administration for Industry and Commerce).

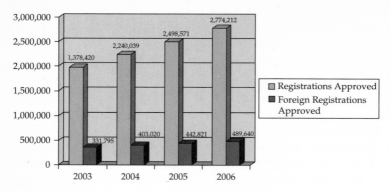

Figure 5.5 Number of trademark registrations, including foreign registrations, approved, 2003–2006
Source: Annual Report on China's Trademarks 2006 (Trademark Office/Trademark Review and Adjudication Board and the State Administration for Industry and Commerce).

in the marks. For instance, Diageo has recently registered the 3-D get up (look and feel) of its Johnnie Walker® Scotch whisky as a trademark. The registration is a very powerful tool in its fight against copycats, who copy the shape of the bottle and the slanted label but use a different brand name.

We recommend that you register as many elements of your brand as possible as a trademark. Be creative; register the words, the logos (including the Chinese versions), and any distinctive elements of the get-up. Consider whether you can register non-traditional elements of your brand. Trademark registrations are the most powerful IP protection in China, and the most straightforward to enforce, so the more elements you can protect, the stronger will be your portfolio. Figure 5.4 shows the total number of applications, including foreign applications, filed for trademark registration from 2003 to 2006, while Figure 5.5 shows the number of trademark registrations, including foreign registrations, approved over the same period.

Protection in China

Unless you have an established presence in China to serve as a contact point (such as a representative office or other FIE), a foreign applicant wishing to obtain trademark rights must lodge an application through a designated trademark agent, which should then be accepted and registered with the TMO. There are now hundreds of these agencies. Given the length of time it is currently taking for marks to be examined, it is important to use a reputable agent who understands the process and will still be around in three years when the application is accepted. There have been numerous examples of companies losing their trademarks because their agent went out of business, and the company was never notified of acceptance and so didn't pay the registration fee. There are also examples of companies whose applications were rejected because their agent was inexperienced in preparing specifications of goods or in arguing around objections to registration.

China is a member of the major international trademark treaties, including the Madrid Protocol and the Paris Convention. International registrations filed under the Madrid Protocol in Geneva may also include China. Marks are registered according to the Nice Classification, which in China comprises 45 classes and their specific subcategories. Separate applications in each class must be sought unless you have been awarded well-known status.

Prior to lodging a trademark application, we recommend that you conduct an official search to determine if the mark you wish to register is available; that is, it hasn't already been registered by another party—and, if it has, in which class of goods and services it has been registered. The search will also identify other trademarks similar to the one you wish to register, which may affect your application. If you know that your mark isn't available, or if it is too similar to an existing mark, then you can decide on an appropriate course of action which may include any of the following: (1) proceeding regardless of the risk; (2) abandoning your mark; (3) changing your mark; or (4) trying to overcome the similar mark by argument or reaching some sort of coexistence arrangement with the owner. You may also choose to lodge an action to cancel the opposing mark for reasons such as non-use or bad-faith registration.

Pepsi was sued by Zhejiang Lan Ye Wine Co. Ltd. for using its registered trademark in a promotion (*Lan Se Feng Bao*®—meaning "blue storm"). Initially, the court said the mark wasn't used as a trademark, so therefore it wasn't misleading to consumers. Pepsi won at first instance, but lost on appeal for various reasons (including use of dominant position). This is a good example of how a simple trademark search would have revealed the pre-existing trademark, which, if known, should have alerted Pepsi to this risk of infringement.

How Long Does Registration Take?

Usually the TMO makes its determination as to whether to allow a mark to become registered or not within about 30–36 months from the date of application, depending on the class. This is very slow, and there has been much discussion on ways for the TMO to improve these time frames.

Trademark rights are granted on a first-to-file basis (rather than a first-to-use basis). The criteria for registration are basically the same as in most countries. After initial checking of completeness of the application materials, the TMO conducts internal checking to ensure that there are no registered marks similar enough, or associated with similar or the same goods or services, which would result in consumer confusion should the mark seeking approval be allowed to register. If this search reveals no potentially conflicting citations, then the application is advertised in the TMO's journal. Publication or advertisement in the gazette, as it is commonly referred to, provides the public with a three-month opportunity in which to oppose the application on various grounds. If no one raises an objection within this period, the TMO will move to full registration and issue a registration certificate for the mark.

Where a mark is rejected due to the prior existence of a similar mark, or where an applicant wishes to oppose or cancel another's mark due to a conflict, a party may take action through administrative channels (through the TMO and the Trademark Review and Adjudication Board). Decisions of these bodies can be appealed to the courts. Marks registered in bad faith can be subject to cancellation at any time. Due to China's first-to-file rule, in the past there was a spate of pirate registrations of famous marks by third parties. The TMO and the courts in the major cities are now well acquainted with such acts and clear cases of pirating of famous marks stand a very good chance of being resolved in favor of the rightful trademark owner.

What Will be the Duration of Protection?

Once registered, a trademark in the PRC is given 10 years of protection starting from the day it is granted. The registration can be renewed for indefinite 10-year periods so long as the renewal procedures are undertaken by the registrant within six months from the date of expiry. Renewal conditions are not onerous and normally require a payment of the renewal fee and proof that the mark has been used in China.

Is My Mark Registrable?

China doesn't grant registration to all marks. Marks precluded from registration include those which:

- are identical or similar to previously registered marks for the same or similar goods or services;
- are purely generic, meaning marks that describe the good or service in respect of which it hopes to be registered;
- are purely descriptive of characteristics, quality, or place of origin of the goods or services to which they are applied; or
- have negative social connotations. This ground for rejection of trademark applications was originally intended to cover marks that may be considered offensive or which may insult religious groups, minorities, or other nationalities. Whether a mark is offensive depends on society at the time and may change as time goes by. For instance, the mark *Da Long Fang*® ("big old house") was registered as a trademark for many years. However, over time the phrase "*da long fang*" acquired a second meaning, referring to the "older wife" or "first wife" of men who had multiple wives. The TMO rejected the renewal of the registration on the basis that it had become a socially offensive term and was inappropriate to be registered as a trademark. However, this ground has been extended by the authorities to be a "catch-all" provision for all cases of bad-faith registration. The law didn't provide for an application to be rejected if it was registered in bad faith, so the authorities stretched the interpretation of this ground to cover not only the negative connotations of the word/image, but also the socially offensive behavior of the applicant. Without this provision, there would be no way to prevent registration of "ghost marks"—that is, applications for other companies' marks with the intention of stopping the genuine owner from registering the mark unless they buy back the registration. (We will discuss these ghost marks further in Chapter 7.) This is particularly important for cases where the mark has a reputation, but doesn't reach well-known status. Under the new draft of the amended Trademarks Law, this provision is split into two sections: (1) the negative connotations of the

word—that is, the initial intended purpose of this provision; and (2) bad-faith applications.

Do I Have to Use My Trademark in China?

Yes. Under PRC law, use of the trademark is required either by the registrant or the registrant's licensee. Three consecutive years of non-use from the date of grant puts the trademark in jeopardy of being cancelled on the grounds of non-use. However, proving use in China isn't difficult; even the occasional announcement in national media such as *The People's Daily* will be sufficient to overcome an action to cancel based on non-use. Use overseas isn't sufficient; the mark must be used in China.

What if I License My Trademark?

The licensing of trademarks is very common in China, particularly given the country's manufacturing capacity and expertise. The law does require, however, that trademark licenses be registered with the TMO within three months of the signing of the agreement. Although penalties for failure to record have been abolished, a recent judicial interpretation by the Supreme People's Court held that neither the licensor nor the licensee can defend against a bona fide third party unless the license has been duly recorded. Moreover, failure to record the trademark license agreement may also result in the licensee's use of the trademark not being allowed as evidence of use in order to overcome an invalidation proceeding based on non-use. The benefits of recording are significant. Short forms of the complete trademark license can be submitted, making the recording process easier. The agreement needs to be translated into Chinese for the record.

Latin Script Trademark or Chinese Character Marks?

Many times we are asked whether a Latin script trademark should be made into a Chinese character trademark for registration and use in China. There is no easy answer to this question, which requires understanding the differences in two fundamental areas: language and consumer behavior.

Chinese language is a character-based script. Each character has a meaning that all Chinese people recognize. However, each character also has a sound, which will differ in different parts of

China. The spoken difference between Mandarin (or Putonghua) and Cantonese is usually described as more different than Italian and Spanish. Characters can also be written in a traditional, more complicated form—as used in Hong Kong, Macau, and Taiwan— and in the simplified style used in Mainland China.

Like all markets, China's consuming public are extremely segmented. Differences exist in where people live, their levels of education, earnings, ages, and so on. Not all people are attracted by the same thing. Some consumers may choose to purchase a product or a service because it is branded in a way that describes its quality, purpose, and function clearly, and in terms they understand and are comfortable with. Others may be attracted to the complete newness of a brand that may not communicate anything about the product. Still others may decide to purchase foreign products because they already know the foreign brand.

The safest course of action when registering your Latin script trademarks in China is to decide whether you should also devise and register a Chinese trademark. There are two good reasons to register a Chinese trademark. First, even if you plan to conduct your marketing under your Latin script trademark, you should remember that the vast majority of China's 1.3 billion people don't read or speak a foreign language. Most may not even be able to pronounce your Latin script mark. Second, if consumers in China cannot pronounce your Latin script mark, then they will come up with their own descriptor for your product and will begin to refer to it by that Chinese word, rather than your Latin script word. Eventually, someone will pick up on this and register those Chinese characters, and may then begin selling similar goods under that Chinese character trademark. Consequently, you may lose market share and have to fight the infringer to get him to stop the infringement. The owners of the famous clothing brand Leonardo® found this when they launched the brand in China under the English trademark, only to find that consumers used the Chinese equivalent of "old man" when referring to the logo, which is an old man's face!

For reasons of public policy, having a Chinese name is a requirement in order to apply for a trademark, as well as for a patent and copyright. The reasoning is that Chinese consumers have the right to know who is responsible for the products they buy. As in most countries, this is especially true for products such as food, beverages, cosmetics, pharmaceuticals and nutritionals, chemicals, and so on, and makes up an important part of labeling and advertising regulations.

The *Starbucks* case is a recent example of what can go wrong. The US-based coffee-shop chain registered its Starbucks® trademark and device in China in May and June 1996. However, it didn't register the Chinese character version of "Starbucks" until December 1999 in class 35 (a class for services) and February 2000 in classes 30 (coffee) and 42 (another service class). In March 2000, a Chinese company was established with a name that included the Chinese characters for "Starbucks," which it proceeded to use on its cafés and goods. Starbucks brought an action against the company in the Shanghai No. 2 Intermediate People's Court. In the end, it won the case on the grounds that the defendant company had registered its name in bad faith, and hadn't provided sufficient evidence of selecting the name independently, and that Starbucks' use of its trademark (though outside China) predated the defendant's (See Chapter 8 for further information on this case).

How is a Chinese Character Trademark Developed?

There are three ways of developing a Chinese character trademark:

- *Translate:* If your trademark describes your goods or services, then you can translate that meaning into Chinese characters. Examples where this has been done in China include American Express, Northwest Airlines, and Black Label®, which is part of the Johnnie Walker® brand. However, sometimes the translation may not be exactly as you mean it to be, in which case you may need to consider if the Chinese is too far removed from your intended meaning. If it is, and if there is no better alternative to choose from, you may want to think of using a transliterated trademark.

- *Transliterate:* Most foreigner trademark owners transliterate their marks into Chinese by choosing characters that (1) sound close to their trademark, and (2) have at least a positive connotation and are sensible when used with each other. Transliteration problems occur when the characters have different sounds when spoken in different Chinese dialects. Sometimes, a chosen transliteration can have a good meaning in the dialect it was selected for (for example, Mandarin or Cantonese), but may have a less desirable meaning in another Chinese dialect (such as Fujianese or one of the minority languages). Your decision should be based on your target market. Examples here include McDonald's (*Mai Dang Lao*) and B&Q (*Bai An Ju*).

- *Create:* When neither the translation nor transliteration options are acceptable, you can simply make up a Chinese trademark. Unlike translations and transliterations, which are often suggested by local Chinese trademark attorneys, created Chinese trademarks are usually the work of branding/advertising agents specialized in the field. You should look for an agency with a proven track record of branding advice that will be able to create a selection of choices for you to consider. Have your trademark lawyers review those you like best and advise you on the likelihood of successfully registering them at the TMO. (If the created mark is not registrable, then it will be of no use to you in China.) Hershey started marketing and selling its chocolates in China in 1995 under the Chinese brand name *Hao Xinshi®* ("good thoughts"), only to find that another Chinese confectioner had already registered the name. The company had to rebrand and find another name—*Hao Shi®* ("good times"). *Sai Bei Wei®* (meaning "tastes better than others") is a good created trademark for Subway® in China.

4. COPYRIGHT

Copyright usually gets the most attention when it comes to pointing out China's IP flaws, and it is mostly because of copyright infringement that China has taken on the image of a "pirate" nation. The first treatment of copyright after 1949 appeared in the 1987 General Principles of the Civil Law, which afforded citizens and legal persons rights of authorship and remuneration for their publications. This was expanded in 1991 when the State Council promulgated the Copyright Law and its ancillary Implementing Regulations. In 1992, China became a member of the Berne Convention for the Protection of Literary and Artistic Works and the Universal Copyright Convention. In December 2001, on its entry into the WTO, China became a signatory to the WTO TRIPs Agreement, which detailed many international copyright standards.

The Copyright Law was subsequently amended in 2001 so as to bring the national legislation in line with China's WTO and Berne Convention obligations, as well as to provide for the rapidly expanding realities of Internet dissemination of copyright works. The 2001 amendments were substantial. Protection was strengthened for public performance rights, compilation works, and the dissemination of works through networks and databases. Copyright license agreements were required to be made in writing, and the previous 10-year term restriction was abolished. Preliminary injunctions and evidence preservation orders were made available to rights owners for copyright infringement, and statutory damages for copyright infringement were increased to RMB500,000. The Implementing Regulations were further amended to incorporate these changes on August 2, 2002.

The next major development for China's copyright regime occurred in 2006, when the country acceded to the various WIPO copyright and Internet treaties. Also of note are the July 1, 2007, Regulations on the Protection of Internet Transmission Rights, which confirmed that the rights of copyright owners included Internet transmission and that failure to obtain consent for use of their works constitutes copyright infringement. The rights and obligations of Internet service providers (ISPs) were also clarified.

Copyright is considered a natural right because it arises automatically on creation of an original work of authorship. Original works of authorship can be books, plays, musical compositions (words and/or music), audio and video recordings, choreographic works, motion pictures, filmstrips, TV programs, photographs, paintings, drawings, maps, architectural designs, jewelry designs, fabric designs, scale models, prototypes, crafts, computer programs, databases, Web sites, and even oral speeches and lectures. However, certain works are not afforded copyright protection in the PRC, such as laws and regulations, official or judicial documents (such as government circulars or court judgments) and their official translations, current news, calendar information, numerical tables, general tables and formulas, and the like.

Protection in China

Unlike patents and trademarks, copyright need not be registered in China for it to exist. There is, as in the United States, a voluntary registration procedure whereby a straightforward form is completed, including details of the author and date of first creation. Since China is a member of the Berne Convention, the work of a foreign author will be automatically protected in the PRC if he or she is from a country that is also a member of Berne or where the work in question was created in a Berne member state. Another requirement for recordal is the deposit of a copy of the work with the National Copyright Administration. This is common international practice, but in China copyright owners are sometimes wary of this, especially in regard to sensitive computer code. This can sometimes be worked around, such as by depositing a selection of code rather than the full code.

Recordal serves as good evidence of (1) subsistence (in that copyright exists in the work and this has been accepted by the government as true) and (2) ownership (by the registrant's name appearing on the recordal certificate). A copyright recordal certificate is useful in terms of more efficient enforcement of copyright. We would rarely advise on administrative enforcement of copyright in China without having a recordal certificate.

Copyright is increasingly being recognized as being applicable to goods that are useful, as opposed to goods that are purely artistic in merit. China recognizes copyright in such works as "architectural works," "graphic works," and "model works." The use of copyright law to enforce intellectual property rights in utilitarian articles such as computer accessories typically foundered on the argument that such useful goods were not works of art and therefore shouldn't be extended copyright protection, but rather needed the protection of design patents. However, using patents was often problematic for rights owners. For instance, the infringing party could counterclaim that the patent was invalid, resulting in a significant delay in enforcement. Furthermore, the registration process for design patents is far more time consuming and difficult than registration for copyright. There have been some recent cases and administrative decisions which we have worked on in favor of confirming that copyright can exist in arguably utilitarian goods, and the United States' "separability doctrine" of being able to confer copyright protection for the aesthetic elements of a functional product now seems to be an acceptable argument.

What Will be the Duration of Protection?

Generally, the term of copyright protection is life of the author plus 50 years. However, in the following instances, the term of protection is 50 years from the date of first publication:

- when the work is a photographic work, or cinematographic, television, or audiovisual work; and
- when the "author" of the work is a corporation.

For a published book or periodical, the publisher will enjoy copyright in the typographical arrangement/design for 10 years from the date of first publication of the work.

What Rights Does a Copyright Owner Have in China?

In keeping with international copyright practice, a copyright owner in China enjoys personal and proprietary rights in the work. The proprietary rights include the right to reproduction, distribution, leasing, exhibition, performance, broadcasting, dissemination through the Internet, adaptation, annotation, compilation, and translation. Personal rights or moral rights include rights of publication, authorship, alteration, and integrity of a work.

Can Anyone Use My Copyright without a License?

Yes, but only in special circumstances. For example, one may use a published work for:

- private study, research, or entertainment;
- quoting a particular part to demonstrate a point in one's work;
- quoting to report current events in newspapers, magazines, or on radio or television;
- translating or reproducing in a small quantity for use by teachers or scientific researchers for teaching or scientific research purposes;
- performance free of charge; and
- copying, drawing, photographing, or recording an artistic work placed or displayed in a public outdoor place.

In addition, government authorities may use copyright works in the performance of their official duties. All such free use as described above must not unreasonably jeopardize the legitimate rights and interests of the copyright owner.

5. TRADE SECRETS

As the scope of manufacturing and production in China increases in sophistication and technological advancement, companies are coming under greater pressure to protect their non-registrable IP rights. The main category of non-registrable IP rights is trade secrets.

Probably the most famous trade secret in the world is the exact formula for the manufacture of Coca-Cola®. Other types of trade secrets include survey methods used by professional pollsters, recipes, a new invention for which a patent application hasn't yet been filed, marketing strategies, client lists, manufacturing techniques, and computer algorithms. A trade secret may be a company's main competitive advantage. For that reason, it may not want to register it, since eventually that registration (a patent or a design) will expire and that advantage will then be public knowledge. The protection lasts for as long as the company continues to keep the information confidential. Trade secret owners who hope to maintain their secret advantage in perpetuity will need to take special care, particularly if they use that secret in China.

Trade secrets (or "commercial secrets") are defined in the PRC Anti-Unfair Competition Law as technology or business information that:

- is not available to the public;
- is beneficial to its owner; and
- the owner of which has taken some measures to keep confidential.

Trade secrets are unregistered IP rights, which means that a government doesn't accept requests for registration of these rights or recognize their existence by way of a certificate. Unlike registered IP rights, trade secrets exist so long as their owner prevents them from becoming known publicly. Under the PRC Anti-Unfair Competition Law, in order for a trade secret owner to sue someone for stealing a trade secret, he or she must prove that the trade secret actually exists (under the three requirements above) and that:

- the defendant knowingly used such "stolen" information;
- the plaintiff has suffered damage; and
- the damage was caused by the defendant's actions.

The Administration for Industry and Commerce, as well as the People's Courts, are authorized to enforce trade secrets under the PRC Anti-Unfair Competition Law.

A possible defense is that trade secrets were acquired through reverse engineering. Reverse engineering refers to the technological process of discovering how something works by taking it apart and analyzing what makes it function the way it does, and then using alternative means to make the same thing in such a way it is not a copy of the original. The court will come to its own view on whether the defense is legitimate on the facts of the case. Where the accused had access to the trade secrets, he or she will have to prove that in fact the know-how to manufacture was a result of reverse engineering and not of improper disclosure of trade secrets.

Protection in China

Disclosure of trade secrets is prohibited in China. Article 10 of the Anti-Unfair Competition Law prohibits business operations from engaging in any of the following acts:

- obtaining the trade secrets of any rightful party by theft, inducement, duress, or other illegal means;
- disclosing, using, or allowing others to use the trade secrets of any rightful party obtained by illegal means; or
- disclosing, using, or allowing others to use trade secrets in breach of an agreement or the confidentiality requirements imposed by any rightful party.

Third parties who obtain, use, or disclose business secrets that they knew, or should have known, to have been infringed by any of the methods outlined above will be deemed to have infringed the trade secrets of the rightful party.

6. OTHER IP RIGHTS

Domain Names

With international assistance in the early 1990s—in particular, from Germany—China began constructing what is soon to become the world's largest Internet capability, with the number of current users estimated to be over 140 million. It will also be one of the largest users and manufacturers of network-related products and services. The proliferation of the Internet and network services has seen a dramatic rise in online businesses in China, and one would be hard pressed to find a business that has no online trading platform of some kind. Online sales of goods and services in China are increasing. China's embrace of the Internet is not without limits, however, as the government maintains a public policy of Internet content control and censorship as a means to maintain a harmonious social order.

China's recently promulgated Internet-related legislation for the most part adequately addresses issues arising from the progress of development. The legal framework is, as in most countries, trying to respond to the phenomenal growth of the Internet and is evolving most interestingly in the People's Courts. Several recent cases have reached contradictory decisions, which makes predicting with any measure of certainty a court's approach to these questions difficult at best. The Ministry of Information Industry (MII) is primarily responsible for Internet control and regulation. On September 28, 2004, the Ministry of Information promulgated its Measures on Administration of Domain Names for the Chinese Internet, which became effective on December 20, 2004. The Measures provide the basic framework for the administration of Internet domain names.

By the end of 2006, China had registered over 1.8 million domain names in the .cn domain space. In addition to MII regulations relating to domain name enforcement, unauthorized domain name registration, often referred to as "squatting," may also be addressed by other areas of Chinese law. The Trademark Law, the General Principles of Civil Law, and the Anti-Unfair Competition Law may all be utilized to strike squatters off a domain name they have registered which is identical—or similar—to trademarks or business enterprise names owned by others.

Under the MII sits the China Internet Network Information Center (CNNIC). CNNIC, established on June 3, 1997, is a non-governmental, not-for-profit body responsible for the operation, maintenance, and administration of China's top-level domain name, ".cn," domain names that are in Chinese characters, and, recently, Internet keywords. While domain name registration applications used to be dealt with online at CNNIC's bilingual Web sites, www.cnnic.net.cn and www.cnnic.gov.cn, all applications are now handled through domain name registration companies.

Previously, individuals weren't permitted to register a domain name in China, which could only be done by Chinese organizations or FIEs. Domain names were also required to be serviced by domain name servers in China. This is no longer the case. The application procedure has been streamlined, and applications are now handled by domain name registration companies, so that the information required is now the same in China as in other countries, namely:

- the desired domain name;
- identification details of the owner;
- host names and IP addresses of the primary and secondary servers; and
- contact details of the administrator.

One important obligation on registration is completion of the domain name registration agreement, which binds the registrant to the various Internet and domain name rules and regulations in China, including CNNIC's Domain Name Dispute Resolution Procedure and Domain Name Dispute Resolution Principles. As with other forms of intellectual property, domain names are alienable in China and can be assigned to third parties so long as this change of information is made according to regulations.

Chinese character domain names can also be registered in China. They are comprised of Chinese character words, or Chinese character words and English words that are used to identify the Chinese character suffixes ".中国" (*zhongguo*, which means "China"), ".网络" (*wangluo*, meaning "web"), and ".公司" (*gongsi*, meaning "company"). When Chinese character domain names were first made available for registration, there was a rush to register for fear of "cyber squatters," but for the most part, the majority of registered Chinese character domains are rarely used. The same is true for Internet keyword domains. Internet keyword domains, like Chinese character domain names, are administered by CNNIC, but registration is handled through commercial registrars. Similar to keywords sold by search engines such as Google or Yahoo!, Chinese keyword domains allow a browser to reach your Web site from the address bar in your browser by simply typing in the keyword (rather than by typing in the full and complete domain name). Both Chinese character domain names and Internet keyword domains require plug-ins available from CNNIC, which makes them arguably less attractive and user friendly.

Registration companies often send out emails in the hope of getting people to register .cn, .hk, or other domains or keywords. There may or may not actually be someone trying to register these domains as claimed. Unless you are seriously interested in acquiring and using such domains, this should not be of concern.

It does, however, raise the issue of "domain name strategy" (or "Intellectual Asset Management") and whether defensive registration may be in order to prevent others from registering domain names incorporating your trademarks (or colorable variations thereof). Different clients do different things, and there is no single correct approach. Our normal advice is to register domains you consider important or where there are local market reasons for doing so. So, if you are operating mainly in Hong Kong or China, we may recommend securing the .hk or .cn domain. Of course, there is also a question of cost of such registrations. So long as you have adequate trademark protection in China and Hong Kong, if a third party registers a similar domain name in bad faith, you would be able to challenge this under the Domain Name Dispute Resolution Procedure, which applies to most domain names, including Chinese character domain names and Internet keyword domains.

Business Enterprise Names

Although a business enterprise name is not an IP right in itself, registering a company name in China is an important step in establishing a presence there. There is an interplay between a business enterprise name and a trademark, but the registration and protection regulations differ and must be considered carefully. China maintains a system of local business name recordal, so if you have registered an enterprise name in a particular province or municipality, it will be precluded from third-party registration only in that particular location. If you want to remove a business name identical or similar to yours, you must attempt to do so on the basis of trademark rights (in the case of a name being identical to the trademark) or unfair competition (in the case of a name being not identical, but confusingly similar).

7. CONCLUSION

As one of the most popular places for foreign direct investment, China must prove that, to a certain tolerable degree, foreigners are comfortable with bringing their IP there. For every instance of IP infringement in China, there are likely to be 10 good examples of foreign IP being protected, achieving its purpose, and contributing to revenues both for the foreign owner/contributor and the Chinese licensee/partner. If the reality was that all IP will be stolen, misappropriated, or otherwise compromised (as, unfortunately, is often presented), we would not be writing this book because there would be no IP deals in China. Successful IP collaborations are those that have been thoroughly planned, taking into consideration all the factors discussed in this and Chapters 2 and 3. Decisions need to be made regarding what specific IP is required to deliver your (and your partner's) goals, as well as to obtain government approval. Careful vetting of potential licensees, manufacturers, partners, and others (including third parties) who may have access to your IP is, of course, critical.

Getting the correct combination of registered and unregistered rights protected in China is a straightforward procedure, so cost cutting and inadequate planning here are easy mistakes to avoid. After these pieces are laid out, understood, and decided on, the various contractual agreements necessary to ensure a balanced, reasonable, and mutually beneficial transaction can be prepared. This formula works, and we have seen success repeated across myriad industries, including clothing, food and beverage, semiconductors, electronics, chemicals, and even in service areas such as education and television content production. IP licensing and technology transfer today remain one of China's primary development goals. Despite the recent downturn in joint venture establishments, their numbers are still impressive, as the small to medium-sized enterprises that are setting up operations in China often find they require the assistance that a local Chinese partner can provide. Even large multinationals such as Pepsi-Cola are entering into a number of JVs every year. As IP lawyers, we have been involved in several contentious IP collaboration matters, but we have come to recognize that usually these problems arise not from some inherent evil plot to steal, but rather from poor planning and miscommunication (on both parts).

The IP environment in China is improving at a remarkable speed. Although the protection of IP rights continues to be a top concern for companies investing and operating in China, the PRC government has made progress in drafting new legislation and enhancing existing legislation in an effort to protect the rights of IP owners and to encourage domestic technological innovation. In China, the safest bet is to take as broad a view as possible of what comprises your intellectual assets, intellectual capital, or simply intellectual property, and then to use every tool available to you to protect it. These tools will be discussed in Chapter 8.

However, this may not be enough to quell rising frustration in regard to the actual enforcement of IP laws, which, by many counts, will remain a key challenge and business consideration for the near future. While the IP laws in China are compliant with the TRIPs Agreement and in fact were basically compliant prior to entry into the WTO, enforcement of the laws remains a challenge in China. Part 3 (Chapters 6–8) examines the most likely types of IP infringements you may encounter in China and offers advice on how to prepare for them.

CHECKPOINT

- What IP do you need to bring onshore to meet your corporate objectives?
- Using a broad definition of IP, what IP do you have?
- How can you best protect your IP in China? What can you do to register it?
- Have you built IP registration into your business structure to ensure you are able to protect inventions early?
- What does your employee inventor reward program look like?
- How can you protect all elements of your brand most effectively as trademarks?

RESOURCES

- www.cnnic.net.cn: Domain name administrator
- www.sipo.gov.cn: State Intellectual Property Office
- www.customs.gov.cn: Customs
- http://english.ipr.gov.cn/en/index.shtml: Government IPR Working Group
- http://sbj.saic.gov.cn/english/index_e.asp: State Trademark Office

Part
3

Protecting your IP in the China market

Companies doing business in China frequently ask: "How do we develop an effective IP strategy in China?" There is no simple answer to this question. Each company's strategy will be different.

The question we like to ask upfront to help you develop the most appropriate strategy for your business, is: "What does success look like?" If you were to stand up in front of senior management and say, "This is what we have achieved," what would you like to be able to show them? With this question in mind, the critical components of a sound IP protection strategy can be broken down into three core categories:

1. "Your company": internal considerations within your company;
2. "Them": considerations relating to the infringers and the infringement; and
3. "What": your enforcement toolbox.

Within these categories, there are eight key components of a sound China IP protection strategy:

- your company's goals;
- your company's management of intellectual property;
- your company's IP rights;
- your team;
- the industry in which you operate;

- the type of infringement;
- the identity of the infringers; and
- your IP infringement toolbox.

We will explore these categories in the following three chapters.

"Your company": Internal considerations

Each IP strategy will be unique, because no two companies will face the same challenges in the same corporate environment. There are steps you can take internally to protect your IP, as well as internal considerations you will need to take into account, when preparing your business line of attack.

As shown in Figure 6.1, the main internal considerations are:

- your company's goals;
- your company's management of intellectual property;
- your company's IP rights; and
- your team.

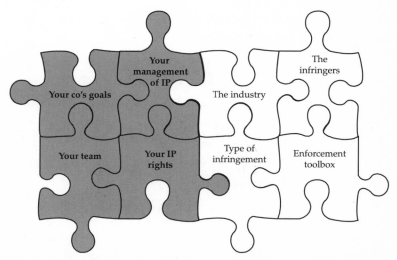

Figure 6.1 Key components of an effective China IP protection strategy: Internal considerations

1. YOUR COMPANY'S GOALS

The companies with the most effective China IP strategies are those whose strategies are intimately linked with their commercial objectives. As a 2005 McKinsey report entitled "Protecting Intellectual Property in China" notes: "Many multinationals in China are losing the battle to protect their IP largely because they rely too heavily on legal tactics and fail to factor IP properly into their strategic and operational decisions." BP is a good example of how this can work (see boxed case study). Diageo, the premium drinks company, has also taken this approach, prioritizing the cities in which it takes action and the brands it monitors, based on its business plan. The steps to follow include:

1. Look at your China business plan.
   - Where are your priority cities?
   - What are your priority products and distribution channels?
   - Who are your partners in China?
   - Are you focused on developing new technology and IP, building brands, or selling existing products?
   - Are you conducting business in China directly or through a partner?

2. Once you have a clear view of your commercial plans, assess where your IP is potentially at risk.
   - Could counterfeit products affect your reputation?
   - Could your brand be diluted?
   - Could confidential information be leaked?
   - Where are the potential leaks in your supply chain?

3. Consider the objectives of your IP enforcement plan (that is, ask: "What does success look like?")
   - Are you trying to keep the retail market clean?
   - Are you trying to stop production of infringing products?
   - What is your company's tolerance for infringements?

4. What resources do you need to deliver this plan?
   - What is your budget for IP infringements in China? ("An effective China IP strategy comes at a price. Recognize this, commit to it, and budget for it!" says Simon MacKinnon, president of Corning China. One of the common challenges

for multinationals is deciding which division covers the costs of IP protection and enforcement, particularly in decentralized organizations where decisions are made—and budgets are controlled—by individual division heads. If one division isn't doing so well, IP costs tend to be one of the first areas for which budgets are reduced. Having a strong core where centralized decisions are made regarding IP will ensure that the budget is controlled and spent in accordance with the business's commercial objectives, rather than on the whim of individual divisions, functional groups, or business groups.)

- What evidence do you need? (We discuss the need for an "evidence bank" later in this chapter.)
- What team do you need? (We will explore this below.)

CASE STUDY: BP—LINKING YOUR STRATEGY TO YOUR BUSINESS PLAN

"China isn't that different from anywhere else," says Sharmini Lohadhasan of BP. *"Break your strategy down into bite-sized pieces and tackle them one at a time."* Many of the companies we spoke to agreed with this advice. It is so easy to be overwhelmed by the size of the challenge and to lose sight of what you can do.

The team at BP (downstream business) set their China IP enforcement policy by asking some key questions:

- *What is our China business plan? What are our business geographic priorities?*
- *What are the risks to this plan? What IP infringements are likely to arise?*
- *What do we want to achieve? What are the objectives of our enforcement strategy?*
- *How do we achieve it? What tools can we rely on?*
- *What resources do we need to deliver these objectives?*

Based on the answers to these questions, BP was able to prepare a strategy that was closely linked with its business plan. The team started with the commercial priority and worked back toward the IP risks. (This sounds self-evident, but many companies lose sight of the importance of linking their IP enforcement strategy to their business objectives.) They engaged the relevant stakeholders *including the regional president, in the process, to ensure high-level commitment to the strategy, and identified appropriate government agencies to work with. They set up a cross-functional team, which included the corporate relations team, to give them the best range of skills and priorities to deliver their enforcement program.*

Once you have developed your long-term plan, it is vital to keep reminding your team of the plan. It is easy to get distracted and to invest resources in activities that are not within your plan but which feel urgent. As Sharmini recommends, you need to maintain the focus internally. This can be challenging when working with a joint venture partner in China. "Find a suitable person within the joint venture team, someone who is on the ground, and invest in developing that relationship. That person will then help keep the rest of the local team focused on the long-term plan and feeding information about IP issues and actions to the IP team."

A few successes under the BP team's belt early on kept the business motivated and focused on the long-term plan. Early successes will not only keep the internal team enthusiastic and focused, but can be leveraged against other infringers, which can be a very cost-effective approach.

One of the most effective strategies that BP employed in its IP strategy in China was to commence proceedings against one of its distributors, who was in breach of his IP contractual obligations. Taking action in this way sends a very strong message to the rest of your supply chain that you won't tolerate infringements of your IP. This is a very effective strategy. Many companies shy away from taking action against partners for fear of upsetting them and losing sales. However, in our view, if these partners are selling counterfeit products and not respecting your IP, are they really appropriate partners for your business in China? In a complex IP market, you want your partners to be supporting your IP protection efforts, not contributing to the problem!

Sharmini's advice to companies developing IP enforcement programs for China is: "Focus, prioritize, and you'll get there!" It certainly seems to be working for BP.

2. YOUR COMPANY'S MANAGEMENT OF IP

The market in China is complex enough for IP enforcement without facing challenges from within your company through elements that are within your control. If you don't get your house in order, the chances of your facing IP infringements will increase significantly.

Employees and IP

One of the biggest areas of IP "leakage" in China is through employees and business partners. This is in part simply because they have access to sensitive information. The keys to minimizing this risk are to build comprehensive IP protection mechanisms into your business structure and HR policies in China, while creating a culture of IP awareness and value within your organization. This strategy will involve two distinct elements: (1) legal protection, and (2) practical protection.

Legal Protection

Run background checks on potential employees

With the current talent shortage in China, many companies are more than happy to "poach" staff from their competitors or to accept a potential candidate's word without checking his or her references. This is a dangerous approach to take in an environment where staff are "job hopping" regularly, having had access to all types of confidential information and often in breach of restraint provisions in their employment contracts.

The depth of the background checks you will need to conduct will depend on the role being recruited. The more senior the role, or the more contact the employee will have with confidential information or the creation of IP, the more research will need to be done into the employee's history. Employers are advised to do the following:

- *Conduct some basic background checks:* This can be done using the candidate's ID card number and full Chinese name. The type of information that can be obtained will vary depending on the area and the relevant authorities. Many companies are now also conducting a brief Internet search on potential employees as a source of information. This can be helpful in identifying connections your candidate may have. In one case, a company discovered that their preferred candidate for managing director in China had been on the board of a state-owned enterprise in the same industry for several years and still held that position at the time he applied for the job. He hadn't disclosed this information, which would have created a significant conflict of interest had he been employed in the position offered.

- *Speak to the candidate's referees:* Ask them specifically about the candidate's IP experience and awareness.

- *Confirm the candidate's qualifications:* A simple call to the university named in the candidate's résumé will usually suffice to confirm that his or her qualifications are genuine. There have been a number of cases of false qualifications being claimed by employees which were not discovered until after the employee had already taken confidential information and sold it to competitors.

- *Speak to the candidate's current employer:* Often candidates are not comfortable with this, as they may not have told their employer that they are looking for another job. However, you need to speak to the previous employer at some stage during the recruitment process to ensure your preferred candidate isn't subject to restraint agreements that would prevent him or her from working for you.

- *Ask candidates about their understanding of IP:* Talk to them about their training, the IP protection mechanisms in their current role, their views on pirated DVDs, and so on, in order to get a sense of the depth of their understanding of IP.

Develop comprehensive employment contracts

The new Labor Contract Law, enacted by the National People's Congress on June 29, 2007, and which came into effect on January 1, 2008, permits employers to include some IP protection clauses in labor contracts. However, we strongly recommend that you develop a sound, comprehensive suite of employment contracts (not just a labor contract) to provide complete protection for your IP (including trade secrets) against employees. A typical package would include:

- a labor contract;
- an IP assignment/work for hire agreement;
- a training contract for any overseas training opportunities for the employee;
- a confidentiality agreement; and
- a non-compete agreement.

To ensure you are able to take action for breach of any of these agreements after the employee leaves, the IP assignment agreement, the confidentiality agreement, and the non-compete agreement should expressly survive termination of the labor contract. Keeping the IP agreement separate allows you to bring an action directly to the IP court if necessary, rather than before a less experienced judge in the general court who is used to hearing primarily labor law cases.

As with other contracts in China, start with your standard employment contract and adapt it as appropriate for use in China. It will be important to have a Chinese-language version to ensure that employees understand the obligations they are agreeing to meet.

Assignment of IP Employees often create IP during the course of their employment, including possibly reports, designs, specifications, software, inventions, and so on, depending on their role and the industry. Ownership of copyright usually falls to the "author" of the work—that is, the person or company that created it. There are exceptions to this rule. In many countries, for example, if a copyright work is created by an employee during the course of his or her employment, copyright will be owned by the employer. In China, however, copyright in works created by employees during the course of their employment is owned by the employees, subject to a couple of exceptions (see below). There are limitations on the employee's rights: (1) the employer has the priority right to use the copyright work within its business scope; and (2) the employee cannot, for two years after creation, license a third party to use the copyright work without consent. Copyright will be owned by the employer, rather than the employee, when it relates to software, maps, product design drawings, and engineering designs when they are created primarily with the employer's funds, equipment, and materials. However, this is a gray area often challenged by employees. The law also provides for copyright to be assigned to the employer by contract. To avoid any issues arising over ownership of copyright, we recommend that all employers have a specific copyright assignment agreement with all employees, covering all copyright works created by the employee during the course of his or her employment.

We discuss employees and the assignment of IP in technical innovations in Chapter 10 in relation to R&D centers and technology transfer.

Confidentiality agreements Having employees sign a separate confidentiality agreement ensures that you can continue to enforce rights of confidentiality regardless of whether the labor contract is terminated. The agreement should be short and specific. It needs to contain a very clear definition of "confidential information"—one that covers the key information to which the employee will have access—rather than a very vague "catch-all" definition, such as "anything that could be considered to be confidential." This makes a breach of the agreement easier to prove in an enforcement claim if required. The confidentiality agreement also needs to set out the employer's expectations as to the control and use of, and access to, confidential information, including any confidential information of third parties (such as customers or clients) to which the employee will have access during his or her employment.

Training agreements Increasingly, employers are sending their employees overseas for training at their headquarters or other facilities, or covering the cost of their further studies. At a time when there is a talent shortage in China, this can be a great incentive and an effective way to create loyal employees. On the other hand, some employees will take the overseas training opportunity and then quit shortly afterward, leaving the employer out of pocket and frustrated at the waste of company resources. Many companies now have employees sign a separate training contract which protects the investment of the employer by providing that if the employee resigns within a certain time after completing the training (a reasonable time frame that will be accepted by the courts will depend on the cost of the training, the role of the employee, and so on), he or she must reimburse the employer for the costs of the training. Although such an agreement may just postpone the employee's resignation until the expiration of the limitation period, it does mean that employers are able to obtain some benefit from their investment in training the employee. The training contract should also contain specific obligations regarding any confidential information (which needs to be expressly defined) obtained by the employee during the training, as often this is where a lot of company information is shared. We also recommend presentation of a training certificate at the end of the course as proof that training was indeed given or received. You should retain a copy of the certificate for your records.

Non-compete agreements Restraints, or non-compete restrictions, are enforceable in China. The new Labor Contract Law provides that employers can include non-competition restriction clauses in labor contracts with employees who have access to trade secrets and other confidential information. The Labor Contract Law provides that the parties may agree to a monthly compensation to include a restriction period (commonly known in Europe and Australia as "gardening leave") on the employee. We recommend having a non-compete agreement, or at least a clause in the labor contract, with all key employees. Employers can then choose whether or not to enforce the restriction, depending on the employee, the access they had to confidential information, and the circumstances of their resignation. The new Labor Contract Law also provides that employees who breach a restraint agreement may be liable for damages. The maximum period of restraint under the law is two years, but the time frame that the court will accept will depend on the compensation, the industry, and the geographical restraints. You should seek legal advice to ensure your restraint will be enforceable in China.

Practical Protection

Contract rights can still be difficult to enforce in China, although the courts are becoming more experienced. So, strong contracts need to be combined with practical mechanisms to prevent disclosure of confidential information and infringement of IP. These practical elements of your IP protection strategy focus on access and control of IP and confidential information. A very effective strategy is to create a culture of IP awareness and respect within your company, so that your employees become a part of the solution to protecting your intellectual assets. Engage your employees and explain how important their contribution to the development and protection of IP is to the success of your business. This can be done through the following means:

1. *Explain your IP policies in an employee manual/handbook:* A detailed employee handbook is a very useful tool for helping Chinese employees understand your business's global expectations. We recommend that you localize it for use in China, and have a Chinese-language version. The

IP section needs to describe the importance of IP for the business, set out the company's expectations in regards to IP protection, and explain the rules for sharing information with third parties (including government officials), ensuring that confidential information is able to be accessed only by the relevant people.

2. *Develop policies and processes for exit interviews:* A representative from Human Resources or a direct line manager should meet with each employee before they leave the company, reminding them of their obligations regarding the confidentiality and use of IP. Such employees should be asked to return all confidential information and to confirm in writing that they are not taking any such information with them. They should also be asked to confirm in writing that they won't use any confidential information with their future employers. We also recommend that you obtain details of the new employer and inform them in writing that the employee had access to confidential information during his or her employment with your company, to put them on notice. If the employee breaches his or her confidentiality obligations, you can then also hold the new employer liable for the breach.

3. *Educate employees about the importance of, and your policies on, IP protection:* It is critical to conduct regular training for all employees on IP awareness and responsibilities, so that they are fully aware of the importance of IP to your business and of your processes for protecting confidential information. We also recommend including IP as a separate session in any induction program for new employees.

4. *Develop trade secret protection policies, including restricting access to trade secrets:* This is discussed below.

Trade Secrets

As trade secrets, or business secrets, are often the most valuable assets of companies venturing into China, and they can be protected only for as long as they are kept confidential, it is absolutely critical to take whatever precautions are necessary to protect the confidentiality of this information. The companies that manage their confidential information most successfully, which constitutes a valuable competitive advantage, are those who cast a wide net in their consideration of what should be kept confidential.

In our experience, the key risk areas for trade secret infringement include:

- new employees, particularly when they are recruited from competitors;
- departing employees;
- electronic communications (e-mails, Web sites);
- insufficient procedural protection in the work environment;
- sharing with third parties—e.g. consultants, vendors, visitors, universities, outside inventors, government; and
- insufficient education of employees.

As mentioned in Chapter 5, in order to seek protection for trade secrets under Chinese law, companies must show the court that they have taken certain steps to maintain the confidentiality of the information. These steps are best practice for protecting this information, in any event. They include:

- restricting access to information to those who require it in order to complete their tasks—i.e. sharing information with employees on a "need to know" basis only;
- physically protecting the information, by keeping it in locked cupboards or on password-protected separate network drives;
- clearly distinguishing confidential information from other information, and marking all relevant documents as "confidential" so that there can be no confusion;
- conducting regular and thorough training for employees on how to handle this information;
- having a clear exit process for departing employees; and
- tracking the flow of confidential information, including restricting the use of flash disks, portable hard drives, and laptops.

It is possible to buy "off-the-shelf" template information management policies and checklists that will give you an indication of the steps you need to take. However, the most effective way to implement these policies is to embed them in your own company culture. The policies need to become an integral part of the daily activities of all employees, and the best way to achieve this is for the documents to be familiar and relevant to them. Ensuring that the policies also apply—and are seen to apply—to senior management sends a strong message to employees. Tolerating breaches by senior managers of protocols with which other employees are required to comply not only puts confidential information at risk, but also sends an inconsistent message to employees about the importance of information control and protection. If management takes ownership of, and responsibility for, complying with the protection policies, this will go a long way toward encouraging employees to do the same.

Companies must also actively control what walks out the door with exiting employees and ensure that non-compete agreements are enforced against key employees.

Sharing Information with Government Authorities

This is a very difficult issue. Many companies have faced challenges to their IP following disclosure of confidential information to a government authority. Rules and regulations in China are often vague and open to interpretation, giving the authorities a very broad discretion to request information from companies before granting approvals. Government authorities will always ask for as much information as possible, and many companies hand it over in the belief that they are obliged to do so. There have been cases where the authorities use the information to levy additional taxes or fines against companies for minor regulatory infringements. However, the biggest risk arises when government authorities use the confidential information or disclose it to third parties.

Companies need to have a very clear, written policy on disclosure of information to government authorities. If requested by the authorities to provide additional information, companies need to assess the value of the information and the risks if it is disclosed. In many cases, providing part of the information, along with an explanation as to why the rest of it is confidential, can be sufficient to satisfy the authorities. Occasionally, the authorities will refuse to issue the requested approval without full disclosure of the information. In such cases, companies need to try to negotiate with the authorities— perhaps allow them to review the information in your office, but not give them copies; or ask them to explain why they need the information, pointing out that the regulations don't expressly require it.

A key risk area is when recording copyright in software. The law requires recordal of the first and last 30 pages of the source code with the authorities, but the authorities often ask for more information than is required. The other key risk area is when seeking approval for pharmaceuticals from the State Food and Drug Administration (SFDA). The authorities will often require pharmaceutical companies to teach them how to create and test the drugs before they will issue their approval. If you are such a company, take care to protect your IP in your pharmaceuticals before submitting them to the authorities for approval. Overall, be alert to requests from government officials, and ensure you have a system in place to deal with such requests and that you don't hand over information immediately.

Managing the Relationship with Your Partners

Many of the above recommendations apply equally to relationships with all your partners, whether they are joint venture partners, distributors, or simply licensees. If you have found the right partners by following the advice set out in Chapter 2, hopefully this won't be such an issue. In summary:

- Create a culture of strong IP awareness within your company, and treat employees as though they are part of the solution rather than a part of the potential problem.

- Have strong agreements with your employees which contain IP provisions, and don't be afraid to enforce them.

- Conduct regular training on your IP protection expectations.

- If you part ways with a partner, conduct an "exit interview" covering the same issues as for employees.

- Put processes in place to control access to, and sharing of, confidential information with partners.

- Require your partners to implement similar systems to protect any confidential information shared with them.

Managing Your Supply Chain

The final area that companies can control internally in an effort to minimize IP risks relates to its sourcing companies and suppliers. As this is a major issue for companies that source from China, as

CASE STUDY: ROCKWELL

Rockwell Automation's IP strategy in China is one of the strongest we have seen. But as Alex Gerasimow, IP counsel at Rockwell, notes: "Our company culture has a strong undercurrent of IP respect, so our China policy is just a natural extension of that." When Rockwell decided to enter the China market, their team were very aware of the unique challenges the move would present to protection of their IP. They took a very proactive approach, as follows:

- *They hired a great team in China who drove the strategy from the China end.*

- *They undertook a benchmarking process to assess any gaps in their IP protection processes in China. This project validated their processes, and no glaring gaps were found. Rockwell is a good example of a company that used in other markets (for example, Singapore) what it learned from tightening its processes in China.*

- *They understood the importance of having senior management buy-in before commencing the project.*

- *They localized their standard international agreements for use in China. For example, they added a non-compete clause into their employment agreements.*

Rockwell also took other creative steps to protect its IP.

- *"Guidelines for the Protection of Company Trade Secrets" were issued to raise the level of awareness among all employees.*

- *A "Relocation Guidebook" contains a checklist of IP issues for management to consider if relocating or expanding the company's business.*

- *"Playbooks" set out what give and take is acceptable when a contract negotiation team is negotiating agreements, particularly in relation to IP.*

Rockwell recognized that if the source code for its software was leaked, this would have a serious impact on its business. As a result, the technical team was involved in moving a part of the company's software business to China. Initially, they trialed their processes by limiting the role of their China technicians to coding upgrades for products where they could control the access to information required to complete the tasks. Programmers working in the software lab can download only those parts of the code they need in order to fix the problem they are working on. The servers are all in the United States, and there is no way that information can be taken out of the lab. There are no printers or CD burners in the lab, and the use of laptops or thumb drives is prohibited. As the technical team became more comfortable with their ability to protect Rockwell's IP, they moved more programming onshore in China.

Rockwell has also moved its pushbutton manufacturing business to China; the center includes an engineering, product development, and manufacturing area. In order to protect the IP in the products and processes, the center in China assembles the products, some parts of which have been produced locally while others have been imported. For example, labels are printed in the US so that the company is able to control the quantities of products being manufactured and access to the confidential elements of the technology. The engineers in China had access only to drawings for the pushbutton business, not the other business lines. This procedure works well in a business where drawings and IP can be segregated between business lines.

Training is an important element of any IP protection strategy in China. Rockwell uses the opportunity when its engineers visit the US for training to include IP training in their schedule. It has also introduced a global IP training policy, so that the Chinese staff didn't feel that they were being singled out. In the past, training programs focused on harvesting inventions. They now have a strong element of trade secret and information management. As a result of these training initiatives, the level of awareness of IP—and of its importance— has increased significantly.

IP strategies will always be a work in progress, as Alex Gerasimow acknowledges: "We are not there yet; there are still things we can do. But we are confident we have a robust IP protection policy in place to allow us to maximize our business in China." Rockwell is now enjoying the rewards of the creative steps it has taken to protect the value of its technology and inventions.

well as those that conduct business there, we have covered the topic separately in Chapter 4.

3. YOUR COMPANY'S RIGHTS

In Part 2 we looked at the importance of identifying what IP you needed to bring to China, and at how to protect and register as much of your IP as possible. We discussed the need to define intellectual property very broadly to ensure that you capture as much of your "intellectual assets" as possible. The stronger your rights, the more options you will have to protect your business from infringers. Your rights will also extend to cover reputation and protection under the Anti-Unfair Competition Law for various elements of your brands, packaging, and get-up.

Companies also need to have best practice use guidelines for their brands, and must use their trademarks carefully to avoid them becoming generic. This is a particular risk in the China market, where consumers are looking for generic terms for newly available products and where many of the terms used in the West don't yet exist. If you are not using your brand correctly and monitoring its use in the market, you may lose it. Pfizer discovered this the hard way when it failed to register its Envacar® mark in China. The trademark application was rejected on the basis that the mark had become a generic term in China for anti-high blood pressure tablets (according to the *Contemporary English–Chinese Dictionary*). Pfizer appealed to the Beijing Intermediate Court, claiming that the mark was registered in many countries, that it was used only by Pfizer, and that the dictionary wasn't authoritative. In rejecting the company's case, the court held that Pfizer didn't adduce sufficient evidence that the brand was used only by its company. This is a good example of a distinctive term that lost its distinctiveness through mistranslation and use.

When determining an enforcement strategy, companies should consider issues such as:

- What registered rights do we have? Particularly given the delays in registering trademarks in China, have our applications proceeded to registration, or are we relying on unregistered rights (which are much more difficult to protect in China and depend on the scope of your reputation)?

- How strong are these rights? Could our trademark registration be canceled for non-use (that is, has it been registered for more than five years, but with a continuous period of three years of non-use)? Could our design patent be invalidated for lack of novelty? A common strategy in the 1990s was for companies to register design patents in China, even though they were vulnerable to cancellation having been released elsewhere in the world prior to the application. This was a useful strategy at a time when awareness was relatively low and having a registration certificate was a powerful tool to stop infringements. However, as infringers become smarter and more experienced, they are increasingly challenging the validity of patents. You need to consider these risks in determining the appropriate steps to protect your rights.

- If the issue involves disclosure of a trade secret, where was the leak? Do we have a contractual relationship we could rely on?

- How strong is our reputation in the relevant brand or packaging in China and globally? Could it be considered a "well-known brand" in China? Do we have the evidence to back up this claim?

4. YOUR TEAM

Obtaining senior management buy-in for your China IP strategy is critical. As Simon MacKinnon, president of Corning China, says: "Companies in which someone at senior management level is responsible for IP have much more robust IP/asset management strategies. Entrusting a board member with responsibility for IP means that all decisions and strategic discussions involve a reflection on intellectual property. IP becomes an integral part of the business's commercial agenda, rather than something managed solely by the lawyers." Currently, this structure is more the exception than the rule, although more companies are recognizing its value. At the very least, it is crucial to ensure that senior management is aligned with the China IP strategy and that the team contains an "IP champion." If the management team is aware of the strategy and has committed to it, the IP champion can assist with keeping IP integral in the broader commercial agenda. It is also important to get the most appropriate and experienced team involved in your strategy. This will include:

- having people on the ground in China;
- having a cross-functional team; and
- getting experienced counsel.

Having People on the Ground in China
It is not possible to manage an IP enforcement strategy in China without having someone on the ground to monitor the

environment and provide feedback on the effectiveness of your program. Ideally, this would be people within your business who are familiar with the industry and your business plan.

Sales teams can make fantastic market monitors as they are out in the market, they are intimately involved with the business priorities, and they are often the ones who make the most noise about IP infringements because they impact on their ability to meet their sales targets. Harness their enthusiasm, and train them in how, and to whom, to report sightings. They should not become involved in in-depth investigations or confront infringers, which could be dangerous. They should simply obtain a sample of the infringing item, or collect as much information as possible through observation and anecdotal reports, and pass this on to the responsible person. Many companies have a standard reporting form for the sales team to use in reporting infringements. At Diageo, the IP team gives the management team regular feedback on the progress of any cases they report, to prove that action is being taken and to encourage them to continue to send through sightings.

You need to have people involved who understand the environment in China and are familiar with the processes, challenges, and locations. If you don't have someone who has local insight and who is able to inform you, for example, that Xinjiang (in the remote western part of China) is often used as a wholesale point for products going into Russia, then you may decide it is not a business priority area and so fail to take action—until your Russian colleagues start complaining that a lot of infringing product is entering their market through Xinjiang. Another effective tool is to send a representative to visit officials and present your commitment to IP enforcement.

If your business is run through a joint venture or licensing arrangement in China, it is important to find a champion in your partner who can act as a conduit for information for you on IP issues. Most companies will have someone who is enthusiastic about IP and happy to take on the responsibility for reporting information and acting as a local contact point. In many of the companies we have worked with, the China IP strategy is run by the IP department at head office overseas, which may have no direct contact with the local business. While not ideal, this system can work if the head office IP team engages with the teams on the ground. In one example, the IP enforcement focus had been on a product design that was a global priority. Much time and money had been spent trying to protect the design from a number of counterfeits and copycats in China. We needed some evidence of use and reputation in the design, and the company eventually tracked down the name of someone in their China business to whom we might speak. When we met with this person and showed him the design we were trying to protect, he said: "Wow, I've never seen this product before! It's quite nice, but we'd never sell it in China because it's too dull!" The company hadn't connected its IP strategy with its commercial priorities, nor had it involved the team on the ground. If it had done so, it would have realized that the product was never going to be commercially viable in China and shouldn't have been a part of its China IP enforcement plan.

Having a Cross-functional Team

In many jurisdictions, it is appropriate to have an IP protection strategy managed solely by the legal team. However, in China, this practice won't enable you to develop a comprehensive strategy. As we discuss throughout this book, the laws on paper are relatively complete. However, their implementation and practical enforcement remains in the early stages of development, which often means that you will need to lobby the authorities to get them to take action or make an informal decision on the meaning of a particular law, as many of the implementing regulations remain internal government documents. Many companies expect their legal counsel to be able to give them specific advice on the law, options, and risks, as they are used to being given in other markets. But in China, answers are often vague and may change from day to day. This is the nature of China, so having a team that can interpret these challenges for you, and which has the experience to brainstorm different solutions, will be significantly more effective. In particular, it is critical to have members of the following teams on your IP strategic team:

- *Your IP/legal team.*
- *Your corporate relations/government relations team.* The lines between legal issues and government relations issues are blurred in China, where the law has a different role to the law in the West. Laws in China are often couched in vague, general terms. The specific interpretation is often left to the broad discretion of the authorities who are responsible for implementing the laws (and, in many cases, this may involve

more than one authority), so it is important to have contacts within those authorities able to provide you with informal advice about their interpretations of the law.

- *Your IT and corporate security teams* are particularly critical when you are seeking to protect technology or confidential information. Often, companies fail to engage these teams, but their ideas and ability to provide practical solutions for managing access to information are an important element of your China strategy.

- *Your supply/procurement teams* are particularly important for managing suppliers' use of IP.

- *Your technical/research teams* will be able to advise on the risk areas. Engaging them also helps to instill the corporate culture of respect for IP, as these teams understand the importance of protecting intellectual assets. You will also need them to assist with assessing whether a product infringes your technology, and with analyzing the content and processes being used by infringers. Some of the most interesting discussions we have had on how to prevent infringers manufacturing counterfeit pharmaceuticals have come from brainstorming sessions with the technical teams on technical packaging solutions to make infringement more difficult (and expensive).

- *Your sales teams*, as we discussed above.

Getting Experienced Counsel

Obviously, having experienced lawyers you trust is vital in any market. However, in China, having experienced legal teams on the ground is even more important. Many companies choose to use their local counsel in their home market, who may have a loose association with a firm in China. While you may be more comfortable with your regular law firm, this approach opens you to the risk of not getting constructive, tailored advice from counsel who understand how China works. Many international law firms support their China practices out of Hong Kong. This can work if they have teams based on the mainland as well. The environment in China is changing quickly, so if you aren't working with counsel who have representatives working on the ground in China you will run the risk of getting out-of-date advice. (Rouse & Co. International, with offices in Beijing, Shanghai, and Guangzhou, has significant experience on the ground in China, enabling the firm to give practical, achievable advice.) Or you may get advice that is legally correct, but which cannot actually be implemented because you haven't realized the necessity of engaging with the authorities to get feedback on how the issue is dealt with in practice.

Companies should also ensure that they use advisors in China who understand their legal and ethical obligations. There are numerous consulting and investigation companies in China offering to conduct investigation and administrative raids at reasonable rates. However, these types of companies are not regulated in China, so make sure you use a reputable one. There are examples of these companies using illegal methods during their investigations to obtain information for their clients. As many companies will take action only when there have been sightings of large quantities of infringing products, there have been examples of consulting companies drumming up business for themselves by placing an order for the infringing product, reporting the order to the local representative of the legitimate owner of the brand, and then offering to conduct a raid. Consulting companies have even been known to fake raids (including providing photographs of the "raid") and to charge the client for the privilege.

Although such cases are in the minority, they do happen. You will need to make your expectations of what is appropriate clear to your advisors. If your targets are based solely on quantities seized, not only will this *not* be an effective way to protect your IP rights, but it may also provide an incentive to your service provider to increase the quantities reported or to create orders themselves in order to meet your objectives. Most such agencies use people who don't have a legal background and whose experience lies mainly in simple trademark infringement cases. Make sure you use a company that can draft submissions to the authorities and can argue more complex legal issues if necessary. When choosing an agency, consider your expectations and objectives for this service provider—what do you want them to deliver? Then select the type of company accordingly. If you are choosing a consulting company, make sure they have the appropriate experience. Can they conduct in-depth investigations to identify distribution chains of the infringements or get to the source? Can they conduct a market survey? This is a very different skill from simply identifying infringements and conducting raids. Do they have experience in conducting raids in the geographic areas of your priorities? Do your IP issues raise complex legal questions requiring involvement of a law firm? Many companies use a combination of service providers—a consulting company for straight counterfeit raids, and a law firm for more complex legal issues, such as criminal cases or look-alike cases. This can be a very cost-effective strategy.

Once you have counsel or advisors you are comfortable with, we recommend that you invest in the relationship by teaching them about your business. The greater their understanding of your business and your priorities, the more effective your program will be. For example, Diageo runs quarterly meetings with its lawyers in China to discuss the priorities for the next quarter's enforcement program on copycat cases, as well as sharing with them information about its priority brands, business plan, and new promotions to assist them in providing advice and results that are tailored to its commercial objectives.

In this chapter, we have examined the way your company needs to operate in order to protect it from IP infringement in China. Once you have the internal structure, you will be better placed to take action against the external risks. In the next chapter, we will examine these external considerations relating to the types of infringements you may face and the likely infringers.

CHECKPOINT

In preparing a sound IP strategy for China, there are eight key areas. In this chapter, we considered the "You" factors—the internal factors.

- *Your company's goals:* Have you matched your company's commercial objectives with your IP strategy?
- *Your IP rights:* Have you checked the strength of your IP rights?
- *Your team:* Do you have the right team in place, including alignment from senior management on the strategy and from people on the ground in China?
- *Your management of IP:* Do you have strong internal processes in place to prevent leakage and infringement from inside your supply chain and your company?

RESOURCES

- www.buyusa.gov/china/en/ipr.html: A US government Web site that contains a China IP toolbox with some interesting suggestions.
- www.ipr.gov.cn: The government's Web site on IP in China contains a number of the relevant laws in English, as well as other resources and links to interesting Web sites.

Chapter

7

"Them": External considerations

Strong internal protection mechanisms are an important preventative measure in your IP strategy for China, as discussed in Chapter 6. However, you are still likely to face challenges from external parties. If you face a number of infringements, how do you determine how to assess the cases and prioritize your actions? In our experience, many companies start spending money randomly as infringement cases come up, without a real strategy as to what they hope to achieve. Others focus on the numbers—quantities of products seized, numbers of raids conducted, and so on. This is an important, measurable objective, but it needs to be part of a broader strategy. As one person noted: "We are not unrealistic. We know

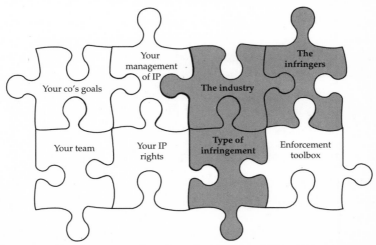

Figure 7.1 Key components of an effective China IP protection strategy: External considerations

that IP infringement is part of doing business in China and that it cannot be eliminated entirely. However, we can and will reduce it to a manageable level." This is the reality of China. With this in mind, in this chapter we look at how to prioritize the steps you take against third parties who infringe your IP in China; otherwise, you could spend all your budget and have no noticeable improvement in the market.

The external environment will provide the background against which you overlay your internal framework. As shown in Figure 7.1, there are three key elements to consider:

- the industry in which you operate;
- the type of infringement; and
- the identity of the infringers.

1. THE INDUSTRY IN WHICH YOU OPERATE

The industry in which you operate will drive the priorities of your enforcement program.

- Is it driven by brand integrity (for example, most consumer goods producers)? If so, your program will most likely focus on the enforcement of trademarks and copyright, as well as reliance on the Anti-Unfair Competition Law. A public relations program to reassure consumers may also be necessary. We will discuss these programs later in this chapter.
- Is it driven by technology (for example, companies in the aeronautical or engineering industry)? If so, there are likely to be more trade secret protection elements to your strategy, as well as a strong patent portfolio.
- Is it driven by a combination of the two (for example, companies in the software and pharmaceuticals industries)?

2. TYPE OF INFRINGEMENT

Working out the basis of the infringement is an important part of determining the appropriate line of attack. There is a saying around Shanghai, "We can copy everything except your mother." This is getting close to the truth! This section examines the main types of infringements companies are likely to face in China.

Common Types of Infringements in China

Counterfeits

A counterfeit good is a direct copy of a product. In the past, these were usually targeted at the luxury goods industry; counterfeits of Louis Vuitton® handbags, Diesel® T-shirts, Mont Blanc® pens, and Rolex® watches were staple souvenirs for visitors to Asia. People knew they were buying "fakes"; that was a part of the fun of it. However, this has now changed. The famous Xiang Yang Market in Shanghai (the "Fake Market") was closed down on July 1, 2006, with great ceremony and claims of IP protection. The day of the closure, the entrances to the market were bricked over and a bright red banner was strung up, proclaiming: "Struggle to Protect the Legal Right of Trademark Obligee and Consumer." The skeptics among us saw the closure of Xiang Yang Market as a publicity stunt combined with a commercial decision that the land was more valuable as the site for a new highrise building than for a market selling fake branded goods! Touts now line the streets surrounding the old market in an attempt to entice tourists into the stores relocated in nearby laneways with their offers of "Watch, bags, shoes, DVDs—cheaper for you." In fact, an advertisement that is run regularly on the front page of the *Shanghai Daily* newspaper claims to be for "the new Xiang Yang Market."

Although these fake souvenirs live on, now almost everything is at risk of counterfeiting—from DVDs, mobile phone accessories, and car parts to pharmaceuticals, alcohol, toothpaste, and baby formula. This shift in counterfeits has changed the rules of the game. The fake products are passed off as genuine products; this not only risks damage to the brand through low quality, but also places consumers in danger from the health risks associated with counterfeit products. Counterfeits generally involve use of registered trademarks (assuming the brand owners have registered their marks), so the fastest way to stop counterfeiters is to take action against them for trademark infringement.

Look-alikes or Copycats

These types of cases tend to result from a crackdown on counterfeits; they are the next phase in IP infringements. They involve infringers trying to trade off the reputation of well-known brands by creating a product that looks very similar to the famous product—in the process, confusing consumers as to the origin of the product. Often, they are a compliment to the brands, as only the market leaders tend to be copied! This has been a common issue in the motor industry, which is surprising given the investment required to copy a car. The Chery QQ is a well-known look-alike of GM's Chevrolet Spark® car. The copycat actually appeared on the market six months ahead of the original, after a Chinese firm obtained the blueprints. Obviously, this example raises issues of supply chain management as well as IP infringement.

In another example, we attended a conference in a major five-star hotel in Shanghai and were given headphones for translation of the Chinese speaker. One set of headphones was branded Sony®; another, almost identical, set was branded Sonia in a very similar font. The copycat headphones were aimed at trading off the reputation in the Sony® brand.

Diageo faced a number of copycats of its Johnnie Walker® Scotch whisky brand in China. Copycats generally have to be attacked by relying on the Anti-Unfair Competition Law, which can be a challenge in China. (More on this later.) Although no one likes to see copycats, they are a sign of the increasing sophistication of China's IP system—and its infringers!

Trademark Infringement

In addition to counterfeits, many companies face use of their trademarks on similar products or services in China by infringers. For example, the Nike® swoosh logo is used on clothing, but not in connection with the Nike® brand.

Vexatious Registration of Trademarks ("Ghost Marks")

A common issue facing companies in China is registration of their brands as trademarks by Chinese companies, often with the intention of extorting the brand owners. As explained in Chapter 5, China has a first-to-file trademark system, which means that if another company registers your mark first, it can be very difficult (and expensive) to get it back. Pfizer Inc. learned this lesson the hard way when the Chinese pharmaceutical company Shenyang Feilong Pharmaceutical Co., Ltd. registered its own version of Pfizer's brand Viagra®—Weige—in China. The Chinese company's registration cost Pfizer a significant amount of money (both in legal fees, while trying to recover the registration, and in lost sales) and has made it difficult for Pfizer to expand distribution of its Viagra® brand in China.

Copyright Infringement

Copyright can be a very complex area of law, particularly in the current environment with the popularity of the Internet. (Many will have read of the recent case against Yahoo! China by the International Federation of Phonographic Industries (IFPI) for illegal downloads of copyright material, such as songs and movies. The record industry recently won the appeal which was lodged by Yahoo! China so it was a very positive case.) High-profile examples of copyright infringement found on the streets of China's main cities include fake DVDs, CDs, and software—even the Chinese version of most of the *Harry Potter* series of books was released before the real thing. But it happens at a general level, too. For example, there have been many suggestions that Chinese companies have brought in a foreign architectural firm to "pitch" for projects, and then have given the project—and the foreign firm's plans and designs—to a local Chinese company to build. Copyright infringement also arises in relation to reports, product designs, logos, articles, and so on.

Patent/Design Infringement

Your patents or designs are most likely to be infringed by third-party competitors, rather than by people to whom you license your rights. This wasn't always the case. In the early days of opening to the West, Chinese licensees or joint venture partners might begin to infringe after being introduced to the patents and learning how they worked. These days, the repercussions of such blatant and conspicuous use are well known, and partners are less likely to steal. With the advances in technology and technical expertise, patent infringement these days is mostly perpetrated by third parties who attempt to reverse engineer your patented invention and produce something different in order to avoid infringement. These scrupulous individuals will likely have gone to impressive lengths to detect any weaknesses in your granted patent rights; then, if you challenge them (hopefully in court, since the adminis-trative authority for patent enforcement is limited in power), they will retaliate by lodging an action with the Patent Office to invali-date your granted rights. Chinese infringers are becoming partic-ularly adept at using retaliatory invalidations to slow down any action the patent owner may take against them. The best advice here is to plan for this, and to have your local PRC patent lawyers draft patent claims that can withstand such challenges.

We are also seeing a growing number of patent cases in China where both parties are foreign. This has long been predicted within the small group of foreign IP lawyers based in China. Just as China's laboratories are a cost-effective way to spin out R&D, so too are the People's Courts a cost-effective way to determine the validity and strength of foreign patents before fighting actions in jurisdictions where real damages can be won (such as in the US or Europe). For example, Honda faced infringement of its design patent by a large domestic manufacturer. The infringer sought—but failed—to invalidate Honda's patent, and Honda succeeded in its infringement action. Be prepared for more foreign competitors to challenge your PRC patent rights in the future!

Internet Infringements

China is struggling to come to terms with IP infringements in the online world, alongside the rest of the international community. There have been a number of high-profile cases relating to unauthorized uploading, linking, and search engines, with inconsistent outcomes, so some clarification will be welcome in this area. Baidu.com, a Chinese search engine, lost a deep linking case instituted by an EMI affiliate in September 2005. It then won a case for single linking in November 2006. In December 2006, the First Intermediate Court fined Soho.com approximately US$140,000 for allowing downloading of movies. Yahoo! China lost a case to the International Federation of Phonographic Industries, which took action on behalf of 11 recording companies (including Sony, BMG, EMI, Universal Vivendi, and Warner Music) for copyright infringement arising from the fact that its search engine linked to sites that contained pirated songs. IFPI appealed the case because the damages granted by the court (RMB210,000) were lower than they had asked for. Yahoo! China also appealed on the basis that search engine operators should not be held liable for content posted on third-party Web sites. The Beijing High Court upheld the original decision in December 2007. Companies also face infringements online through offers for sale of infringing products.

Trade Secret Infringement

Trade secret infringement usually comes from either employees or business partners, as the infringer must have had some access to the information to be able to disclose it. The most high-profile trade secret case in China didn't involve a foreign company. Three former employees of Shen Zhen Huawei Co., Ltd. had been intimately involved in R&D within Huawei. Huawei had taken a number of steps to protect its confidential information—for example, the employees had been required to sign confidentiality agreements and labor contracts. They had also signed agreements when they left Huawei, agreeing not to take confidential information with them. However, the three soon started their own company, in which they used information taken from Huawei. Huawei sued the former employees for theft of its business secrets, and won. The employees were fined and received jail sentences.

Unauthorized Registration of Trading Names

In China, as in many countries, trading names are not checked for infringement of registered trademarks before they are registered. If the name being registered is a famous name, the Administration for Industry and Commerce may challenge the company's right to register the name, but in most cases it rests with the trademark owner to monitor the market and take action to remove trading names that infringe its name. This issue is becoming increasingly important in China, where the authorities/factories require evidence of the right to manufacture a branded product. Companies have been known to register a trading name using the brand, and then to issue an authorization letter from the company giving them the right to produce the company's products. Chinese entities are increasingly using Hong Kong-based entities for this as well, to give them more credibility. These Hong Kong companies are often called "shadow companies," and we'll explore them further in the next chapter.

Domain Name Infringement

Cyber squatting is a global problem associated with the huge popularity of the Internet and its increasing importance both as a marketing tool for communicating with consumers and as a business platform. Many companies have faced the challenge of recovering their .com.cn domain names following registration by a cyber squatter, often long before the company even considered entering the Chinese market. IKEA, the Swedish furniture giant, discovered in 1997 that the ikea.com.cn domain name had already been registered by a third party. The registrant was a well-known cyber squatter who had registered a number of foreign companies' brands as domain names in China. IKEA had to commence litigation against the registrant to recover the name.

Image, or Celebrity, Rights

Celebrities often try to protect the use of their images through a right of publicity (for example, in the US) or a right to privacy (in the UK). These are hotly contested areas of the law globally. In China, the Chinese General Principles of Civil Law provide all Chinese citizens with the exclusive right to use their portrait or image. It is generally only those celebrities who see value in commercializing this right who take action to protect it. The key case that considers this right is known as *The Tea House* case, as it involved an actor who played a leading role in a well-known Chinese film of the same name. The actor, who never appeared in commercial advertisements, discovered that a five-star hotel in Beijing was using an image of him from the film (with two other actors) in its promotional materials, giving the impression that he had been paid for the commercial. The actor demanded damages and an apology from the hotel. When they refused, he took them to court. Although the hotel's lawyers argued that the image from the film was a matter of copyright, which belonged to the film's producer, rather than a matter of infringement of the portrait rights of the actors, the court found that use of the image without consent infringed the actor's IP rights. The court held that the image clearly identified the actor, and so his right of portrait wasn't undermined by the fact that he appeared as a character in a film. Companies will need to be aware of the scope of this right in China, where more Chinese celebrities are discovering the value of commercializing the use of their images, and more companies are wanting to use celebrities' images to promote their own products and services through sponsorships. We will discuss this issue further in Chapter 11, in relation to sporting celebrities in China.

Identifying Key Risk Areas

You need to identify where your company's key risk areas lie by asking questions such as:

- How is the infringement affecting your company's bottom line?
  - Is the infringement a counterfeit (that is, a direct copy of your products) sold through similar distribution channels,

so that it competes directly with sales of your products? This is often the case with alcohol, automobile oil products, and food and beauty products, for example.

- Are the counterfeit copies being sold through different distribution channels, so that consumers know they are not buying a genuine product (for example, Rolex® watches being sold by hawkers in known fake markets, or DVDs bought on the streets)?

- Does the infringement involve technology belonging to your company? That is, does it involve a loss of crucial confidential information that creates a significant loss to your business?
- Is the infringement a copycat or look-alike product, which dilutes your brand or may confuse consumers but doesn't generally result in a direct lost sale for your company?
- Where are the infringing products sold? Is it through the same distribution channels as your products?
- Is it possible that the products are overruns or midnight runs from your suppliers?
- Are the infringing products competing with your genuine products?
- Are the infringing products parodies of your brand? For example, a company in Hong Kong regularly uses parodies of well-known international brands in its clothing line—such as the name "McSlavery" used with the Golden Arches made famous by McDonald's. If the parody suggests a connection with drugs, sex, or something else not in line with the brand values, you may wish to take action to stop the parody.
- What types of IP rights are involved? This will help you to determine which of the tools in your IP toolbox you should use (see Chapter 8).

3. IDENTITY OF THE INFRINGERS

Knowing the identity of infringers and having knowledge of their operations will assist you in determining the most appropriate strategy for your business. This is often the most difficult information to obtain, and will require an investment of both time and money to acquire. However, having collected and analyzed this information, you will be able to target your approach at the most effective level of the infringing supply chain. The following questions will be helpful in obtaining the information you need to consider:

- What type of company is the infringer? Is it a retailer? A trading company? A wholesaler or distributor? A manufacturer?

- Where is the infringer located? Is it in a known infringement hotspot? Is it in an area that suffers from protectionism by the authorities? Is it in a location where the courts are IP aware and experienced? Is it in an area where your company conducts business?

- Does the infringer supply the infringements only to the domestic market, or does it export the products overseas?

- Does the infringer have any assets?

- Is the infringer known to the authorities or other brand owners as a repeat infringer?

Many companies target their enforcement programs at the retail end—"cleaning up the market." (This is obviously important for strategic reasons, but it won't stop the infringement.) For example, Dunhill took action against Parkson, in Shandong, for selling counterfeit bags and packs without permission. Parkson is a well-known, well-respected department store chain in which consumers may expect to be able to buy the genuine product. Thus, Dunhill felt it was important to take action, in order to send a message to consumers that these types of stores are safe for buying genuine products.

Generally, though, identifying the "driving force" behind the infringements will allow you to direct your enforcement budget at the most valuable targets. In some industries, the driving force will be the manufacturers, who sell their products through business-to-business Web sites. In other industries, it may be being driven by the "middle men"—businesses that design a product which infringes a third party's rights and offer it for sale at trade fairs, online, and so on. Once they receive an order, they find a manufacturer to supply the product for them. These types of cases are difficult, because there will often be no stock of infringing products to justify a raid. This is often the case with design patent infringements, where offering the product for sale isn't an infringement; it is the *act of manufacture or sale* that infringes the rights. Sending the infringer a letter asking them to remove the images from their Web site or other sites, or taking action at trade fairs to get them to remove images from their catalogues, may provide some relief. Some companies place trap orders to identify the factories and then conduct a raid. However, unless the target is a major or strategic one, this approach simply gives the target confirmation that there is demand for the products!

In some industries, the counterfeit supply chain is becoming increasingly decentralized, rather than consisting of single, self-contained operations. For example, printer cartridges are often refilled in one place, packed in another, and then warehoused in a third, making it more difficult to take action. Creative action will be important in dealing with this type of environment.

Once you have identified the type of infringement and the infringer involved, you need to determine which action will be most effective in stopping the damage to your IP. This requires you to consider your enforcement toolbox, which will be discussed in Chapter 8.

CHECKPOINT

In preparing a sound IP strategy for China, you will need to consider the eight key areas identified at the start of Part 3. In this chapter, we have considered the "Them" factors—the external elements—that will impact on your strategy.

- *Your industry:* Have you assessed the industry in which you operate, and the specific options and opportunities it creates?

- *The infringers:* Have you investigated and gained a firm understanding of the infringers? Who is the driving force, and how does the supply work?

- *The type of infringement:* What type of infringement are you facing? Have you considered the strongest approach for dealing with it?

RESOURCES

- www.ipr.gov.cn: The government's Web site on IP in China contains a number of the relevant laws in English, as well as other resources and links to interesting Web sites.

- www.cnnic.net.cn: China Internet Network Information Center.

- www.buyusa.gov/china/en/ipr.html: A US government Web site that contains a China IP toolbox with some interesting suggestions.

- www.chinaiprlaw.com/english/default.htm: A Chinese Web site with some interesting resources on IP run by Judge Jiang Zhipei, one of the IP judges of the Supreme People's Court in China. The site contains numerous English case briefs and many of the IP laws.

Chapter

8

"What": The enforcement toolbox

The third phase of developing a China IP strategy is to look at your enforcement options—the enforcement toolbox (see Figure 8.1). In this chapter, we will outline some of the traditional tools—as well as alternative channels—for protecting your rights.

1. ADMINISTRATIVE ACTION

The options for IP enforcement in China include taking action through the administrative authorities. This route for enforcement was extremely popular up until the last couple of years, when

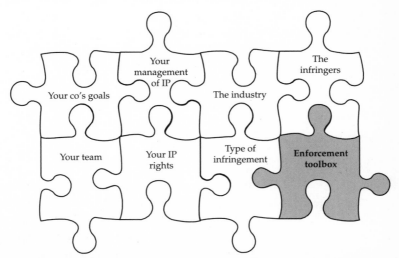

Figure 8.1 Key components of an effective China IP protection strategy: Enforcement toolbox

Table 8.1 Responsible authorities for various IP rights

Authority	IP right
Administration for Industry and Commerce (AIC)	• Trademarks • Unfair competition actions • Trade
Technical Supervision Bureau (TSB)	• Labeling, advertising, anti-counterfeiting, product quality issues
Intellectual Property Offices	• Patents (including design patents)
National Copyright Administration	• Copyright

close to 90% of IP infringement matters in China were handled through the administrative agencies. These authorities still offer an effective and economical means to investigate and stop the piracy or unauthorized use of IP rights. They also generally accept a lower threshold of evidence than the People's Courts.

Areas of Responsibility

There has been some tension among the authorities over which authority is responsible for different types of IP infringement actions. As we have discussed elsewhere in the book, the matrix of responsibilities for IP in China is confusing and the lines are blurred. Table 8.1 sets out the responsible authorities for each action.

The effectiveness of these authorities, and their willingness to take action, varies considerably depending on a number of factors:

• the location;

• the authority;

• the infringer; and

• the amount of information and evidence available.

The overlap between the Administration for Industry and Commerce and the Technical Supervision Bureau has historically been the cause of much tension. The AIC has been plagued by conflict between its commercial and IP responsibilities. When it was unwilling to take action, the TSB, which is responsible for overseeing consumer protection issues such as product quality and national standards, stepped in to oversee counterfeits. (Arguably, the low quality and inherent consumer risks of counterfeit goods bring them within its remit.) The TSB is far less weighed down by conflicts and resourcing issues, and is grateful for the case fees it can earn from counterfeit cases.

Location

Authorities in the major cities and some other key areas have a much higher awareness of IP than do those in more remote areas. In some areas, there are also higher levels of protectionism than in others. This is particularly the case in areas where there is a high dependence on a certain industry for taxes. (Some parts of the country are still very reliant on counterfeiting to support local businesses.) In some provinces, particularly where there is a high level of foreign investment, the authorities will be more active in protecting IP rights in order to encourage more investment.

The Authority

Some of the authorities have few resources for IP enforcement. The Copyright Administration has a very limited budget for enforcement, and its understanding of the intricacies of copyright law is very varied. In some areas, the authorities will take action only in the case of a direct copy of a copyright work, rather than focusing on whether a substantial part of the work has been copied. The issue of infringement of a work of applied art (as discussed in Chapter 5) is also one the authorities generally don't understand. With the increased sophistication of infringers, who are now often challenging the decisions of the authorities, the officials are becoming even more reluctant to take action to protect an IP owner's rights.

There are also cases where the authority has internal conflicts of interest. For example, the AIC regulates all commercial activity, including responsibility for the enforcement of trademarks and unfair competition cases. There is often a conflict between management of the market (that is, the IP side, which takes time and resources and, increasingly, risks violence from infringers) and the regulation of enterprises (that is, business licenses and registration for which they collect fees, which is much less likely to be dangerous). The officials will be reluctant to shut down businesses that provide the government with a steady flow of income through taxes or other payments, in order to protect IP rights—particularly the rights of foreign companies.

In some areas, the administrative authorities are quite proactive in conducting raids to seize infringing products. The more steps you take to educate these authorities about your brands, and to show them how to distinguish a genuine product from a counterfeit one, the more likely it is they will proactively take action to protect your IP. However, in general the authorities take a more passive role in investigating infringements only on the request of rights owners, except in cases where the infringed goods pose a public health or safety threat.

The Infringer

If the infringer is a well-connected or well-known company that provides a steady source of income to the government, the authorities may be less likely to take action for infringement, particularly if the infringer also contributes significant taxes to the local authority.

The Amount of Information and Evidence Available

The likelihood of the authorities following up on a request to take action over an infringement will depend on their resources, the amount of information the IP owner can give them about the infringement and the infringing company, as well as the amount of evidence of the infringement. The amount or type of evidence required by the authorities will depend on the location of the infringement and the particular authority. Some authorities, such as the Patent Office, require notarized evidence; others may accept a sample purchase and an indication of quantities.

The Complaint Process

The process for reporting an infringement to the administrative authorities varies depending on the authority involved, but generally you will need the following documents:

- A submission should set out the claim, with details of the infringer and the rights being claimed.
- Prima facie evidence of the infringement will be required, such as an investigation report. Some authorities require

this evidence to be notarized and legalized, which can create challenges in patent cases (see below).

- You will need to produce copies of the registration certificates (if any) on which the claim is based. Although recordal of copyright is technically not required for protection in China, many of the Copyright Administration offices won't take action without a copyright registration certificate. An unfair competition claim will usually require sales data and other evidence that your product is well known in China. The more evidence you can give the authorities of your reputation, the more likely it is they will take on the case.

- A power of attorney (POA) will be required if you are using an agency or law firm to lodge the complaint. Some authorities will require the POA to be notarized and legalized; others require it only to be signed. In order to ensure that you have the POA ready in case you need to take action, we recommend that you prepare it in advance once you have selected your agency. The POA can be granted to cover multiple actions for a specific time frame.

Usually, once the authorities receive a submission, they will then meet with the claimant's agents to confirm the details of the claim and the strategy for the enforcement action. Ensure that your agent or lawyer advocates zealously for you at this meeting, particularly in marginal cases or where your evidence may not be complete, in order to convince the authorities to take up your complaint immediately.

After accepting your submission, the authorities will sometimes conduct their own investigation to confirm the infringement and then organize a raid. During the raid, the officials will visit the premises of the infringer and search for the infringing products. In patent cases, the authorities don't have the power to seize the infringing products or materials; they will simply seal and inventory them, and leave them on the premises, although usually with an undertaking from the suspected infringer not to move or otherwise dispose of them. In most other cases, the authorities will seize the products and take them to a warehouse for storage pending the outcome of the case.

The authorities also have a fairly wide discretion to ask for information about the infringing products, including their source (if the infringer is not a manufacturer) and the name of the customer who placed the order. Often this information isn't available, but it is always worth asking the authorities to try to obtain as much information as possible. One of the benefits of having a representative attend the raid is that it ensures the products are accurately counted and seized, and that any other relevant information is collected. It can also be helpful in cases where the infringer argues with the officials that his or her products don't infringe the IP rights being claimed, or that he or she has authorization to produce/sell the products. There have been cases where the infringer has produced a trademark registration certificate or a letter that purports to authorize their use of the IP involved. Although there may be an argument between the officials and the infringer over such claims, the officials may be reluctant, unless the IP owner's representative is present, to risk having a claim made against them later by the infringers for the losses they suffered as a result of the raid. Infringers are increasingly using this tactic—in particular, having a fake authorization letter (often from a shadow company in Hong Kong, as discussed further below) to present to the authorities—to try and get around raids.

The authorities will then review the evidence and the quantity of product seized, and issue a punishment decision to the infringer. This usually imposes a fine and orders destruction of the infringing products. We recommend following up with the authorities regularly to ensure they issue the punishment decision in a timely manner. The fine is meant to be imposed based on the value of the seized goods, but there is often debate around whether the relevant value is that of the genuine product or the counterfeit product. We'll discuss valuation issues further in relation to criminal cases.

Effectiveness of Administrative Action

In the past, administrative action was the fastest, most cost-effective way to take action to prevent infringement of IP. This was particularly the case as infringements tended to be counterfeits (direct copies), which were easy to identify. However, as the IP environment changes, so does the effectiveness of administrative action as a deterrent to infringement. Its value also varies depending on the type of right being enforced. It tends to be more effective for trademark infringement and some straightforward unfair competition cases, but more complicated and expensive for copyright and patent cases due to the complexity of the rights

Table 8.2 Advantages and disadvantages of administrative action as a tool in an enforcement regime

Advantages	Disadvantages
• Generally fast and relatively cost-effective, particularly for trademark infringement cases	• The fines and seizure of products tend to be of low deterrent value which are often built-in as an expected "business cost" by infringers.
• Useful for collecting intelligence against other targets and evidence for civil litigation action	• For copyright and patent rights, the authorities may not have the resources or experience to take on cases. Often, it takes more time and evidence to convince them of the infringement and to take action.
• Can be used to send a strong message to the market and to keep the market clean of infringements while action is taken to stop infringement at the source	• Local protectionism still exists in some areas.
	• Tends to be a short-term solution
	• The increasing sophistication of infringers means that they are aware of the law and engage in activities that are arguably infringing but more complicated. Infringers also often challenge the validity of raids and threaten to take action against the authorities for unfair action. This creates an environment of reluctance and caution by the officials in more complex cases.

involved and the inexperience of the authorities in determining infringements.

Table 8.2 sets out the advantages and disadvantages of administrative action as a tool in an enforcement regime.

2.   CIVIL LITIGATION

Up until recently, foreign companies were reluctant to use the civil litigation mechanism to enforce their rights in China. This

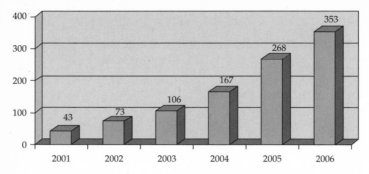

Figure 8.2 IP litigation cases involving foreign litigants, 2001–2006
Source: Supreme People's Court.

was partly for very good reasons. The courts weren't experienced in hearing complex IP infringement cases, the judges weren't trained in the relevant laws, and there was still corruption and protectionism in the courts. However, the value of launching civil litigation is becoming stronger and increasing numbers of foreign companies are turning to the courts to protect their IP from infringement in China. As Jiang Zhipei, the chief justice of the Intellectual Property Rights (IPR) Tribunal of the Chinese Supreme People's Court, has famously said: "Foreign companies should take their complaints to courts rather than to the newspapers or their politicians" and "Foreign companies should complain less and act more." According to many lawyers in China, their foreign clients are now willing to engage with the court system to resolve ongoing issues, and there has been a steady increase in the number of IP litigation cases involving foreign parties (see Figure 8.2). Recent high-profile cases include the highly publicized luxury goods companies' victory over the landlords of the Silk Market in Beijing, and Starbucks' victory in Shanghai over a persistent infringer that was using the international coffee chain's Chinese name, "Xingbake."

The numbers of cases in Figure 8.2 don't give a complete picture, because they don't include companies that are registered in China (that is, foreign-invested enterprises) and often cases are commenced by foreign companies' Chinese entities. To give a more accurate indication, from January to October 2006, 533 IP cases were lodged and 308 were concluded; of those, 207 involved a foreign litigant (including FIEs). These cases mostly involved trademark rights, followed by patent and copyright cases.

CASE STUDY: STARBUCKS AND XINGBAKE

Starbucks sued the Shanghai company Xingbake for trademark infringement and unfair competition for use of an identical Chinese trade name, as well as a similar logo to Starbucks' famous green and white logo. Shanghai No. 2 Intermediate Court awarded RMB500,000 (approximately US$60,000) in damages and ordered the defendant to apologize. It held that (1) the registration of the enterprise name was in bad faith because, being in the same industry (coffee), they must have known about Starbucks; and (2) the association caused confusion as to the origin of the services and as to whether a relationship existed between the companies, resulting in unfair competition. The court also declared Starbucks and its Chinese name, Xingbake, to be well-known trademarks due to Starbucks' international reputation and extensive promotion in Chinese-speaking territories. This decision was upheld on appeal.

The case was noteworthy not only due to its high-profile nature, but also because the court set out some very practical and helpful considerations to take into account when determining well-known trademarks. By making it clear that prior trademark rights prevail over subsequent rights in an enterprise name, pirates are prevented from taking advantage of the vagueness of the law and the loophole in the system, which fails to require the Trademarks Office to check trade name registrations.

The courts are becoming increasingly transparent. The proceedings are now usually open to the public (including foreigners, who, until recently, were not able to attend court without special permission). All judgments are now published on the Internet in Chinese, and some are being published in English. All the relevant rules and regulations are published and available to the public. The Supreme People's Court is also encouraging the lower courts to follow best practices in IP by selecting "The Top Ten Cases" each year. In 2006, one such case involved Sony and a Guangzhou company. The Supreme People's Court used this case as an example to encourage the lower courts to overcome their conservatism in reviewing and granting preliminary injunction applications.

Although there are still occasional suggestions of instances of the National People's Congress leaning on the courts to

```
┌─────────────────────────────┐
│ SUPREME PEOPLE'S COURT      │
│ (1 court)                   │
└─────────────────────────────┘

         ┌─────────────────────────────┐
         │ HIGH PEOPLE'S COURTS        │
         │ (Provincial level—31        │
         │ courts, all with specialist │
         │ IP divisions)               │
         └─────────────────────────────┘

              ┌─────────────────────────────┐
              │ INTERMEDIATE PEOPLE'S       │
              │ COURTS                      │
              │ (In major cities—376 across │
              │ China, 172 of which had     │
              │ specialist IP divisions in 2006. │
              │ Hear cases at first instance) │
              └─────────────────────────────┘

                   ┌──────────────────────────────────┐
                   │ DISTRICT-LEVEL PEOPLE'S COURTS   │
                   │ (25 have power to hear           │
                   │ non-patent IP cases)             │
                   └──────────────────────────────────┘

              ┌─────────────────────────────┐
              │ PRIMARY PEOPLE'S COURTS     │
              │ (Over 3,000 courts; 25 had  │
              │ specialist IP divisions as  │
              │ at April 2007)              │
              └─────────────────────────────┘
```

Figure 8.3 Courts with jurisdiction to hear IP cases

tactically release decisions to coincide with important IP days, the process is improving, making it a worthwhile option for foreign parties to consider enforcing their IP rights in China.

Courts with Jurisdiction to Hear IP Cases

Most of the People's Courts have some ability to hear IP-related cases (see Figure 8.3).

The People's Courts are qualified to handle IP questions dealing with a range of issues, including judicial review of revocation of IP rights in Beijing courts, IP infringements, unfair competition, technology contracts, and declarations of non-infringement. Of the Intermediate People's Courts, as of April 2007, 64 had been designated with authority over cases of patent infringement, 43 for integrated circuit infringement, and 38 for infringements of new plant varieties (of which there have only been two cases to date).

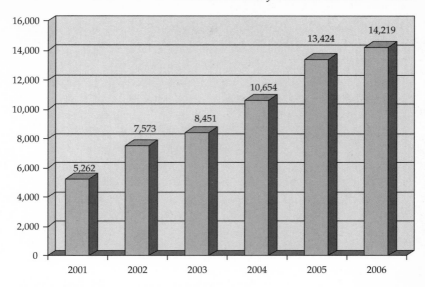

Figure 8.4 IP civil cases in China, 2001–2006
Source: Supreme People's Court.

Number of IP Cases Heard

There has been a significant increase in the number of IP cases filed since China's entry to the WTO in 2002 (see Figure 8.4). Between 2002 and 2006, the People's Courts received 54,321 first instance civil IP cases; a year-on-year increase of just over

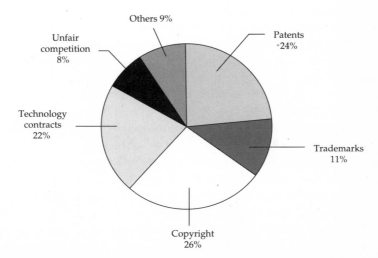

Figure. 8.5 IP infringement civil cases by type, 1985–2006
Source: Supreme People's Court.

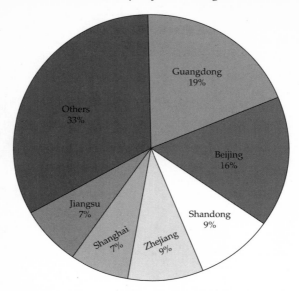

Figure 8.6 IP infringement civil cases by province, 2006
Source: Supreme People's Court.

17% and a considerable 145% increase as compared to similar received cases between 1997 and 2001. Of these cases, 52,437 were concluded; a year-on-year increase of over 19% and, again, a massive 141% increase over similarly concluded cases handled between 1997 and 2001. Roughly 52% of the cases were mediated or reconciled.

Figure 8.5 sets out the breakdown of civil cases lodged by IP right. The number of trademark cases is relatively low, as many of these cases are actioned through administrative action. The percentage of copyright cases has increased rapidly due to the difficulty of taking administrative action to protect against copyright infringement.

It is interesting to note where the majority of these cases were filed (see Figure 8.6). Most were filed in the coastal areas—that is, the more developed parts of China. The "others" in the chart are mainly inland areas. When it comes to finding a jurisdiction in which the courts are likely to have more experience in hearing IP cases, these statistics are very telling. A court will have jurisdiction to hear an IP case if there is a connection with the geographic locality. This can be either through the location of the defendant, or the manufacture or sale of the infringing products. Some provinces and cities have more experience with IP cases and a greater awareness of the issues. It is important when considering civil litigation to try to obtain evidence of sale or distribution of the infringing products in the most appropriate jurisdiction. This can often be achieved through joining a distributor or retailer as a party to the proceedings.

Laws Binding on the People's Courts

There are a number of legal instruments that are binding on the courts:

- laws—which are passed by the National People's Congress;
- administrative regulations—which are passed by the State Council;
- local regulations—which are passed by the ministries and local governments (mainly at the provincial level); and
- judicial interpretations—which are passed by the Supreme People's Court and the Supreme People's Procuratorate (discussed below).

There are also local rules, passed by the ministries and local governments, which are binding only on the relevant local court, but are used for reference by other courts.

Judicial Interpretations (JIs)

The Constitution empowers the Supreme People's Court and the Supreme People's Procuratorate to pass JIs. China operates a civil law system, which means there is no doctrine of precedent. Although the lower courts tend to follow the decisions of the higher courts, they are not required to do so. The laws were passed very quickly and are very general, leaving many of the specific details to the courts to determine. JIs provide guidance to the courts on how to interpret the laws. As one judge said, they provide the "meat" of the laws. The JIs have had a great impact on the development of China's IP laws.

JIs tend to be inspired by real cases as well as international best practice, and deal with issues raised by implementation of the laws. They are drafted by the judges and specialists and then referred to the Judicial Committee for discussion and decision. The majority of the JIs are passed by the Supreme People's Court, which issues approximately 10–20 JIs per year. Between 1978 and 2006, there were approximately 50 IP-related JIs issued by the Supreme People's Court, most of which remain in force.

Table 8.3 Process for civil actions and time taken

Step in the procedure	Timing	Court
Pre-trial provisional measure	48 hours	Intermediate Court
Commencement of proceedings	If judge grants pre-trial measures, IP owner must commence proceedings within 15 days.	Intermediate Court
First instance trial	Six months to conclude case from acceptance of case. (Six-month extension for complex cases.) This only applies to domestic cases, not "foreign-related cases." However, in practice, most courts treat them the same and so they can be concluded within a "reasonable term."	Intermediate Court
Appeal	Judgment: 15 days Order: 10 days	High Court
Second instance trial	Judgment: 3 months Order: 30 days	High Court
Application for retrial (discretion of the court as to whether to accept)	Two years	Supreme People's Court

Procedures for IP Actions before the People's Courts

The People's Courts hear three types of cases concerning IP:

- civil actions—between IP rights owners and infringers;
- judicial reviews (for example, challenges to the validity of IP rights)—between the IP owners or infringers and the administrative authorities; and
- criminal actions—between the public prosecutors and infringers, and victims and infringers.

Each of these is discussed in some detail below.

Civil Actions between IP Rights Holders and Infringers

Court action in China is relatively fast compared with many jurisdictions (see Table 8.3).

Pre-trial preliminary applications

Three types of pre-trial applications are available in IP cases in China:

- *Preliminary injunctions:* to stop the infringing behavior. This is the equivalent of an interlocutory injunction in many countries.
- *Pre-trial property preservation order:* to freeze the infringer's bank accounts and other relevant property that may be used to pay any damages awards. It is the equivalent of a freezing order or a Mareva injunction in many countries.
- *Pre-trial evidence preservation order:* to protect any evidence that the IP owner cannot obtain without the court's intervention. This is often accounts and evidence of profits. This is known as a search order or an Anton Piller order in many countries.

These preliminary orders are available for trademarks, copyright, and patents (some under the Civil Procedure Law and some under JIs), but only the property preservation orders are available for unfair competition cases at this stage. The applicant has to pay a guarantee to the court for any preliminary order granted to cover any losses incurred by the other party if the case isn't lodged or if the plaintiff loses the case.

Grounds for preliminary orders

Under the law, in order to successfully obtain a preliminary injunction or a property preservation order, the applicant must prove that:

- there is an ongoing or imminent threat of infringement; and
- irreparable harm will be caused by the actions.

The JIs set out the factors for the courts to consider when determining these orders. These include:

- likelihood of infringement;
- irreparability of the losses;
- the guarantee; and
- public interests (for example, consumer safety).

The courts tend to be quite cautious in granting these orders, focusing on the likelihood of infringement. If companies can convince the court that the infringer will continue to infringe their rights pending final judgment in the infringement action, the courts will often grant the injunction. It does depend on the location of the court (Beijing courts tend to be more conservative than those in Guangdong and Shandong) and the type of infringement. If it is a patent case, for example, where increasingly infringers are challenging the validity of the patent registrations when faced with an infringement claim, the chances of obtaining a preliminary order are much lower.

For property preservation orders, the grounds as set down under the law are that:

- the order is necessary to stop the infringement; and
- the evidence will possibly be destroyed or lost or be difficult to obtain in future.

The JIs set out the factors to be considered, which include:

- the likelihood of infringement; and
- a reasonable explanation to show that evidence controlled by the accused is unable to be collected by the claimant but is crucial for the case and may be destroyed.

The Supreme People's Court's attitude is that, given the parties' difficulty in collecting evidence of the profits of the infringer, the courts should actively try to grant these orders if possible, particularly in patent cases.

These preliminary orders were introduced into the law in 2002. By October 2006, 430 applications for preliminary

Table 8.4 Preliminary injunctions for patent cases filed up to October 2006

Applications filed	258
Applications concluded	252 (22 of which were foreign-related)
Applications granted	136
Applications dismissed	29
Applications withdrawn (or other)	87

Source: Supreme People's Court.

Table 8.5 Preliminary property preservation orders and evidence preservation orders applications filed up until October 2006

	Property preservation orders	Evidence preservation orders
Applications filed	218	642
Applications concluded	208 (5 foreign-related)	607 (9 foreign-related)
Applications granted	171	506
Applications withdrawn (or other)	30	61
Percentage granted	96%	93%

Source: Supreme People's Court.

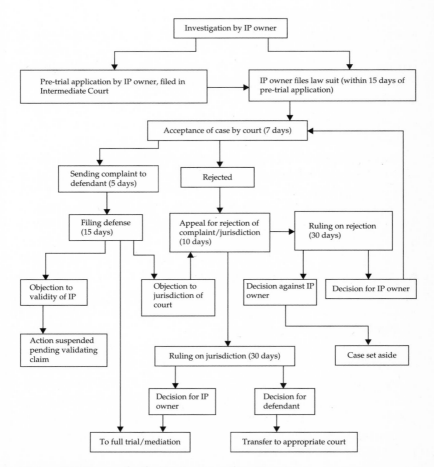

Figure. 8.7 Process for first instance civil cases

injunctions had been received by the courts (32 of which were foreign-related), 425 of which were concluded. The court granted 257 of these applications, which is an 83% approval rate (relatively high for preliminary orders). It dismissed 52 applications, and 116 were withdrawn (or other). In patent cases, there was also an 82% success rate for preliminary injunctions. The statistics for patent cases up until October 2006 were as set out in Table 8.4.

For preliminary property preservation orders and evidence preservation orders, the statistics are as set out in Table 8.5.

Process for first instance civil cases
Figure 8.7 shows the process for first instance civil cases.

Process for second instance civil cases
Parties can lodge an appeal against a first instance judgment within 15 days. The court will send the appeal to the respondent within five days, after which the respondent has 15 days to file a defense. If the original judgment is overturned, the appeal will be executed immediately.

Process for retrial by the Supreme People's Court
An application for retrial to the Supreme People's Court, based on either an error of law or an error of fact, can be made by either party within two years of the second instance decision. In 2005, of the 13,424 first instance decisions, only 23% were appealed to second instance and of those only 45 (0.33%) were appealed for a retrial. Certain other courts or representatives of the courts (such as the president of the original court with the approval of the Judicial Committee or the Supreme People's Court) may opt to retry a case. This very rarely happens in practice.

IP Rights Revocation Applications
If a party wants to challenge a registered IP right such as a patent or trademark, it may make an application to the relevant re-examination board. (For patents, this is the Patents Re-Examination Board, and for trademarks, the Trademarks Re-Examination Adjudication Board.) Parties can appeal the Re-Examination Board's decision to the Beijing Intermediate Court. There is some uncertainty as to which division of the court will hear the appeal. Generally, if there is another civil litigation

case pending relating to the relevant IP right (for example, an enforcement action), the appeal will be heard by the IP Divisions. Otherwise, it will be heard by the Administrative Division of the court, as the Re-Examination Board will be a party to the proceedings. This creates an inconsistency in the decisions, because the Administrative Division will look only at the procedural issues before upholding the Re-Examination Board's decision, whereas the IP Division will examine the validity of the right. This can be important to keep in mind when challenging a Re-Examination Board's decision.

In a challenge to the validity of a trademark registration, the court will tend to continue to hear any infringement action that is on foot while the validity challenge is taking place. However, where the validity challenge involves a patent registration, the courts tend to stay proceedings pending the outcome of the validation action. Chinese parties in patent infringement actions are increasingly filing invalidation claims as a response. They know that this will then stay the infringement proceedings pending the outcome of their challenge, during which time they can often continue to sell the infringing products (unless the IP owner can obtain a preliminary injunction, which is very difficult in patent cases). This is an ongoing challenge for enforcement of patents in China and often results in owners looking for alternative methods of enforcing their rights in the meantime. It also highlights the importance of having a proper Chinese translation of your patent specifications before filing them in China, to ensure that your patent is valid and strong when you seek to enforce it as it is likely to be challenged.

Remedies

The People's Courts may, in addition to the pre-trial remedies discussed above, make the following orders:

- apology;
- rectification;
- compensation (if damages cannot be ascertained, the maximum compensation the court may impose is RMB500,000 [approximately US$60,000]); and
- confiscation of the infringing products, the tools and equipment for making the same, as well as the unlawful profits.

Evidence in IP civil litigation cases

One of the biggest difficulties associated with enforcement of IP rights in China through civil litigation is the standard of evidence required. In China, there is no contempt of court, or punishment for lying in court. This means that there is a presumption that evidence is forged or fake unless it is independently validated. In practice, this raises the standard of evidence required and increases the hurdles parties have to overcome for their evidence to be accepted by the courts. Increasingly, infringers are challenging every piece of evidence that IP owners put forward in infringement actions, as a tactic to slow down proceedings. In one case, the infringer even challenged the validity of a trademark registration certificate issued by the Chinese Trademark Office! The judge lost his patience at this point and the tactic began to work against the infringer. This is an extreme example, but it is a common issue that adds pressure to foreign companies when collecting their evidence. Often, it means that the courts require notarized evidence (that is, the evidence must be authenticated by a registered notary public). Although there are numerous notaries in China, it can be difficult to obtain notarized evidence of an infringement, particularly in patent cases.

There is no discovery process in civil litigation in China. The parties can apply to the court for the collection and investigation of evidence in certain circumstances, including: (1) where the documents are held by the state authorities and must be collected by the courts; (2) where the evidence involves state secrets, trade secrets, or individual privacy; or (3) where collection of the evidence is beyond the party's capacity due to objective reasons. This third circumstance is very subjective and often difficult to obtain in practice.

Evidence must be adduced either as the parties agree, or no less than 30 days before the hearing. Only evidence that is considered "new" will be accepted after the deadline. "New evidence" includes evidence that has been newly discovered after the deadline, or which could not be provided earlier for objective reasons. Although lawyers often debate what this means, the courts' approach is generally quite flexible in allowing in additional evidence.

In most IP cases, whichever party makes a claim must adduce the evidence to support the claim. This is in line with the usual burden of proof. There are some exceptions to this rule; for example, in a process patent infringement claim, if the infringer is proved to be selling an identical product to the IP owner's product, the infringer must prove that its product is manufactured using a different process to the IP owner's patent.

The Supreme People's Court is also in the process of shifting the burden for proving illegal gains to the respondent. This is due to the fact that there is no discovery, and thus it is very difficult for IP owners to prove the illegal gains of the infringers.

The challenges with collecting strong evidence for IP cases are ongoing. It is particularly strenuous in cases where IP owners are trying to prove that their trademarks are well known. The courts require evidence that is independently verifiable, as Chinese parties often fabricate evidence of use. We have seen cases where infringers went to the trouble of printing an entire fabricated newspaper that included an advertisement containing the design in question in the case and which just happened to pre-date the IP owner's design patent by two weeks. The IP owner eventually managed to track down an original copy of the newspaper, which didn't contain the supposed advertisement! Cases such as this make it harder for genuine companies to produce evidence that is acceptable to the courts.

One of the elements that many companies struggle to produce is an independent audit report of their promotional and marketing spend. Most companies' audits don't break down this spend by brand and by market, as it is not a mandatory element of audits. In this case, companies need either to invest significant amounts of money in an independent audit, or to try and adduce invoices and contracts with marketing agencies that show how much they have spent.

Evidence banks

Due to the high threshold requirements for valid evidence in civil litigation cases in China, we strongly recommend that companies develop an "evidence bank." It doesn't need to be terribly sophisticated, but it will help to overcome some of the hurdles. An evidence bank could contain items such as:

- original advertisements and promotional materials (for example, the original magazine or newspaper, or at least the full page on which the advertisement appears as well as the front cover showing the date);
- photos of promotions and billboards;

- invoices for marketing spend;
- dates on which all campaigns were run, including dates on which television commercials were shown;
- other marketing materials, such as catalogues, sales presentations, trade fair materials, and Web site printouts;
- dates of first use globally and in China of trademarks, patents, copyright, etc.;
- samples of products;
- details of any awards the products or company has won;
- brand awareness/product quality/consumer satisfaction surveys;
- evidence of market share and sales figures;
- advertising campaign plans;
- punishment decisions against infringers;
- copies of any newspaper or magazine reports (including the full page and the front page of the publication);
- details of any sponsorships involving the brand;
- details of any steps taken to protect a trade secret (for example, copies of sample employment agreements, policy documents, employee handbooks, etc.);
- copies of any agreements with partners, licensees, and manufacturers; and
- any other materials that show your use of and reputation in the product, brand, process, etc.

If your IP enforcement program is run from outside of China, you will need to make sure you have someone on the ground who is collecting these materials for you. Many law firms or consulting companies will do so for a fee, if you don't have business people on the ground who are willing to help.

Having this information prepared in advance will not only enable you to take action more quickly and efficiently, but it will also ensure you have strong evidence that cannot be challenged by the infringer.

Trap purchases

The use of trap orders or trap purchases to obtain evidence against infringers is a contentious issue that requires careful consideration. If you are simply purchasing a sample of a product that is offered for sale to be used as evidence, this is generally accepted as valid and ethical. The debate centers around placing orders where the infringer has offered to supply the products but doesn't have stock ("made to order") or, at the other end of the spectrum, asking an infringer if they would be prepared to supply a product they haven't offered and then placing an order. Some companies will undertake the first scenario if necessary to obtain evidence against an infringer. (For example, often an infringer manufactures to order, and so placing an order is the only way to obtain evidence.) The second example is more likely to be an issue both ethically and legally. There is no clear guidance on the legality of placing trap orders, so companies need to be aware of the risks. Some companies approach the authorities first to confirm that they will accept the order as evidence for the purposes of conducting an action, which can give some comfort, although it wouldn't necessarily be accepted by the courts. There was a case in Beijing in which an IP owner bought hardware with software loaded to prove software infringement. The IP owner had offered to buy the hardware *only if the software was loaded by the supplier*. The case was retried by the Supreme People's Court, which looked at the social interest and value of allowing the evidence. The court considered the evidence might be acceptable if it couldn't be obtained without the order. At the end of the day, companies have to determine their own comfort levels in relation to the use of trap orders in China.

Civil litigation strategy

Civil litigation now forms an important part of any successful IP protection strategy in China. The more foreign companies that engage the court system, the stronger it will become. The courts really are trying to come to terms with IP infringements. Many judges have traveled overseas for training, and more are studying IP to ensure they are completely up to speed on the issues and the law.

In order to make the most use of this tool in your IP enforcement toolbox, before taking action, consider:

- How strong are your rights? If they are challenged, can you overcome the validity claim?

- How strong is your evidence? Do you have notarized evidence of the infringement and of your reputation, if necessary?

- Which jurisdiction is the best for your action? Do you have sufficient evidence to commence proceedings in this locality?
- Do you have sufficient evidence for preliminary applications?
- What is the purpose of your action? Is it to obtain a judgment, which can be used as a deterrent to other infringers? Is it to obtain damages? Is it to immediately stop the infringement?

3. CRIMINAL ACTION

As IP owners continue to complain about the lack of deterrence associated with administrative action or even civil action, criminal prosecution becomes even more important. There are three areas of criminal liability for IP infringement: (1) IP offenses; (2) substandard products; and (3) illegal business operation (see Table 8.6).

Table 8.6 Areas of criminal liability for IP infringement

Type of offense	Scope	Laws and JIs
IP offenses	Includes trademark counterfeiting, counterfeit trademark labels, sale of counterfeit goods, trade secret infringement, copyright violations, sale of infringing products, patent counterfeiting	Criminal Law (sections 213–220) and the Judicial Interpretations on IP Crimes (2004 and 2007)
Substandard products	Fake and inferior goods generally, and particularly fake pharmaceuticals, substandard food and medical equipment, cosmetics, pesticides, and electrical appliances	Criminal Law (sections 140–150) and Judicial Interpretation on Substandard Product (2001)
Illegal business operation	Conducting other illegal business activities that seriously disrupt the market order	Criminal Law (article 225)

There is currently no criminal liability for an unfair competition action. There has been much debate around whether this would be appropriate. It would send a strong message to infringers who seek to trade off the reputation of well-known brands and packaging, particularly in a complex IP environment such as China. But activities that "sail close to the wind" of the unfair competition regime are common antics between competitors and companies globally, particularly in the environment of own-name brands that are sold by retailers. To turn this into a criminal offense raises concerns among such companies. This debate continues and is unlikely to be resolved any time soon.

Thresholds Required to Trigger Criminal Liability

Although the threat of jail time is a strong deterrent, the number of criminal prosecutions for IP infringements is relatively low. This is because the thresholds required to trigger criminal liability are still very high, despite being reduced in December 2004. The JI set out criteria for convicting someone of the IP crimes listed in Table 8.6. People who are convicted of an IP crime will be liable to imprisonment if their turnover of the illegal products reaches RMB50,000 (approximately US$6,600) or if their illegal profit reaches RMB30,000 (approximately US$4,000). The threshold for companies is RMB150,000 (approximately US$18,000). Prior to these changes, the authorities needed evidence that the counterfeiters had sold RMB200,000 (approximately US$26,600) worth of fake goods (RMB50,000 for individuals) before they could bring a criminal action against an infringer. The distinction between liability for individuals and for companies has been criticized as making it easier for infringers who set up a simple front company through which to trade to ensure they are subject to the higher thresholds.

Infringers use these thresholds to their advantage by ensuring that they store the infringing products in different locations, or by shipping smaller orders to avoid being subject to a raid that would allow seizure of a quantity that would exceed the criminal liability thresholds.

The valuation of the counterfeit products remains a hotly debated issue. Usually, the valuation of the counterfeit products is calculated as follows:

- for goods sold, based on the price at which the goods are actually sold;

- for goods that are not sold, based on the quoted price or actual price at which the goods are found to have been sold after investigation; and

- for goods without quoted prices or for which the actual price is not possible to ascertain, based on the market price of the genuine goods.

In some cases, it may be more favorable to the IP owner to use the illegal income made by the infringer to determine criminal liability, as the criminal threshold for illegal income (profit) is RMB30,000.

If the infringer is a "multi-infringer" (that is, has counterfeited two or more trademarks or rights), the threshold is reduced to RMB30,000 for the value of the goods and RMB20,000 for the illegal income.

A third threshold that can subject an infringer to criminal liability is based on the quantity of products sold: over 20,000 counterfeit labels or trademark representations, or 10,000 pieces of pirated copies (books, DVDs, software, and so on).

Although these thresholds remain, there is significant lobbying to have them removed.

The Process

A criminal case usually is heard following an administrative raid or a seizure by Customs. If the value of the products, the quantity of the products, or the illegal income from the products meets the thresholds, the case may be transferred to the Public Security Bureau (PSB) for investigation. The more evidence of the infringement and the infringer that IP owners can provide to the PSB, the more likely it is to take the case. This evidence will usually include:

- a statutory declaration on the price of the genuine goods;

- a statutory declaration verifying the counterfeit nature of the products. Both of these documents will need to be notarized and then legalized by the local Chinese consulate or embassy if they are being executed by a foreign company;

- evidence relating to the IP owner, its brands, and the relevant trademark or patent registration certificates;

- samples of the infringing product, details of stock levels, and other details relating to the infringers; and

- any punishment decisions issues against the infringer by the administrative authorities.

In the past, it was very difficult to successfully transfer cases for prosecution to the PSB. In 2004, for example, only 86 cases were transferred from the relevant authorities to the PSB, which was only 2% of copyright cases and less than 1% of trademark cases filed. In 2006, this number had risen to 252. Companies needed to actively lobby the administrative authority that conducted the initial raid to prepare the case for criminal prosecution, and then the PSB needed to be lobbied to accept the case. This process was slow and uncertain. In March 2006, a new opinion came into effect, which made the process easier. It requires "prompt transfer" of cases from the administrative authority to the PSB for investigation. If it is "obvious" that the quantities seized in an administrative action meet the criminal thresholds, the case must be transferred "immediately." The PSB then has 10 days to decide whether to accept the case. If it is a "complicated" or "serious case," the PSB has 30 days in which to make a decision.

It is still often difficult to transfer cases from the administrative authorities to the PSB. The Technical Supervision Bureau and Administration for Industry and Commerce are reluctant to transfer cases, as they don't want to lose the fines or the income from counterfeiters if their business is closed down. The PSB is also often not interested in taking a case unless the chances of success are very high. They don't want to send cases back to the AIC, as this can be seen as a loss of face to the PSB. However, there are an increasing number of cases where the PSB is proactively getting involved and is conducting its own detailed investigations into infringers. In a recent case the PSB not only arrested an infringer within a couple of days of receiving the complaint, but it also decided to investigate the buyers of the infringing products, who had been identified by the infringer, and eventually took action against the entire distribution chain for the sale of counterfeit products. Such cases are becoming more frequent.

If the PSB refuses to take a case, the administrative authorities may request a reconsideration of the case. If the PSB still refuses, the administrative authority may make a "suggestion" to the Public Prosecutor, requesting that it exercise its supervision over the case. The Public Prosecutor may determine that the case should be filed for criminal prosecution and may send a notice to the PSB requesting it to prepare a submission. If the Public Prosecutor issues such a notice, the PSB must file the case within 15 days. Although this rarely happens in practice, it can be useful to be aware of the options for lobbying other authorities to put pressure on the PSB if it is refusing to take action in a case.

Once the PSB accepts a case, it will conduct a criminal investigation into the infringer's business and activities. This may include interviewing witnesses, inspecting the suspect's business and other related premises, seizing relevant documents and evidence, and freezing the suspect's bank accounts. It may invite experts to examine relevant evidence as well. The PSB may also take "compulsory measures," such as taking the infringer into custody pending further investigation, or placing the suspect on bail or under house arrest. Foreign suspects may also be subject to these compulsory measures, but the PSB must notify the suspect's embassy or consulate in China and must allow embassy or consular officials access to the suspect on request. There has been at least one high-profile case involving two American citizens who were arrested and eventually sentenced to jail for selling counterfeit DVDs over the Internet in 2005. The mastermind of the business, Randolph Hobson Guthrie III, was sentenced to 30 months' jail and fined RMB500,000 (approximately US$60,000). This case is often touted as having been politically motivated at a time when the United States was putting pressure on China over its IP regime. Either way, it shows China's willingness to take action against foreigners who are engaged in IP-related crimes in China.

If the PSB is satisfied that there is a case to answer, it will prepare a brief for the Public Prosecutor. This process usually takes between two and 10 months, depending on the complexity of the case and the manpower of the relevant PSB.

The Public Prosecutor will confirm whether a crime has been committed and whether someone should stand trial for criminal actions. It will also confirm that the PSB's investigation was conducted legally. It may request the PSB to conduct further investigations if required. This process can take up to five months. If the PSB accepts the case, it will file a "Bill of Prosecution" with the court. The case will then proceed through the People's Courts in a similar way to the process for a civil litigation case (described above). Criminal IP cases are usually heard by the Criminal Chamber of the district courts and then by the Intermediate Courts if the initial decision is appealed.

Punishments

If found guilty of a crime, a suspect may be sentenced to up to three years' imprisonment. A higher punishment of three to seven years may be imposed if the value reaches five times the threshold; or it may be even higher if it relates to substandard goods that may affect people's health and safety (for example, counterfeit pharmaceuticals).

Private Prosecutions

The law does allow for an IP owner to file a private criminal prosecution with the court if the Public Prosecutor doesn't file a case. This can be a useful tactic to threaten infringers and encourage them to mediate and settle cases. It gives the IP owner more control over the process than a case taken by the PSB. It can also create trouble for infringers, stopping their ongoing infringement. However, without the public support of the Public Prosecutor and the PSB, with rights to conduct searches and arrest suspects, it can be difficult to obtain evidence and proceed to trial.

A Real Deterrent?

Although criminal prosecutions for IP infringements are becoming increasingly popular as a stronger deterrent than administrative action or civil litigation, are they a real deterrent to infringers? Two cases we came across in our research are of interest in this respect. Both involved foreign IP owners that had invested heavily in investigating counterfeit operations in their industries. One was in the computer components industry and the other in pharmaceuticals. They finally managed to uncover the masterminds behind the operations and in both cases successfully had the suspects arrested and sentenced to time in jail for their IP-related crimes. However, they noticed that the levels of infringements continued to increase. On further investigation, they realized that the infringers were making strong connections in jail, which enabled them to expand the scope of their counterfeiting business. One IP owner continued to take action to try to identify and arrest other members of the gangs involved. The other took a different approach, lobbying to have the infringer released early from jail on strict bail terms. He was learning more skills, and was a greater danger to the IP owner, in jail than he was on the streets! This case illustrates that you need to be both open-minded and creative in your IP enforcement program in China. Don't assume you have solved a problem and move on. You will need to remain diligent and be prepared to reassess your strategy if it doesn't appear to be working.

4. MEDIATION

In many cases, using mediation to explore means of resolving an IP dispute can be an effective option in China. There is a long history of mediation in China, where the culture focuses on relationships and maintaining face. Whether mediation is appropriate will depend on the type of dispute and the other party involved. Mediation with a business partner may be appropriate as a way to retain the relationship. Some cases against third parties are also appropriate for mediation. For example, one company mediated a dispute in a case that involved a smaller competitor. The IP owner's rights were quite weak, relying on the Anti-Unfair Competition Law, but they were keen to move the competitor away from the similar packaging. Through mediation, the parties were able to brainstorm solutions to find one that met both parties' needs and resolved their concerns. During the process, the IP owner was able to educate the competitor as to more effective ways of communicating than trying to trade off the reputation of the well-known international brands.

The People's Courts will often recommend that parties to a civil litigation mediate a dispute in an attempt to reach a mutually agreeable resolution that the court will then accept and enter on to the record. There are several mediation centers in China set up to assist foreign companies mediate disputes. Try to ensure you choose a mediator who is experienced in IP issues.

5. CEASE AND DESIST LETTERS

The value of cease and desist letters tends to cause a divide among lawyers in China. People usually have a very firm view one way or the other. In our experience, cease and desist letters can be a useful tool when used strategically. They can be used as a "litmus test" of whether the infringer will stop if asked. We agree that sending a standard letter in English on a foreign law firm's letterhead is ineffective and will most likely end up in the garbage bin of the recipient's receptionist. We came across an example of a German company that was sending letters in German, on a German law firm's letterhead, citing German law, to Chinese infringers identified at a German trade fair. The company approached a law firm in China in frustration when the Chinese party continued with their infringement. They eventually investigated the company in China and followed up with an administrative raid against them and an undertaking that had the infringer agree not to exhibit the infringing products at trade fairs abroad in the future. Alternatively, they could have taken action against the infringer at the German trade fair and negotiated with them from that end.

Cease and desist letters can be effective in cases where:

- your rights are not very strong and you want to put the infringer on notice that you are watching them—what we call a "this far, no further" letter;
- the quantities the infringer is selling are low and don't justify an administrative raid;
- you are following up on an administrative raid;
- the infringement is in a catalogue or on a Web site, and no evidence of actual manufacture can be obtained;
- you want to negotiate with the infringer to assign certain registered rights to you;
- you are looking for a cost-effective approach to put infringers on notice; or
- the infringement is a concern, but is not a priority in your IP strategy (such as branded merchandise which you don't sell but which contains your brand).

A cease and desist letter should always:

- clearly set out your rights;
- include photos of the infringing products;
- be in Chinese and sent from a Chinese law firm;
- contain an undertaking that the infringer should sign and return to you (unless you are simply seeking to put the infringer on notice of your rights);
- contain a response date if undertakings are included; and
- be followed up immediately.

You may even consider including a final notification that failure to respond will result in a copy of the letter being sent to the appropriate local AIC or other relevant authority.

6. CUSTOMS

Working with the Customs authorities in China to prevent the flow of infringing products either into, or more usually, out of the country can be a very effective means of removing infringing IP products from the market. This is particularly important if the products are heading for one of your company's main markets. It is common for companies to find that infringing products turning up in their home markets or other overseas markets are originating from China. Often, products can be seized as they arrive in a foreign port; however, it is preferable that they are proactively seized by China's Customs Authority.

There are a number of things you can do to get the best value out of working with Customs in China, including:

• recording your rights with Customs;

• having in place a verification and bond payment process; and

• conducting training on your company and your rights.

Recording Your Rights

Trademarks, copyright, and patent rights can be recorded with Chinese Customs. Trademark rights are the easiest for officials to recognize and action, as infringement is relatively easy to determine, particularly when it involves identical copies of the mark. For copyright and patents, it can be difficult for Customs officials to determine infringement, and they will need to be trained to do so (see below). Recordal is a relatively straightforward process that can be done online. The more information you can give Customs, the more likely they will be to proactively watch for your rights. For example, you can provide them with samples of your products so that they can compare these with infringements. Also, providing details of companies that have the right to import or export products bearing your company's brands or IP—for example, licensees, distributors, exporters—can help to determine whether a company is authorized. For some companies, this is relatively straightforward, as only a limited number of companies may be authorized to use their marks on certain products, or they may have only a couple of authorized manufacturers. In these cases, those names and addresses should be provided to Customs. This also helps to avoid the seizure of genuine products, which can be frustrating to your business teams. Companies with complex distribution models, or that don't have a tight control over their supply chain, may find it more difficult to supply Customs with a complete list of authorized companies. Incidences of Customs officials mistakenly seizing genuine products from an exporter whose name was omitted from the IP owner's list of authorized companies are not uncommon. Not only does this cause commercial frustration and embarrassment, but it can also mean that the officials are reluctant in the future to seize products that infringe your rights because they are concerned about being sued for unauthorized seizure.

If you have knowledge of a shipment that will be leaving China, file a report with the Customs authority, providing as much information as possible. In most cases, action will be taken to seize the products. There have been a few cases, though, where the infringer had strong contacts within Customs, which resulted in a large shipment of infringing products being released. In one such case, the IP owner had given Customs not only the quantity of products, a sample, and details of both the exporter and the receiver of the shipment, but also the destination of the products, the name of the ship on which they would be traveling, the container number, and its position on the dock. When, after two days, the IP owner followed up with Customs, the officials said they "could not find the container." It turned out that the infringer was an ex-official, who was able to convince the Customs officials to let the shipment go. The IP owner notified Customs at the ship's destination and the shipment was seized when it arrived in Germany.

Having in Place a Verification and Bond Payment Process

If suspected infringing products are seized by Customs, companies have three days in which to verify whether the products are authorized. According to the General Customs Administration, a high proportion of IP owners fail to respond to a seizure notice within the given time periods and many companies fail to respond at all. This will only mean that the Customs officials will be less likely to report seizures to you in the future. Customs in China are largely under-resourced, and they won't waste resources on companies that don't bother to engage them or respond to their notices. Even if the quantity being reported is low and appears not to be worthwhile pursuing, it is important to respond to Customs and to show your appreciation for their support for your IP. This will encourage them to continue to monitor shipments for infringing products on your behalf.

Companies need to pay a bond to Customs for any products seized. This is to protect the other party in case of loss due to a groundless seizure. The bond needs to be paid within the three-day deadline, so it is important to have a payment process in place. Under the new regulations, a bank guarantee will suffice in place of a bond. The amount of the bond required will depend on the value of the goods seized:

- Less than RMB20,000 (approximately US$2,500): 100% of the value of the products.
- Between RMB20,000 and RMB200,000 (approximately US$2,500–$25,000): 50% of the value of the products.
- Over RMB200,000 (approximately US$25,000): 10% of the value of the products.

At the end of its investigation, Customs will issue a punishment decision and return the bond. It will also arrange to destroy the infringing products. There are currently no regulations as to the time frames for finalizing a case, and some ports are notoriously slow, which increases the storage costs for the infringing products (which must be covered by the IP owner) and ties up your bond. The situation is improving, however. If Customs determines that the products are not infringing, they will release the shipment to the owner of the products unless the IP owner commences proceedings against the infringer.

Conducting Training on Your Company and Your Rights

One of the most critical elements of a Customs enforcement program is the need to conduct training on your company and your rights for the officials in the key ports from which infringing products are likely to be shipped. Customs officials see thousands of shipments go through every day; if you don't train them in how to identify an infringement of your rights, they are likely to let infringing products leave the country. This can be done through a simple presentation that clearly sets out your rights and explains—using images and examples—how to identify an infringement. This training will help to keep your company in the officials' minds and increase the chances of them identifying infringements of your rights. It can be organized very cost-effectively through organizations such as the Quality Brands Protection Committee (see Chapter 9) or in conjunction with other IP owners.

Increasingly, counterfeits are being mixed in with genuine shipments to throw off Customs seizures. This is known as "seeding" a shipment, where a layer of legitimate product is laid across the fake product. Training Customs to look deeper, as well as to look for proper paperwork, will help overcome this issue.

7. TRADE FAIRS

Infringers often use trade fairs to promote their products. Monitoring trade fairs for infringements and to check the activities of known infringers is an important part of a China IP strategy. Prepare a list of all the key fairs for your industry at which infringements may occur. If your representatives in China (often sales and marketing teams) are attending the fairs, brief them as to what information you need (for example, details of the infringement, a copy of the catalogue if relevant, a business card, the location of the infringer's stand). Otherwise, you can brief your counsel to attend and provide a report.

In March 2006, China introduced new Measures Regarding Intellectual Property Rights Protection at Exhibitions and Trade Fairs. These Measures provide a framework for protection of trademarks, copyright, and patents at trade fairs. If the exhibition lasts longer than three days, the organizers must set up an IP Complaints Office to deal directly with infringements detected during the exhibition. Complaints received must be passed to the relevant authorities within 24 hours of reporting, and the authorities must promptly make a decision as to whether to take action. Any cases that are not finalized during the exhibition will be transferred to the authorities for further investigation. Possible punishments for an IP complaint at a trade fair include an order to stop the infringing activity, confiscating or destroying the infringing goods and promotional activities, and imposing of fines. Exhibitors that commit infringements twice will be banned from participating in further exhibitions.

In order to ensure that you are able to take action during a trade fair, if it proves necessary, we recommend that you have all the relevant documents prepared in advance, including:

- copies of the relevant IP registration certificates;
- basic information about the infringer and the infringement for cases where you are aware of the infringers; and
- a notarized, legalized power of attorney for your agent.

As we discussed earlier, taking action against the middlemen who put suppliers together with customers can help to remove the demand for infringing products in many cases. They are also a useful source of information about what Chinese parties are offering in your industry, and thus are worth monitoring.

8. TARGETING OTHER LEVELS OF THE INFRINGERS' SUPPLY CHAIN

One strategy that has been very effective is to target other levels of the supply chain—for example, the landlords, transporters, internet service providers (ISPs), financiers, the printers of the infringing packaging, and the factory workers/shop assistants—for their role in the production and sale of counterfeits. This will send a very strong message to all levels of the chain that you are serious about taking whatever action is necessary to protect your IP rights. It can also be a useful source of information on the driving force behind the infringements, as these entities are more likely to provide information in exchange for a settlement on any claim against them.

Some luxury goods companies have successfully held the landlords of infringers criminally or civilly liable for the IP infringement. For example, five luxury goods and fashion brands took the landlords of Beijing's famous "fake market," the Silk Market, to court for IP infringement. The Beijing Intermediate Court held them jointly and severally liable for failing to stop infringements after having been notified of them. The decision was upheld on appeal. These IP owners have now leveraged this victory to convince landlords in other infamous fake markets to clamp down on infringements by their tenants, often by including a warranty in their leases that tenants will not infringe any IP rights.

Taking action against printers of packaging and labels can also be a useful approach. Chinese companies engaged in printing materials must comply with the Regulations on Trademark Printing, which require that printers identify their customers and confirm the customer's rights in the trademarks. Customers must provide a copy of their business license as well as the trademark certificates or evidence of a license agreement. There are criminal sanctions for breach in serious cases, which enables companies to lean on printers to obtain information about the rest of the supply chain.

In a 2006 case involving refilling of genuine Hennessy®, Chivas®, Martell®, and Remy Martin® bottles with counterfeit liquid by a syndicate in Zhongshan, the mastermind behind the syndicate was sentenced to seven years' imprisonment and fined RMB400,000 (approximately US$54,000). The landlord of the premises where the products were made was sentenced to one year in prison and fined RMB40,000 (approximately US$5,400), and the workers and transporters received between 18 and 42 months in prison and were fined between RMB30,000 and RMB80,000 (approximately US$4,000–$11,000). This is a great example of successfully including the whole supply chain in an action.

9. DOMAIN NAME RECOVERY

China has the third-highest number of alleged cyber squatters in domain name dispute resolution procedures, according to WIPO statistics. Prior to the introduction of China's .cn Domain Name Dispute Resolution Policy (.cn DRP), at a time when cyber squatters were running riot over famous brands as domain names in China, brand owners had to rely on contacts at the China Internet Network Information Center (CNNIC), China's domain name administrator, to take action, or resort to the courts. In the early years, a complaint very similar to an opposition before the Trademarks Office would be prepared and delivered to CNNIC—often personally. Although CNNIC administrators had no authority to take on such disputes, they did so because there was no other government agency that would accept them. There were several early notorious cyber squatters in China who had registered every famous brand or company name imaginable, including those belonging to Chinese companies. The ever-helpful CNNIC administrators, often computer techies who understood that there was little they could do until regulations were passed enabling them to take more action, would sometimes call contacts when a suspicious application was lodged, so that a representative of the rightful owner could lodge their own application, which would be fast tracked before the squatter's application would be considered.

If CNNIC couldn't help, then that left only trademark arguments to be put before the Trademarks Office, or unfair competition arguments on unauthorized use of a business enterprise name to be made before the AIC, or civil litigation. Such actions would usually take a long time to resolve because of the unknown and misunderstood nature of the Internet and its relationship with traditional trading. The most well known such case involved IKEA, the Swiss furniture giant. The case received a great deal of publicity at the time because the Chinese party had registered many widely known names, apparently with the intention of vacating them in return for a fee. Other similar cases involved cartier.com.cn, dupont.com.cn, and tide.com.cn.

Today, however, disputes are dealt with by Domain Name Dispute Resolution Institutions (DNRI), which are authorized by CNNIC. There are currently two authorized DNRI—CIETAC (the China International Economic and Trade Arbitration Commission) and HKIAC (the Hong Kong International Arbitration Centre). The .cn DRP is modeled closely on ICANN's (Internet Corporation for Assigned Names and Numbers) Uniform Dispute Resolution Policy (UDRP) procedure, with minor variations that favor the complainants slightly more generously than the UDRP rules.

A complainant must show that:

- the disputed domain name is identical with or confusingly similar to the complainant's name or mark in which the complaint has civil rights or interests;
- the disputed domain name holder has no right or legitimate interest in respect of the domain name or major part of the domain name; and
- the disputed domain name holder has registered or is using the domain name in bad faith.

The .cn DRP rules were amended in March 2006. There were three major changes:

1. *Institution of a two-year bar:* Complainants cannot take action if a domain name has been registered for more than two years. In these cases, a complainant will have to go to court to recover the name.
2. *Clarification of how the registrant can claim a legitimate interest:* The registrant must show that they have either (1) used the domain name in good faith to provide goods or services; (2) acquired a certain reputation through use of the domain name; or (3) legitimately used the domain name for commercial or non-commercial purposes without the intention of obtaining a commercial gain or misleading the public.

3. *Narrowing of the bad faith provision:* Complainants must now show evidence that the registrant offered to sell, rent, or transfer the domain name for profit and it must be directed at the complainant or its competitors. In the past, companies used to send an investigator on a no-names basis to try to recover the domain name and this would be used as evidence in a .cn DRP action later if the recovery was unsuccessful. Under the new rules, companies must send a cease and desist letter asserting their rights and offering to buy back the name at cost. If the registrant asks for a higher amount, this will constitute evidence of bad faith.

A DNRI panel is made up of one or three experts who are selected from a list DNRI publishes regularly. The applicant will select one expert and pay the fee, unless the respondent seeks three experts to hear the dispute, in which case the fee is split. The fee is approximately RMB4,000 (approximately US$540) (or RMB7,000—approximately US$950—for three panelists). If you use a law firm to prepare your complaint, this will obviously cost extra.

Once a complaint is lodged, the registrant has 20 days to lodge a response. The DNRI has five days to appoint a panel and then 14 days to issue its decision. There is a 10-day window before the decision is finalized and published on CNNIC's Web site. The domain name registration service must then effect the DNRI decision within 10 days of receipt of a copy of the decision. Currently, DNRI decision authority is limited to (1) revocation of the disputed domain name, or (2) transfer of the domain to the applicant. Arbitration or court proceedings may be lodged to stay DNRI resolutions.

The .cn DRP process appears to be quite a successful way of recovering domain names that have been registered by cyber squatters. Of the approximately 540 disputes lodged up to the end of 2006, around 400 were found for the complainant.

Below are a few case examples:

- Hugo Boss recovered the boss.cn and boss.com.cn domain names from a Wenzhou company through the .cn DRP. The domain names were not used, and the panelist found that the registrant must have known of the trademarks when they registered the domain names.

- Anheuser-Busch Inc. recovered the budweiserbeer.com domain name in Chinese characters after a panel held that the name was registered in bad faith, as it was registered to create confusion and to mislead the public.

- Google wasn't so fortunate when it tried to recover the google.com.cn domain name from a cyber squatter. In March 2003, the panel held that it hadn't registered its trademark prior to the registration of the domain name and hadn't adequately proved that it had a legitimate right on which to base its claim. It was reported that Google had to pay a very large sum of money to "buy back" this domain name.

Keywords

The CNNIC has introduced a procedure for registration of keywords in China. In order to use these keywords, Internet users must download a plug-in from CNNIC. They can then enter keywords into the plug-in and go straight to the registrant of the keyword's Web site. Currently, there isn't much demand for keywords and consumers don't use them, so their usefulness as a marketing tool is limited.

Some companies have taken the view that they should register the relevant keywords to prevent others from obtaining them, despite the fact that they don't use them in their own business. Other companies have adopted a "wait and see" approach— deciding that they will take the risk and not register the keywords at this stage but will take action if their brands are registered by a third party and used in a way that affects their business or reputation.

Scam or Warning?

There is a common scam going around that is being used by unethical registrars to drum up business. Local businesses send e-mails and faxes to foreign companies, claiming to be registered CNNIC agents, and warning them that someone has sought to register their brands as either a domain name or a keyword. The warning tells the brand owner to respond immediately and to register the names, keywords, or "Internet brands" (another term for "keywords") itself or the registrations will be given to the third party. This generally creates panic initially. Chances are, the threat doesn't exist and the e-mail or fax can usually be ignored.

10. TRADEMARK CANCELLATION: RECOVERING A MARK REGISTERED BY ANOTHER PARTY

As awareness of IP in China has increased, so have the chances of Chinese parties filing trademark applications for well-known international brands. There was a spate of these types of vexatious registrations a few years ago which are now being discovered by brand owners. As discussed above, not only do these registrations prevent the foreign company from registering these marks and so protecting their brands from use by third parties; they can also prevent the foreign companies from using their own brands in China until they recover the marks or cancel the registrations.

There are a couple of options for cancelling a registered trademark:

- *Non-use cancellation:* If the mark has been registered for over five years and has not been used for a continuous three-year period, it is vulnerable to cancellation. Often, this can be determined by an investigation into the registrant of the trademark. Once a cancellation action is filed, the owner of the registration has to provide some evidence of use in order to overcome the claim. In the past, the majority of these cancellation actions were successful. However, Chinese parties are now often seeking legal advice from cheap local firms that advise them to provide some evidence of use. The threshold requirements of use are very low, and often these parties are fabricating the evidence to overcome the claim. Unfortunately, the Trademarks Re-Examination Adjudication Board is accepting this evidence without assessing its authenticity and so many of these cancellation actions are being rejected. It is possible to appeal the decision to the People's Courts, at which time the courts will be more likely to examine the evidence in depth and will be open to considering arguments of its authenticity.

- *Cancellation based on prior rights or similarity to an existing or well-known mark:* A registration can be challenged within five years of registration if it was registered in bad faith or otherwise breaches the Trademark Law. If the challenge involves a well-known mark, the five-year limit doesn't apply. A party can file a cancellation action with the Trademark Review and Adjudication Board (TRAB). As we have discussed, the decision of the TRAB can be appealed to the Intermediate Court in Beijing. A cancellation action currently takes approximately three years to be finalized, and the current owner can continue to use the mark in the meantime. Many foreign parties file the cancellation action and then approach the current owner to attempt to negotiate a settlement to recover the registration. As Chinese parties realize the value of these registrations, the costs have gone from a couple of hundred dollars a few years ago to much more significant requests. We heard of one case where the registrant asked the foreign company for €2 million to assign the mark, which wasn't even a well-known international brand. A more reasonable price can sometimes be obtained if the Chinese party is approached on a "no names" basis by a third party who indicates their interest in acquiring the brand, without indicating their connection with the foreign brand owner. This will obviously depend on the brand involved.

11.   INTERNET ACTION—TAKE-DOWN NOTICES

The continued development of technology creates new challenges for IP owners. The Internet provides an environment in which copying is easy, cheap, and fast, allowing rapid sharing of material. It also puts suppliers in touch with buyers much more easily than in the past. There are a number of business-to-business Web sites in China that offer to supply a broad range of products, providing an environment ripe for IP infringements, particularly as the Internet can offer complete anonymity if required. For example, there has been an increase in the number of cases relating to:

- uploading of copyrighted material;
- linking;
- search engines providing links to copyrighted material;
- domain names being registered by cyber squatters;
- offering for sale online, or online promotion of, infringing products;
- Internet caching;
- games software;
- search engines and their result listing order; and

- unauthorized use of another Web site's information for commercial purposes. (One US strategy consulting company, Technomic Asia, discovered that a company called Hainan Sunshine Investment had copied its entire Web site—everything from the look and feel, to the content, right down to the testimonials from clients! The only change was the company name.)

In 2006, China introduced its Internet Copyright Regulations, which allow ISPs to delete objectionable material on receiving a complaint from an IP owner. This can provide a useful option for copyright owners to have infringing material removed from the Internet, particularly when it relates to copyright material or the offering for sale of infringing products. Otherwise, companies usually need to depend on civil litigation to resolve Internet-related disputes. We strongly recommend that companies monitor the Internet regularly to ensure they are aware of the scope of the infringements and how the products are being offered. There are specialist companies that offer this service, and most consulting companies and law firms can provide reports and sightings.

12. PRODUCT LIABILITY/PRODUCT SAFETY/ PRODUCT RECALL

We discussed the laws and issues associated with this current hot issue in Chapter 4. However, it is important to keep it in mind as a tool in your enforcement toolbox. It can be particularly useful in convincing authorities to take action against an infringer for breach of the relevant safety laws in cases where you cannot obtain the required evidence to take action against them for IP infringement. It sends a message to the infringer and can create added costs for them in their business.

13. BREACH OF CONTRACT AND ARBITRATION

The courts in China are much more experienced in hearing contract infringement claims. If you have a contractual relationship with an infringer, it can be easier to stop them based on a breach of contract claim rather than infringement of IP rights. This may be action against:

- a partner;
- a distributor;

- an employee;
- a licensee;
- a manufacturer or supplier;
- a third party who has signed a non-disclosure or confidentiality agreement with your company for some reason; and
- a third party infringer who has signed undertakings agreeing not to infringe your rights again in future.

Obviously there may be other considerations before taking action against many of these parties, such as the relationship with them moving forward, but this option can be a very powerful strategic one for sending a strong message to your partners, and to the market, of your intention to protect your IP.

This option also highlights the importance of having infringers sign an undertaking agreeing not to infringe your IP rights again in future, either when sending them a cease and desist letter or after an administrative action. This can provide a relatively quick and cost-effective way of taking follow-up action if necessary.

Many companies provide for arbitration as the dispute resolution option in their agreements in China. With the uncertainty of the courts and enforcement of rights, arbitration can give companies a greater sense of comfort about their ability to protect their rights. The China International Economic and Trade Arbitration Center (CIETAC) is the main arbitration center in China. Its rules are in line with generally accepted arbitration rules and it has internationally experienced arbitrators. In the past, companies complained that CIETAC was slow and the process cumbersome, but it has amended its rules to incorporate time frames and to overcome some of the tedious procedural requirements. Arbitration can be conducted in Chinese or any other major language, depending on what is provided for in the arbitration clause in the agreement. Some companies prefer to choose arbitration through the more experienced Hong Kong International Arbitration Centre (HKIAC). The best option will depend on the location of your business in China, your partner, the type of IP involved, and other factors such as a willingness to arbitrate in China. Arbitral decisions from HKIAC are enforceable in China and, although some argue that an award from CIETAC will be easier to enforce as it is a Chinese center, there are examples supporting both arguments.

14. **HONG KONG AS A CREATIVE OPTION FOR ENFORCEMENT AND DEALING WITH SHADOW COMPANIES**

Hong Kong's IP regime is older and stronger than China's. As many infringers in China have some connection with Hong Kong and as many infringing products pass through Hong Kong on their way out of China, using Hong Kong's enforcement options can be a very useful supplement to a China IP strategy. Investigations in China will often lead to an export company in Hong Kong. Action can be commenced against this company in Hong Kong, and a damages award or an Anton Piller order or Mareva injunction obtained to protect evidence and assets. This may provide access to more information that can be used in a case in China. If the company is simply a shelf company with no assets, it may be more difficult to obtain information or a damages award, but often the Hong Kong entities have more assets and more to lose through litigation. A cease and desist letter may be taken more seriously in Hong Kong, and the threat of civil litigation (being cautious of Hong Kong's protection against unjustified threats) will often mean that you can use negotiations in Hong Kong to stop action in China.

As mentioned above in relation to the types of infringements that you may face in China, there has been an increase in the number of "shadow companies" being registered in Hong Kong. These are companies registered in bad faith, which contain famous brand names. They are used to provide authorization certificates or license agreements to companies in China that are manufacturing infringing products, to give them an air of authenticity. A number of well-known international brands have fallen prey to this tactic, including Anheuser-Busch®, Panasonic®, Sony®, and adidas®. As at the time of writing (November 2007), Anheuser-Busch has successfully taken action against nine such companies in Hong Kong. But having them removed from the register isn't always easy. The Hong Kong Companies Ordinance allows the Registrar of Companies to strike names from the register if they are too similar to the name of another registered company, but the Registrar interprets this right to strike off names under the ordinance very narrowly. The Registrar can also strike off dormant companies, but the level of evidence required to show the company is being used is very low and evidence of business activity in China is sufficient.

Companies need to take action against the directors of the infringing companies (and their shareholders), obtain a judgment against them, and then take this to the Registrar to have the names struck off. Although this approach is time consuming and costly, it has been successful. A number of companies are lobbying for an amendment to the ordinance to provide a process for objecting to company names that incorporate a third party's registered trademarks, to make it easier for these companies to be removed. This is unlikely to happen for a couple of years, but in the meantime litigation provides one option for dealing with these shadow companies.

15. BUILDING UP STRONG RELATIONSHIPS WITH THE AUTHORITIES

Strong relationships with the authorities are a critical element of a China IP strategy. There are many examples of when having a contact within an authority can assist with action or advice, from administrative action, to Customs, to the Public Security Bureau. That is definitely not to suggest that companies should engage in unlawful activities. The authorities are often under-resourced, but keen to assist; if IP owners can find a way to recognize or "give face" to authorities that support the protection of IP, this encourages all officials to be more diligent in taking proactive action to eliminate IP infringements. The Quality Brands Protection Committee (discussed in Chapter 9) has set up an annual Top 10 IP Enforcement Cases award for the authorities that have demonstrated initiative, effectiveness, efficiency, and innovation in combating IP infringement. The competition to win one of these awards has provided positive developments toward stronger IP protection.

The authorities also appreciate publicity for the administrative actions they take. Depending on your policy on publicity for enforcement, allowing the authorities to invite the media to attend raids can encourage them.

Approaching the authorities to organize raids or to destroy seized products around International IP Day can be effective, as they are often looking to showcase how active they are in IP enforcement. For example, on World IP Day in 2007, the authorities destroyed 120,000 counterfeit DVDs in Hubei. The owner of the illegal DVD factory had discouraged curiosity about the factory by spreading rumors that it was being used to study bird flu! International IP celebrations can also be a useful time to conduct difficult cases.

Having a contact in an authority who is able to confirm the authority's view on a regulation or opinion on a potential infringement can mean that companies are able to prepare for action in a more informed way. Organizing training sessions and inviting the authorities to attend can be a useful way to raise their awareness both of your IP rights and the support you need from them.

At the end of the day, there is a balance to be struck: IP enforcement in China requires contact with the authorities; and the stronger the relationship, the more able you will be to take effective action. On the other hand, there must be no suggestion of foreign companies engaging in improper actions in dealings with the authorities.

16.   OTHER REGULATORY OPTIONS

In addition to the above-described tools in your enforcement toolbox, there are a number of other options in China for taking action against IP infringers. These options may not always stop the IP infringement, and in many cases they can be fixed relatively easily, but they create added business costs for the infringer, which can give you leverage to negotiate a resolution with them. These options include drawing officials' attention to the infringer's:

- non-compliance with regulations covering warehousing and handling of goods;
- breaches of complex labeling regulations;
- non-compliance with the Advertising Law of the People's Republic of China and associated regulations;
- failure to lodge audit documents and annual reports with the AIC; and
- non-compliance with labor laws.

If, during your investigations, evidence of these other areas of non-compliance is obtained, retain it and consider these options as part of your strategy for dealing with infringers.

17. PUBLICITY

Use of publicity in IP enforcement strategies can send a powerful message to the infringers that your company will take action to protect its rights in China and to protect consumers from counterfeit and dangerous products. You just need to work out how best to harness the media. In some cases, you will have no control over the media involvement. (The authorities are increasingly inviting the media to be present at administrative actions in order to increase their profile of being proactive in the protection of IP.) You will need to engage your public relations team in advance and be ready with a statement if the media becomes involved.

Some companies use publicity very actively in their enforcement campaigns, with consumer hotlines set up for reporting infringements and regular promotional activities. These companies see the role of publicity as reassuring consumers that they are taking action to protect them from counterfeits or dangerous products. They use the opportunity to educate consumers on how to distinguish a genuine product from a fake one, and about the benefits of demanding the real products along with the dangers of buying unauthorized products. Other companies prefer not to attract publicity at all, concerned that it sends a message to consumers that their brand has a counterfeit problem. They focus instead on advertising the benefits and quality features of their products to help consumers correctly identify them.

There is no one correct publicity strategy. Publicity can be a powerful tool if used carefully, but it can also be very damaging if you are not prepared for the consequences.

18. FINDING CREATIVE SOLUTIONS TO IP INFRINGEMENTS

China's fledgling IP regime comes with its challenges. But it also comes with opportunities to be creative in finding solutions to IP infringements. Some of the most successful strategies in China are those that don't limit themselves to using the traditional tools for enforcement. The movie industry is a good example. There is a very high demand for pirated copies of movies, because there is limited access to genuine products. This is due to the fact that:

- the authorities allow in only a limited number of foreign films every year, and those are significantly censored;

- the authorities impose "blackout dates" when foreign films cannot be shown; and
- there is only a limited number of movie theaters in China, and they are expensive for most consumers.

These restrictions allow pirates, rather than the industry, to follow the demand. The authorities launch campaigns every year in an attempt to clean up the market, but there are still significant quantities of pirated DVDs sold on the streets throughout China. In fact, many of the more established stores that sell fake DVDs take the opportunity to "close for renovations" during the annual campaigns!

Some of the creative strategies the movie industry has used to try and overcome these challenges include:

- partnering with local companies and setting up cinemas equipped with the latest technology, to enhance the viewing experience;
- supporting the development of the local film industry through providing scholarships for film directors and other such initiatives;
- launching films in China at the same time as the international launch to maximize profits before the fake DVDs hit the streets;
- adding extra features to genuine DVDs to encourage consumers to buy the real products; and
- selling the genuine products at a much lower price than in most markets, better to compete with the fakes.

Although they have a long way to go, these creative approaches have helped the process and will hopefully soon start to pay off for the film industry.

An international power tools company provides another great example of creative thinking. Many of the products it sells in the second-tier cities in China are from its older ranges of products, which are no longer protected by patent rights. This situation created a challenge for the IP owner, which wanted to stop counterfeits being sold in these developing mini-markets in China. Even when the authorities managed to conduct administrative action based on trademark infringement, they would often return the seized counterfeit products to the infringer as they were reluctant to destroy them. To overcome this problem, the IP

CASE STUDY: MARS, INC.

Mars, Incorporated has taken a very proactive and educative approach to protecting its portfolio of confectionery and pet care brands in China. Mars' marketing property manager for Asia Pacific, Rhonda Steele, comments that "there is no global one size fits all IP policy; you need to have a strategy that is tailored for emerging markets."

Rhonda has four golden rules for Mars' successful IP program in China:

1. ***Get the basics right:*** *"The benefits of registered trademarks cannot be overestimated," says Rhonda. "It only costs a few hundred dollars and it is so important to get it right." Mars has been very proactive in not only registering its core brands and logos, but also in stretching the limits and trying to register less traditional elements of its brands as trademarks—for example, the colors that form such a critical element of its Whiskas® and Pedigree® pet care brands. This approach gives them a very strong foundation on which to base their action.*

2. ***"Education, education, education!":*** *This is Rhonda's core advice to those trying to protect IP in China. "Not just the government, consumers, and your employees. Educate yourself. It's not just a one-way street. Learn about your options, what systems exist, and who can help you along the way." And given the pace of change in China, this is an ongoing process—learn something new about China every day. Education of others is also an important element of Mars' strategy. As IP in China is so new, Mars has been very active in lobbying for stronger laws and practical implementation of the existing laws. In 2006, Mars was a very active player in a project to take various judges and officials to Europe to educate them on registration of non-traditional trademarks—in particular, the use of color as a trademark. This project involved working closely with a number of other companies; some in different industries (for example, Orange and BP) and some fierce competitors (Cadbury). As Rhonda says, sometimes you need to come together with your competitors for the greater good. Mars has also actively engaged the enforcement authorities, inviting them to training sessions on Mars' IP rights to raise awareness about the issues being faced by foreign companies in China.*

3. ***Understand your supply chain:*** *"It isn't good enough to sign an agreement and close your eyes. You need to understand how*

it works and then take steps to minimize the risks." Mars has employed a number of the options outlined in Chapter 4 to come to terms with the China supply chain for its licensed products and to minimize the IP leaks.

4. ***Stay focused on your strategy:*** *Mars has been very consistent in selecting strategic targets against which to take action. This may include repeat infringers and/or targets in troublesome jurisdictions where it wants to send a strong message. In the early stages of their strategy, they looked for "slam dunk cases," as Rhonda describes them; for example, strategic targets where they could take administrative actions through the AIC, recheck whether the targets were continuing to infringe their rights, and, if they were, then Mars commenced civil litigation action against them. Every couple of months, they analyzed the statistics (including punishment decisions issued) and selected a couple more strategic targets against which to take tougher action. Once Mars had taken civil litigation action against a couple of "slam dunk cases" in one difficult area (Fujian province) and publicized these successes, a number of the outstanding targets they had commenced action against approached them to settle the disputes. One mistake that a lot of companies make is to lose focus and take action against non-critical infringements. Mars has an active licensing program in the US for its well-known M&M's® characters on a wide range of non-food items; however, this program is not currently active in China. Initially, the temptation was to take action against the non-food infringements of its M&M's® characters (for example, T-shirts, plush toys, etc.) in China. However, they were fighting a losing battle and spending a lot of their IP budget on non-core products that were not then hitting their bottom line in China. The decision was taken to refocus priorities on the core products—in this case, confectionery—while at the same time investing the resources into management of their supply chain to reduce the infringements on the non-food side. Rhonda's advice: "Get a strategy, get alignment from all the core stakeholders, and then give it time. Don't get distracted."*

Mars' China IP policy leads the way on creative, strategic actions. Rhonda Steele continues to push boundaries and to strive for the more effective solutions to infringements. Other companies can learn a lot from Mars' approach.

owner included the trademark on all key parts of the products. The infringer then had to do the same if it wanted to pass the products off as genuine. This change made it easier for the IP owner to convince the authorities to destroy the seized products, as it wasn't possible to remove the trademark from all the components.

This same strategy of including the trademark on all key components of a product means that subcontractors will be infringing trademark rights if they manufacture these parts, making it easier to take action against them. Otherwise, counterfeiters often assemble the products in one location and simply add the final trademark as the very last step (often by the customer) to avoid being caught with branded products, which can be seized.

Xerox also adopted a creative approach when it found fake parts were being produced for its copiers, which were damaging the machines as well as being dangerous. They invested in training their technicians to tell the difference, and also in training consumers to recognize the value of the genuine products. They also set up a toner phone hotline and cooperated with the government in taking action against infringers.

Top 5 tips for enforcement

1. Align your IP enforcement strategy with your commercial business plan.

2. Engage in civil litigation.

3. Practice what you preach—take steps to manage IP internally and with partners, and don't permit employees to buy counterfeit products!

4. Budget for in-depth investigations to gain a sound understanding of the business models of the infringers before taking action.

5. Identify the "driving force" of the infringements and focus your actions on dealing with them.

CHECKPOINT

In preparing a sound IP strategy for China, there are eight key areas. In this chapter, we considered the "What" factors:

- *Your enforcement toolbox:* Have you considered all your "tools" for dealing with the infringement? Overlay these with your responses to the "You" factors (see Chapter 6) and the "Them" factors (see Chapter 7), and be creative with your strategy for protecting your IP rights.

RESOURCES

- www.ipr.gov.cn: The government's Web site on IP in China. It contains a number of the relevant laws in English, as well as other resources and links to other interesting Web sites.
- www.cnnic.net.cn: China Internet Network Information Center (CNNIC) Web site.
- www.cietac.org: China International Economic and Trade Arbitration Commission (CIETAC).
- www.hkiac.org: Hong Kong International Arbitration Centre (HKIAC).
- www.buyusa.gov/china/en/ipr.html: A US government Web site that contains a China IP toolbox with some interesting suggestions.
- www.chinaiprlaw.com/english/default.htm: A Web site with some interesting resources on IP, run by one of the IP judges of the Supreme People's Court in China. The English version is out of date, but it has some old cases and many of the laws.

Part
4

Looking to the future

China's IP regime continues to develop alongside the country's rapid economic growth. These changes present a great opportunity for foreign companies to support implementation of the laws in order to provide a fairer competitive environment that no longer allows Chinese companies to trade off the reputation and IP of other companies. Lobbying for change with the Chinese authorities is an important element of a comprehensive Chinese IP strategy, and Chapter 9 explores the ways in which companies can use this opportunity to their best advantage. In the following chapter we consider China's future transition from world's factory to a country that develops and exploits its own IP through local research and innovation. In the final chapter, we will consider the possible impact of the 2008 Olympic Games on China's IP regime as the world's eyes turn to watch the sporting spectacle in Beijing.

Lobbying for change

1. SETTING THE SCENE

China's IP legislation was put into place very hurriedly, partly in order to satisfy China's obligations to join the World Trade Organization. The sheer pace of development in the country over the past 20 years also means that some of the laws that were initially passed, and the infrastructure put in place to manage them, no longer satisfy the needs of a country that has its eyes on moving from being the world's factory to a serious global economic player. This, coupled with the ongoing challenges of enforcement of the IP laws, the immature nature of China's IP protection system, and the relative inexperience of the officials and judges who are responsible for enforcing IP in China, means that an important part of many companies' IP protection strategies in China involves lobbying for change. Whether this is lobbying for a change of legislation, for better enforcement of rights, or for changes in the infrastructure to meet the changing needs of companies in China, getting the right lobbying channel with the best lobbying partners will be crucial in successfully creating change. The good news is that, with the right strategy, creating change is possible in China as, on the whole, many of the authorities are open to learning and to implementing international best practice as they develop a solid IP protection regime.

2. PREPARING TO LOBBY

Do You Need to Lobby for Change?

Many companies' first thought when they face rampant infringement of their IP in China is that they need to report it to their home government and put pressure on them to lobby the Chinese government for change. Political pressure can definitely be a powerful method for facilitating change, but on its own it won't be effective in creating real change in China. Companies need first to look at whether they have engaged the right tools from the enforcement toolbox outlined in Chapter 8, and at whether there are other ways of effecting change without relying solely on their government.

The Lobbying Matrix: Getting the Strategy Right

There are a number of elements that will impact on a successful IP lobbying strategy in China. They include:

- *What types of change are you trying to make?* Is it a legislative change, or a change in the practice of the judiciary or the local officials?

- *Where does the issue fall in the Chinese government's priorities?* Is it a piece of legislation currently under review, or an issue set out in the current IP Working Plan?

- *Which government authorities are involved?* Which levels of officials need to be engaged?

- *Does this issue impact other companies?* Or is it an individual issue unique to your company?

We will explore each of these elements below.

What Types of Change Are You Trying to Make?

Companies need to categorize the issue they are facing. What exactly is the root cause of the issue? It may be a combination of factors, or there may be one obvious challenge.

- Is the current legislation inadequate? For example, the current Trademark Law doesn't provide for protection from dilution (that is, protection against use of well-known brands on different products—for example, the use of the Coca-Cola® brand on cosmetics).

- Could the issue be resolved though amendments to the various implementing regulations? For example, the current Trademark Law provides for trademark applications to be examined within "a reasonable time." This provision is in line with the global standard. However, in practice, the current waiting time is over two years, which is by no means reasonable; it not only prevents companies from being able to enforce their rights in the meantime, but in some cases it prevents them from selling their products in China until the mark is registered. For example, in the pharmaceutical industry, a drug cannot be sold in China unless the name has been trademarked or the drug has received approval from the State Food and Drug Authority (which will only approve drugs that are new to the market). Another example is in the retail industry, where many department stores are now requiring a trademark registration certificate or trademark license recordal certificate (which can only be obtained for registered trademarks) before they will lease out retail space to brands. A change to the legislation stating a specified time frame would resolve the issue, but this will take time. An alternative approach is to lobby the State Trademarks Office to implement a change in its regulations to provide a limit on the time in which applications will be examined, which would have the same effect.

- Is the issue with implementation/enforcement of the laws by the authorities? For example, the relevant regulation provides that the standard for determining "confusion" under the Anti-Unfair Competition Law is "the likelihood of confusion"; however, many of the local authorities responsible for enforcing the law apply the standard as "actual confusion," which is extremely difficult to prove and effectively prevents brand owners from taking action against copycats in some provinces. This is more an issue for the authorities, both locally with training and at a state level, to ensure that the local authorities are effectively enforcing the law. The central government's focus on IP is definitely improving, but most enforcement issues occur at the local level.

- Is the challenge associated with engaging local officials to take action to protect your company's rights? For example, local Price Evaluation Bureaus are responsible for calculating the value of infringing goods seized during the course of administrative raids, but sometimes they won't calculate semi-finished goods into the overall figure. If so, it might be appropriate to engage the local officials with some training and brand awareness to help get them focused on your company's challenges and the proper handling of the issues under law.

- Is the issue associated with court decisions? For example, the court requirement of having to obtain notarized and legalized evidence, discussed in Chapter 8, can often prevent companies from taking action in a timely manner—or at all, in some cases. This issue may be best addressed by engaging the People's Courts directly.

Coming to terms with the specifics of the issue being faced and the change required to resolve it ensures that you focus your lobbying efforts on those who have the ability to influence the changes you need.

Where Does the Issue Fall in the Chinese Government's Priorities?

If the issue is one that is currently under review by the Chinese government, or which has been included in their current priorities, this can often be a "fast-forward" pass for lobbying. The government department or authority responsible for the priorities will be more open to receiving feedback on the issues. (In fact, they may even be seeking it.) To identify the latest government priorities, check http://english.ipr.gov.cn/en/policy.shtml for the latest IPR Action Plan.

If the issue is one that has recently been explored and settled by the authorities, they may be more reluctant to reopen it and a different tactic may be necessary.

If it is an issue that is not on the radar of the authorities, the process is likely to be slower and will require more education prior to more structured lobbying.

Which Government Authorities are Involved?

China's government structure for IP issues is confusing, and in some cases there is substantial overlap between the authorities' responsibilities. This situation can create challenges for lobbying efforts, as identifying the department with the authority to make the changes you need isn't always straightforward.

This structure is overlaid against the need to determine whether to engage the state/national, provincial, or local authorities. For example, it may be that the issue is a local one, but that engaging the provincial authorities may be more effective than approaching the local officials only. However, companies need to be careful of the issue of "face," which is critical in China, and not go above a local authority without giving it an opportunity to respond to the issue directly. It is usually local-level officials that your business will need to work with most closely to obtain the various required business approvals and operating licenses.

If, by going above them, you directly suggest to their superiors that they are not satisfying their legal obligations, your business may find itself facing sudden audits and other challenges from the local authorities.

In some remote areas, there are still cities that rely on counterfeiting for their livelihood, so a very compelling case is going to have to be made to convince the local authorities in those cities to take action. We have explored potential ways around this issue in Chapter 8.

If the issue is widespread, or relates to legislation, going straight to the state/national-level authority will be more effective provided you engage the right partners.

Does this Issue Impact Other Companies?

This is an interesting question and one that many companies don't ask during their preparatory work. They assume the issue is widespread; but when they try to engage others to lobby with them, they find it appears to be unique to them.

There are several levels to this question that you will need to address:

- Is the issue unique to your company? Does it involve a very specific regulation that your structure or product doesn't satisfy? Or is it a decision by a particular authority that your product doesn't satisfy the requirements for IP protection? This is often the case in the more highly regulated industries and in relation to copyright and unfair competition cases.

- Is it an industry issue? For example, refilling of bottles with counterfeit liquid is an issue faced by the whole alcohol industry, as well as the automotive oils and photocopier toner cartridges industries.

- Is it a wider issue that affects all businesses, including Chinese brand owners? For example, the issue of delay in examining trademark applications will affect Chinese companies and international companies equally.

- Is it an issue that affects foreign brand owners/companies only? For example, until recently, foreign representatives were prohibited from attending IP court proceedings.

Once companies come to terms with the extent of those impacted by the issue, it will assist with determining the appropriate lobbying partners.

Preparing a Lobbying Paper

Having considered the four elements above, we recommend that companies put together a briefing paper that clearly outlines the issue you are facing, the reasons for the problem, and the solution you would like to see, together with an assessment of the above areas. This is a crucial step with a number of benefits:

- It will help you to determine whether in fact you need to lobby for change, or if you can try another approach first.

- It will enable you to get alignment from all your stakeholders internally, including your local team in China, your legal/ IP team, your corporate relations team, and the management team. Companies that have had the most success with their lobbying efforts are those that make the best use of their internal resources (such as relationships with government officials) before looking externally.

- It will help with prioritization of the issues.

- It will provide all the information needed to determine the best partners and approach to effect the change required.

- It will be a useful briefing document for any partners in the lobbying efforts.

Finding the Best Lobbying Partners, or Going it Alone

The old adage that there is strength in numbers is often the case with lobbying to change the IP environment in China. As the Chinese government's primary goal is to develop the country as quickly as possible, it continues to seek foreign investment, which gives foreign companies a strong bargaining position from which to create change in the level of protection for IP rights in China. However, power at the moment comes from showing the Chinese authorities how a stronger IP protection regime would benefit their own local entities as they grow and begin to develop valuable brands and other IP of their own. It is also important to keep in mind that the Chinese government will often have vested interests—such as social control, access to goods and services, generation of taxes, and development of export markets— contributing to its willingness (or sometimes apparent lack thereof) to accept change. One commonly heard explanation for why the mass availability of fake DVDs is allowed to continue is that if the government were suddenly to crack down entirely on their availability, it would create substantial unrest among those who cannot afford the genuine goods. Another argument runs that the ongoing tight censorship regulations in China mean that the demand for foreign films won't be met through government-sanctioned films, and so the government allows the manufacture of fake DVDs for a wider range of films in order to keep consumers happy while maintaining the stance that all access to films in China is strictly controlled. Interestingly, another argument from years past was that foreign production companies didn't want to invest in the high-tech movie theaters needed to screen blockbusters in China. Cynical as these arguments may be, the reality is that the government has to balance many competing interests as challenges are thrown at it by the rapid pace of growth in China.

Potential Lobbying Partners

Government

Sometimes, leveraging political power can be the most effective method of effecting change. Australia, for example, is currently negotiating a Free Trade Agreement with China and is seeking input from Australian companies on the types of IP challenges they face in China so that these can be taken into account during the negotiations. The US government, through its Joint Committee on Commerce and Trade (JCCT), meets with the Chinese authorities every quarter to discuss a number of issues, one of which is IP. It regularly seeks feedback from US companies conducting business in or with China on the IP challenges they face, although currently it seems to be focused more on currency valuations rather than IP infringements. Providing this feedback, and allowing the governments to lobby the issue on your behalf, can be useful. However, it tends to be slow. It also means that you lose control over your input and the resolution requested. The foreign governments will always be seeking feedback and examples that justify their position, so if you have a different view, your opinion is likely to be disregarded.

Chambers of Commerce

The Chambers of Commerce in China can be very effective lobbying partners. They have been active in the country for many years and have developed strong relationships with various levels of government. They are often actively solicited for their input by the government. For example, with the Franchising Regulation that was finally implemented on May 1, 2007, following years of debate and delays, it was the European Union Chamber in Beijing that was first approached by the authorities to provide feedback. Each year, many of the Chambers prepare a white paper for the government on the priority challenges facing their members in their businesses in China, and they are often invited to discuss the issues raised in these papers with the relevant officials. The white papers are, on the whole, very practical; they offer solutions to the government that balance the needs of the Chambers' members with the realities of the government's agenda, giving them added credibility with the authorities. If you conduct business in China, contributing to these white papers can be a very effective way of getting immediate access to the officials through the Chambers' relationships. Research the Chamber that is the most appropriate to your issues. Most of the major foreign players have a Chamber in each of the main cities in China. A list of some of the key Chambers is set out in the "Resources" section at the end of this chapter. Follow these guidelines to determine which is most appropriate:

- Start with your home country's Chamber in the key city in which your business operates.
- Ask them what their IP lobbying efforts entail and about their approach. Some Chambers are more focused on IP than others; some have stronger contacts with IP officials. Find out who in the Chamber drives the IP agenda—is it industry-driven or driven by IP professionals?
- Review their latest white paper and assess whether the challenges identified there match with your priorities.
- Discuss with the IP champions in the Chamber the process for preparing the white paper, how easy it is to get involved, how they choose which issues are included, etc.

Assess all these factors in terms of your lobbying paper to find the Chamber that is most appropriate for you.

China Business Councils

Most countries have a business council with China. The majority of these offer business advice and support services, as well as organizing trade missions. But only a few of them are actively engaged in lobbying activities in China. One of the strongest business councils for lobbying is the US–China Business Council

(USCBC), which was established in 1973 to try to fill the void at a time when there were no formal diplomatic relations between the United States and China. Their IP agenda is quite substantive. The USCBC's approach is to work as a service provider to its members. Members are invited to share their issues in China with the USCBC, which will then research the issue, approach the authorities, and advise on the appropriate strategy for proceeding. If the issue affects a number of members, the USCBC will begin to advocate the issue on behalf of its member companies through written submissions and meetings with its contacts in both the US and Chinese governments.

Industry organizations

Often IP issues are common across an industry, so exploring the option of teaming up as an industry to lobby the government can be a useful approach. Whether this is done formally through an industry body, or informally through a coalition, will depend on your industry and whether there is an industry body in China able to lobby the government. Convincing leadership to work with your company's competitors can be a challenge. This is where your lobbying paper can be a powerful tool. At the end of the day, it is an individual decision. However, an industry approach will be more powerful than a single entity, and having a strong IP protection regime will benefit all market players across the board. The *Silk Market* case in Beijing run by the luxury goods industry, discussed in Chapter 8, is a great example of how it can work.

Quality Brands Protection Committee

The Quality Brands Protection Committee (QBPC) was established in March 2000 with a vision "to work cooperatively with the Chinese Central and local governments, local industry, and other organizations to make positive contributions to intellectual property protection in the People's Republic of China." As a result of its high-profile and creative campaigning, it is now seen by the government as a very strong partner in creating an international IP protection regime in China.

QBPC is a good example of cooperating with the authorities (a "we're all in it together" approach), rather than pushing for change, which can create defensiveness. The annual QBPC Awards for the best cases of the year are hotly contested, and a suggestion that a case may qualify for one of the awards can often help convince the authorities to take action. There are seven committees, each with a different primary focus. (Their names can be misleading, so find out which committee is responsible for the area in which you are interested.) For example, the Patent Committee is running an IP Civil Litigation Project in conjunction with the Supreme People's Court to provide training programs, mock trials, and joint conferences as opportunities for members to engage with the judiciary on some of the common issues faced in IP litigation in China. The comparative IP law conference held in Chongqing in September 2006 created a great opportunity for discussion between international experts, foreign rights holders, and local judges and authorities. A similar, expanded conference was held in Beijing in October 2007.

The Legal Committee, which maintains close relationships with the relevant committees in the National People's Congress, focuses on administrative actions and criminal enforcement of IP but has also been lobbying for greater transparency of laws and procedures through English versions of laws, judgments, court procedures, and so on. One of the most active committees is the Customs Committee, which regularly organizes opportunities for members to meet with Customs officials in various areas and to conduct brand awareness training to familiarize the officials with their IP issues. The need for this, as discussed in Chapter 8, is an important part of most IP protection strategies. However, QBPC's 176 members are mainly global corporations with a lot of power in their own right. It isn't always a useful lobbying tool for smaller companies whose voices may be lost among the big players who were founding members and have run the organization since its inception.

One Size Doesn't Fit All

There is no right or wrong way to find the right lobbying partners. We have had numerous clients ask us, "What's the best organization to lobby through?" and the answer is very individual to a company's needs. Review your lobbying paper; the answers it provides to the questions set out above will provide you with the information you need. Other issues will also play a role in your decision:

- Do you have people on the ground in China able to drive your lobbying efforts?
- What is your budget for lobbying?

- Do you have the time to be actively driving your lobbying agenda?
- Are you prepared to compromise on the issues to get an outcome? (This may be required if you lobby through an organization.)
- How important is achieving this change to your future business plans?
- Have your key stakeholders bought into this process?

Going it Alone

Some companies wish to maintain complete control over the lobbying and the approach, as well as the requested solutions. They have strong contacts on the ground in China and so mainly do their lobbying independently. This can be a very effective approach, with creative solutions much more possible than in group lobbying. The following are some examples of where independent lobbying was done:

- Prior to choosing a province in which to invest a substantial amount of money in a new plant, a global manufacturer of electronic products successfully used the approach of engaging the local governments in the key provinces it was considering to sign a Memorandum of Understanding that committed them to take active steps to protect the foreign company's IP. It then negotiated the best deal to protect its IP. As mentioned in Chapter 2, the provinces and municipalities are often so keen to attract foreign investment that they will compete to show their commitment to protecting your rights. A conference on IP rights held in Hangzhou in March 2007, organized for its clients by Latham & Watkins, a foreign law firm, successfully enabled the Zhejiang authorities to showcase the steps they have taken to provide a strong IP protection regime in order to attract foreign investment into the province.

- The movie industry concluded that a new approach was required, as efforts to clean up counterfeit DVDs were not having great effect. They decided to support the development of the domestic film industry, realizing that with a strong domestic industry putting pressure on the authorities, more action was likely to be taken. They awarded scholarships to film students, set up cinemas, and sponsored movie premieres, for example. This approach also showed the authorities that the industry is committed to China's future, which spurred them to take action against DVD pirates.

- Microsoft entered into an agreement with the Shanghai government to legitimize every piece of software in government offices in Shanghai. It has now expanded this approach with other governments in China, but this independent lobbying approach gave the company a strong platform on which to base its business in China.

The best examples of independent lobbying are non-confrontational and cooperative with the authorities, focusing on the mutual benefits to be gained from an increased awareness and enforcement of IP in China.

Other companies may prefer just to lend their voice and support to organizations that are lobbying for similar issues, and which are not so attached to the specifics of the outcome. At the end of the day, you need to come up with an approach that suits *your* company's needs. In most cases, a combination of working with organizations as well as individual lobbying will be the most appropriate solution.

CASE STUDY: BAYER—PARTNERSHIPS WITH UNIVERSITIES AS LOBBYING

Bayer depends heavily on its technology and IP. Without it, it couldn't deliver the success it does across its three core business units—Bayer Healthcare, Bayer MaterialScience, and Bayer CropScience.

A few years ago, Bayer set up a project to look at its IP processes and options in China. One of the first things that became obvious during this project was that the company needed to have someone on the ground to manage its China strategy. Traditionally, its IP in China had been managed and controlled out of headquarters in Germany, where management weren't in very close contact with the business teams on the ground, especially regarding day-to-day issues. Bayer quickly realized that China was different, and the company hired an IP lawyer to create a robust, localized IP protection program that was better placed to deal with the unique challenges of China's environment, including the establishment of a local IP function in China staffed with local lawyers.

In April 2006, Bayer announced that it was establishing the Bayer Chair in Intellectual Property Rights (IPR Chair) in conjunction with the Department of Economic Law of the Chinese-German School for Postgraduate Studies (CDHK) of Tongji University, Shanghai, with the aim of:

- *increasing the awareness in China of IP as a value asset;*
- *promoting education with regard to IP issues; and*
- *encouraging discussion of and comparative studies in IP.*

Many industries have sponsored chairs at universities (for example, engineering chairs) as a way to connect with potential employees. However, the IPR Chair has a different focus—general IP awareness and education—in an attempt to change behavior and attitudes toward IP. The IPR Chair organizes regular small seminars targeted at particular issues. Bayer and Tongji have also run an annual IPR Forum. It was first run in Shanghai in October 2006 as a platform for dialogue and exchange of ideas among experts, with the target of discussing and formulating recommendations for improved IP protection in China. It is a unique forum in that it brings government officials together with both Chinese and foreign companies as well as students. In China, the IP regime isn't easy to navigate as the local regulations are complex. The Forum is aimed at providing a sophisticated level of debate and the means to share and exchange ideas. The first Forum focused on the third amendment of the Chinese Patent Law, with small working groups focusing on inventor remuneration, grace period, and protection of drugs. As Lisa Haselhorst, the head of IP for Bayer in Greater China, commented: "These smaller group workshops create great open discussions and debate."

Bayer recently ran its second annual IPR Forum, which was focused on patent and trademark enforcement. Again, there were international experts present, as well as local and multinational companies alongside government officials. The morning consisted of presentations by Chinese officials and foreign experts on patent issues. The afternoon focused on trademark issues; later a podium discussion provided an opportunity for attendees to address some more specific topics in greater depth. Bayer is not unrealistic as to the outcomes of these Forums. It doesn't expect immediate change. But this cooperative, ongoing approach can be expected to start to change attitudes and raise awareness.

This is a great example of how lobbying can be done creatively in China. It doesn't need to be the traditional approach of meeting with government officials at a high level. Through the IPR Chair, Bayer has created a platform for contributing to change among all the relevant stakeholders.

Lisa also recommends two other lobbying strategies that Bayer has found useful in China:

- **Involve the appropriate team:** *In many companies, the lobbying platform is managed by the Corporate Relations or Government Relations teams. The involvement of these teams is critical. However, often these people are not experts in the relevant areas being lobbied. Chinese government officials are now well educated about IP issues and are very familiar with the relevant foreign laws. They will ask quite detailed and interesting questions which require a sound understanding of the commercial issues, international laws, and the practical problems and solutions. If the team who is managing your IP lobbying strategy isn't able to respond to the officials' questions, the discussions will tend to be superficial and less effective. Involving your IP team, your technical teams, and your researchers can send a much stronger message to the authorities about the issues affecting businesses on the ground, and will enable a more in-depth and engaged discussion to take place.*

- **Working with competitors:** *As we have discussed, industry lobbying can be a very powerful tool. Lisa believes that working with competitors to send an industry message can be a powerful approach. In order to manage the push back from the commercial teams, companies who work well with competitors often have a relationship between the legal and IP teams who drive the lobbying agenda on IP issues together. Obviously, there will be company-specific issues and concerns that need to be dealt with separately, but in most industries there are general issues facing the industry as a whole. Working side by side and speaking with the same voice sends the message to the authorities that this is a broader issue that they need to address, rather than a unique issue being faced by one company. If competitors don't address the same issues, the authorities will often respond to requests for change with the claim that the problem may be an internal one, unique to your company and which your company needs to deal with, rather than an issue that needs to concern the authorities.*

3. IMPLEMENTING YOUR LOBBYING STRATEGY

Once you have determined the best approach for your lobbying efforts in China to achieve your desired outcomes, there are a couple of golden rules to consider in implementing it:

- *Be patient:* Achieving change can take time. Sometimes, if a stalemate has been reached, the best approach is to let the issue rest for a while and revisit it in a couple of months.

- *Be creative:* The Chinese authorities, in general, are very keen to learn and develop a strong IP protection system in China. They are enthusiastic and often easy to engage. This presents great opportunities for companies to be creative in coming up with innovative ways to work with the authorities to achieve the desired outcomes.

- *Constantly reassess your goals and your progress:* Some companies become so focused on their lobbying that they forget to stop and check their progress against their objectives. The business reason for the lobbying may have dissipated, or priorities may have changed. Or you may have made more progress than you think you have, despite the fact it feels like there is a deadlock. Taking a step back and evaluating your progress is an important part of the lobbying process.

4. EDUCATION AND TRAINING AS LOBBYING

Many of the issues that companies face in protecting their IP in China may not require a change to the legislation or regulations, but, rather, more education and training to increase awareness. Given the short history of IP in China, it is understandable that officials are not always well equipped with expertise at this stage. Engaging with the authorities, and helping them to come to terms with the laws, can be a very fruitful approach.

The following are some of the many ways in which companies can engage authorities, officials, consumers, and suppliers in order to increase awareness of IP as a critical step in the implementation of the IP laws in China.

Training of IP Officials
Many companies have engaged the officials currently responsible for implementing and enforcing the IP laws in China to help

increase awareness of the intricacies of sound IP protection. For example, Bayer has taken a very active approach to increasing awareness of IP in China, but with a focus on the relevant IP authorities. In June 2007, it organized an IP Forum in conjunction with Tongji University to provide a forum between Germany and China to discuss the IP challenges in China and to share the German experience. One group of companies organized a visit by Chinese trademark officials to the EU, to meet with IP officials in various offices there and to explore the complex issue of registration of colors as trademarks. As we discussed in Chapter 5, this is a new and highly controversial area of trademark law everywhere in the world, so inviting the Chinese officials to study the issues enabled them to share in the international best practice being developed, resulting in the brand owners in China being able to lobby for amendments to the trademark practice to allow for registration of single colors as trademarks. Many companies also conduct training on their brands and IP rights for Administration for Industry and Commerce officials, to assist the officials with administrative enforcement actions. Often, this can be organized through associations or with groups of companies.

Training of Customs Officials

As discussed in Chapter 8, training of Customs officials is a key part of any Customs strategy to stop counterfeits and other IP infringements from crossing into or, more likely, out of China. The authorities are so under-resourced, and they face such large quantities of shipments passing though every port daily, that unless you engage them in some training to increase their aware-ness of your company's IP rights, just recording your marks with them won't be terribly effective. QBPC, as discussed above, has a very active Customs training program for its members. This is a cost-effective way of engaging Customs officials, the majority of whom, in our experience, welcome the opportunity for training to help them identify IP infringements.

Training of Judges

A number of delegations of Chinese judges have traveled overseas to work with foreign courts and judges as a way to increase their understanding of the intricacies of IP judicial practice. There have also been examples of high-profile foreign judges working in China directly with Chinese judges. Sir Hugh Laddie, a retired

English High Court judge, was invited to China by Rouse & Co. International to meet with Chinese IP judges and discuss some of the challenges they are facing. The result was some very engaging debates and questions from the Chinese judges and companies operating in China, resulting in an increased awareness on both sides of the issues and challenges each faces in making sound decisions. The US Patent Office and the European Patent Office have also conducted training sessions with the State Intellectual Property Office.

Training of Future Generations of IP Professionals and Business Managers

Some companies have opted to focus on multi-levels of increasing awareness, but particularly on helping to train future IP officials, professionals, and business managers by working with universities. Philips, the consumer electronics products manufacturer, has also established a number of IP Academy projects in China aimed at sharing international best IP practice with Chinese students through three universities—Renmin and Tshinghua universities in Beijing and Fudan University in Shanghai. The company brings in IP experts from the EU and the US, as well as Philips IP experts, to teach the students. Philips has also organized, together with various government agencies, IP awareness courses for Chinese companies. These activities are excellent examples of the creative approaches that can be taken to IP lobbying in China. They will increase IP awareness among young Chinese people and Chinese companies, as well as increase the awareness of Philips' products and of its commitment to the development of a strong IP system in China. As mentioned above, Bayer, in addition to its IP Forum, sponsors the IPR Chair position at Tongji University as a conduit for conducting further research and education on IP awareness in China.

Increasing Consumer Awareness

In order to create a shift in the moral context in which IP operates in China, many companies are focusing their lobbying efforts on increasing consumer awareness. Some companies distribute pamphlets that introduce their brands and their IP rights following a market sweep. Manchester United has publicly appealed to its fans in China to demand genuine merchandise in support of the popular football club. As mentioned in Chapter 8, some companies set up a consumer hotline for reporting of counterfeits.

Others take the opposite approach, not wanting to admit openly to any counterfeit issues they are facing and preferring instead to focus on marketing the quality benefits of their products and then engaging officials for the educative side of their lobbying strategy. Even Jackie Chan, the famous Hong Kong action movie star, has been involved in the fight against IP pirates by appearing in public service announcements in a campaign called "Fakes Cost More." The program is aimed at educating consumers as to the damage caused by IP infringements and suggesting that buying counterfeits may indeed be supporting child labor or other forms of criminal activity.

CASE STUDY: DISNEY

Disney's promotion to entice consumers to buy genuine product— by including a unique code that consumers needed in order to claim prizes—had the unanticipated, but welcome, side effect of encouraging consumers to report counterfeit products to them for action. Consumers were so keen to get their codes that Disney was able to generate a very high level of awareness of IP infringements with consumers, to increase brand loyalty, and to create a very effective network of "investigators" through its fans to report infringements. A very successful consumer awareness campaign!

CHECKPOINT

- Do you need to lobby for change?
- Have you prepared a lobbying matrix?
  - *What types of change are you trying to make?* Is it a legislative change, or a change in the practice of the judiciary or the local officials?
  - *Where does the issue fall in the Chinese government's priorities?* Is it a piece of legislation currently under review, or an issue set out in the current IP Working Plan?
  - *Which government authorities are involved?* Which levels of officials need to be engaged?
  - *Does this issue impact other companies?* Or is it an individual issue unique to your company?
- Have you prepared a lobbying paper?

- Have you selected the appropriate lobbying partners (or does lobbying alone better reflect your goals)?
- Have you built an education component into your lobbying strategy?

RESOURCES

- www.acbc.com.au: Australia China Business Council
- www.ccbc.com: Canada China Business Council
- www.cbbc.org: China-Britain Business Council
- www.eucba.org (which has links to the individual country associations): EU-China Business Association
- www.comitefrancechine.com: Comite France Chine
- www.dcw-ev.de: German-Chinese Business Association
- www.china-italy.com: Italian-Chinese Chamber of Commerce
- www.sctc.se: Sweden-China Trade Council
- www.uschina.org: US-China Business Council
- www.qbpc.org.cn: Quality Brands Protection Committee (QBPC)
- www.dfat.gov.au/geo/china/fta: Australian government Web site for the Australia–China Free Trade Agreement

R&D centers and technology transfer in China

1. SETTING THE SCENE

As discussed in Chapter 3, due diligence is key to minimizing risks when obtaining the fruits of China's growing research and development efforts. China's commitment to technological development and innovation is not only fostering a shift from "Made in China" tags to the more quality-indicative "Made by China" labels, but is also making local technologies targets for acquisition by foreigners. Developed and incubated in state-funded, private, and Sino-foreign R&D centers, these technologies are often discovered by foreign enterprises as they conduct due diligence on Chinese targets for acquisitions, joint venture partnerships, and even contract-manufacturing arrangements.

Such discoveries of local technology shouldn't be surprising. With China's large and highly skilled research and scientific community, low costs for research and manufacturing, sophisticated laboratories, and government incentives for creation and innovation that were first instituted in the early 1990s and show no signs of abating, the pace of China's climb up the technological ladder should only increase. What *is* surprising, however, is the fact that many of these technologies are for sale. In China's case, there may still be some Rembrandts in the attic.

Commitment to Technology and Innovation

China's success with cheap export manufacturing in the 1980s and 1990s helped to fill government coffers with the financing it needed to improve research infrastructure. Technology, innovation, and laboratories were pegged to be recipients of this new cash, especially once the government realized that low marginal returns on low-tech goods wasn't a sound long-term policy. Foreign collaborations were encouraged and IP laws were strengthened. Technology and innovation became very hot.

China's new commitment to the development of innovative technologies is mostly addressed in its Five-Year Plans (FYPs), which regularly emphasize technology creation. In addition, many recent national programs are designed to encourage development in technological fields. These include the Major Science and Technology Projects of the 11th FYP (2006–2010) and the National High-Tech R&D Program (also known as the "863 Program").

To implement these and other plans, PRC ministries and agencies often issue opinions and development guidelines. One of the latest was unveiled in July 2006 to encourage innovation and technology transfers into China. The Opinion on Methods for Promoting Technology Transfers and Innovations and Encouraging Changes in Foreign Trade Growth focuses on biotech, telecom, petrochemicals, civil aviation and aerospace, environmental protection, and renewable energy. Although most of the Opinion discusses how domestic companies can achieve the goals set out by Beijing, it also encourages foreign companies to create partnerships with local companies, R&D centers, and universities in their research endeavors. The Opinion also indicates that PRC tax authorities will study ways to adjust income taxes levied upon royalties that foreign companies earn from technology transfers from overseas to China.

These types of government pronouncements are common in state-controlled economies. While they are not effectively laws that officials must recognize and enforce, a foreign investor can rely on them in order to convince officials to make favorable decisions. They should be understood and mentioned in negotiations and referenced in correspondence with authorities to remind them that the central government is committed to innovation and that Beijing acknowledges that foreigners have a role to play. Market access and good cheap labor will continue to be the bartering tools for foreign cash and technology which China admittedly needs in order to develop its research base.

What is the Current State of China's R&D?

Statistics compiled by the PRC Ministry of Science and Technology show that during the 10th FYP (2001–2005), the number of full-time personnel engaged in basic research in China rose from 78,800 in 2001 to 115,400 in 2005, a jump of 46.5%. The country now has roughly 200 national labs in operation and an expanding network of satellite field research stations. The amount of government funding for science and technology has also significantly increased in the past few years, from RMB54.4 billion (US$6.6 billion) in 1999 to RMB133.5 billion (US$16.1 billion) in 2005.

Beijing's financial support is one factor to consider when evaluating China's R&D commitment. Another encouragement is the government's support for the patenting of new technologies not only from government-supported R&D centers, such as universities and government labs, but also from state-owned and private enterprises. In terms of numbers, these efforts appear to be paying off as domestic patent applications are increasing dramatically in China (see Chapter 5). The important role that Chinese companies have to play in China's continued development and desire to become more technologically sufficient is a cornerstone of the National Working Group for IP Protection. This was announced by Vice Premier Wu Yi at a conference in Beijing on April 24, 2007. Wu Yi has been charged with leading the National Working Group after her success with guiding the country through the SARS crisis of 2003. Her responsibility for IP protection and for developing China's IP strategy shows the central government's commitment to addressing issues effectively. Though China's R&D strength may not yet match that of Western economies, it is clear that the PRC government has and will continue to consider technological development a national priority and use the state guiding hand to help it expand further.

Foreign R&D Centers in China

As a result of tax incentives, encouragement by government investment authorities, the Chinese consumers' demand for innovations, and the overall globalization of technological development, many foreign enterprises in China have set up R&D centers. According to the PRC Ministry of Commerce (MOFCOM), about 46% of multinational corporations (MNCs) operating in China established R&D centers by 2005. Reports also indicate that China could currently have more than 750 foreign-invested R&D centers, the vast majority of which are located in Beijing, Shanghai, Shenzhen, Tianjin, and Zhejiang, where talent is readily available and cheap. This is a significant increase from the numbers widely reported in 2000 of approximately 40, and about 400 in 2003. While the majority of these centers focused a few years ago on technology research in sectors such as automobiles, chemicals, information technology, and medicines, today's labs have expanded into more diverse sectors including biotechnology, telecommunications, and agriculture.

Despite estimates, the absolute number of foreign R&D centers or facilities in the PRC is unclear. Recent Chinese news articles put the number at anywhere between 120 and nearly 400 foreign-invested R&D centers spread throughout the country (though it is not known what methodology or criteria were used in calculating these totals). Another recent study conducted by the Chung-Hua Institute for Economic Research on Taiwan estimates that there are 148 foreign high-tech R&D centers located in the PRC.

Other accounts that break down the numbers by region are similarly difficult to assess. The Xinhua News Agency counts "at least 40" such centers in Shanghai in 2001, but reports in early 2003 state that "more than 80 foreign-invested enterprises have established research institutions in Shanghai" (a remarkable rate of growth, if accurate). Industry and academic experts estimate the number of foreign R&D centers in Beijing and Shanghai at approximately 50 in each city, while one source suggested there were 300 in Shanghai alone (presumably including small and medium-sized firm R&D activities). At the same time, the head of an R&D center in Beijing claimed there were only 50 "real" foreign-invested R&D centers in all of China.

How Did R&D Centers Become so Important?

During the course of the "deal fever" that swept through China in the early to mid-1990s, many provincial and national approval authorities encouraged R&D center add-ons to JV and WOFE establishment deals as a means to show commitment and contribution to the country's technological development. Beijing encouraged foreign investors to vie against each other for positions. For example, the competition in the late 1990s among foreign auto companies to establish the last Sino-foreign automotive joint venture to be approved for several years in Shanghai led to an unprecedented level of foreign investment and technology transfer commitments—including a joint R&D center—with General Motors ultimately winning the bid.

Despite attitudes then that these "back of the house" labs would likely never make any commercially viable technological achievement, today's reality proves that this would not be the case. These centers are developing creative technologies for both domestic and foreign applications.

In addition to patentable technologies being born in the labs, foreign investors recognize other additional benefits. With a Chinese market that possesses qualities and characteristics usually different from Western traditional notions, many companies see their Chinese R&D centers as critical to their future success in the country. This is particularly true in such sectors as pharmaceuticals, where treatments for ailments more common among the Chinese are better developed than in countries where that disease is less prevalent, compared to software which, of course, has a language-specific agenda.

Once thinly staffed and effectively ignored, these research centers are now considered important training grounds for the technical skills the company will need in the future in China. And then there is cost. By most estimates, R&D centers in China are about one-tenth the cost to operate similarly set-up labs in the United States or Europe. With a wide range of necessary laboratory equipment enjoying duty-free import, capital costs are also kept low. For this reason, along with lower salaries, construction loans, additional tax incentives in encouraged areas of investment, and some ability for these centers to engage in production and sale of goods or the provision of technical services, it makes good sense to choose to set up a lab in China.

In a survey conducted in 40 cities in September 2006 by the PRC National Bureau of Statistics, about half of the 1,600 enterprises surveyed said that they prefer collaborative research projects rather than going it alone in China. State-owned enterprises said they prefer collaboration with universities or science and research institutes, whereas foreign companies prefer R&D collaboration with clients or investment partners, rather than with Chinese academic institutes. Collaboration with universities, however, does foster other benefits, such as talent generation, improved relations with regulatory authorities, and relationship building. By the end of 2005, 97 MNCs had set up around 20 collaborative R&D centers with 36 universities in China.

Who's in the Game?

US computer companies were among the first foreign enterprises to operate in China following its opening to the West in the 1980s. In 1985, IBM became one of the first US computer companies to set up shop on the mainland. Hewlett-Packard (HP) also entered the China market that same year, establishing the first official Sino-foreign, high-tech JV. Since then, these multinationals have been joined by numerous other high-tech companies from around the world who are drawn to the mainland by the dream of capturing a piece of this dynamic and sizeable market.

Today, high-tech MNCs from around the world are establishing growing numbers of R&D centers, programs, and labs in China. HP established what is considered by foreign R&D managers to be the first true foreign-sponsored high-tech R&D center in China in the mid-1990s. Similarly, IBM established its China Research Lab in Beijing in 1995 "to focus initially on creating software and applications that are especially relevant to China … [including] digital libraries, speech recognition for Mandarin, machine translation, Chinese language processing, multimedia and the Internet." Often accompanying these R&D programs and other types of investment are various forms of traditional technology transfer, such as education and training programs, licensing agreements, contract research, and equipment donations.

Other technology companies working on advanced research projects in China include Motorola, Lucent Technologies, Intel, Bayer, Rohm & Haas, and Corning.

In August 2006, US engine designer and manufacturer Cummins Inc. and Dongfeng Motor Corp. established one of the newest collaborative R&D centers in China, the country's first collaborative engine R&D center. While many domestic enterprises are setting up their own R&D centers in China, often by forging relationships with other companies, universities, or foreign partners, large Chinese MNCs have also set up centers overseas. For example, Haier Electronics Group Co., Ltd. and Lenovo Group Ltd. have centers in the United States, while Huawei Technologies Co., Ltd. has set up in India.

2. KEY RISK AREAS

Setting up a Collaborative R&D Center

Current PRC laws and regulations allow for foreign-invested laboratories or technology centers to be established as equity joint ventures, cooperative joint ventures, wholly owned foreign enterprises, or even branches of existing foreign-invested enterprises. In addition to the myriad of legislation relevant to establishing these types of vehicles in China, the Questions Relating to Foreign Investors Investing and Establishing Research and Development Centers Ministry of Foreign Trade and Economic Cooperation (MOFTEC) Circular 2000 must also be considered. There may also be specific local regulations to comply with, as is the case in Beijing and Shanghai, which issued their own rules in 1999 and 2000, respectively.

There is a minimum investment of US$2 million, specifically allotted for R&D purposes, but this doesn't have to be in the form of registered capital. R&D centers must have a defined focus and specific projects as well as a permanent site, equipment, and other facilities necessary to support the R&D work. According to a September 1999 State Administration of Taxation circular, firms that incurred at least 10% more in R&D expenses than in the previous year can deduct an additional 50% of the R&D expenses incurred in the current year when determining taxable income.

Who Owns R&D Center Results?

These labs' innovations belong to the companies that fund them. A company that invests in the research owns the intellectual property created. However, the law requires that the patent applications for technology developed in China be filed first in China.

According to article 20 of the Patent Law, any Chinese individuals or legal entities (and this includes both JVs and WOFEs, as described in Chapter 2) shall file their first patent application or Patent Cooperation Treaty international application in China. After this first China filing, filings can then be made in other countries. In an official interpretation by the Law Department of the Patent Office, this regulation is actually to protect the right of Chinese patent applicants/inventors. There is no penalty if the application is first filed abroad. Foreign-invested labs may already be filing abroad for technologies developed in their Chinese labs and thereby bypassing article 20. However, there have been no reported cases of any refusal by the China Patent Office when that overseas filing is extended to China. Current draft amendments to the Patent Law seek to close this "no penalty" loophole, however.

The main purpose of article 20 of the PRC Patent Law is to protect the national interest. If the patent is first registered in China, then it would first become a Chinese patent. The assignment or licensing of a Chinese patent requires the approval of relevant Chinese governmental departments, which enables the Chinese government to have some control over what kind of patent can be registered overseas, either by separate applications in other countries or via Patent Cooperation Treaty international applications. How to speed up the registration procedure isn't the main concern here. If the invention is completed in China by a Chinese entity or individual, the applicant would have no choice but to lodge an application with the Chinese Patent Office first.

3. SOLUTIONS

Transferring China Technology out of China

The term "technology" can mean different things to different businesses. A widely accepted definition is elusive, but it is commonly thought to encompass science, engineering, and human resourcefulness. (Don't think, though, that animals aren't capable of resourceful reactions to their environments.) "Technology" can refer to material objects of use, such as machines and products, but can also encompass broader themes such as techniques, systems, and methods of organization. If yours is a manufacturing business like the big auto companies or a small holiday goods maker, then you may recognize technology in your supply chain when you use specific techniques to source components or distribute your products in a timely and cost-efficient manner. IT businesses such as Bloomberg would identify their software, their news collection capabilities, and delivery systems as technology. Chemical companies may see technologies existing in their businesses in the form of newly synthesized compounds or molecular modifications to make new products. What seems to be a common factor in all "technology" businesses is their emphasis on intangible assets such as intellectual property, rather than on fixed assets such as factories or land.

The Regulations on Administration of Import and Export of Technologies, issued by MOFTEC in 2001, govern technology transfers into or out of China. These regulations define technology transfers to include patent assignments, patent prosecution

rights assignments, patent licenses, technological secrets transfers, technology cooperation, and provision of technology-related
services.

The control of these types of technology-related licenses,
assignments, cooperations, and services into or out of China is
a relatively straightforward procedure whereby the technology
is categorized according to where it falls within the Catalogue
of Export-Prohibited and Export-Restricted Technology and
the Catalogue of Import-Prohibited and Import-Restricted
Technology promulgated by MOFTEC and the Ministry of
Science and Technology on January 1, 2002. For some ideas on
what China classifies as restricted and prohibited technologies,
see the appendix at the end of this chapter.

In China, the import and export of technology is also under
government control under the same principle of protecting the
national interest. If the technology (including patent) falls into the
prohibited category of export, it won't be allowed to be exported
overseas or transferred to a foreign entity or individual. If the
technology (including patent) falls into the restricted category
of export, then it needs to be reviewed and approved by the
government before being exported or assigned overseas. If the
application for technology transfer isn't approved, then the title
to the technology would remain with the foreign-invested entity
as its property, but the FIE can only transfer this technology to a
Chinese entity if it doesn't want to retain the ownership of the
technology. If the technology (including patent) doesn't belong to
the restricted or prohibited category, then the assignment of the
technology can be completed by going through a simple recording
procedure with the government. This is the free category of
export, and most technologies fall under this classification.

The Regulations for the Administration of Technology Import
and Export specify the procedures for government review and
approval of technology acquisition deals in China. Technology
in the prohibited category may not be exported, so an agreement
involving this kind of technology is illegal.

Restricted technology can be exported, but only after obtaining an
export license from the government. The detailed procedure is as follows: the Chinese entity files an application for technology export
with MOFCOM, which, along with the Ministry of Science and
Technology, reviews the technology and decides whether to
approve the export. After both ministries agree to grant an approval,

MOFCOM issues a formal approval opinion for the technology acquisition. Only after receiving such an approval can the parties begin substantive negotiations and conclude the acquisition agreement. After finalizing the agreement, the PRC entity applies for a technology export license with MOFCOM by presenting relevant documents such as the agreement and the list of relevant technologies. The ministry then reviews the authenticity of the agreement and decides whether to grant a technology export license. After obtaining the export license, the PRC entity should register the agreement online via the Web site of the China International Electronic Commerce Center (CIECC). An agreement that involves restricted technology export takes effect when the export license is issued.

An agreement relating to free technology, which constitutes the bulk of technology acquired from PRC entities, only needs to be registered. After the parties sign the acquisition agreement, the PRC entity applies online to register the deal via the CIECC Web site. After the online application, the PRC entity delivers the relevant documents—such as the application form, the agreement, and certain supporting documents—to the local authority in charge of foreign trade. The local officials review the documents and may require amendments. After the review is completed, the local authority issues a registration certificate. An agreement that involves free technology takes effect when it is executed.

If the owner of a technology is a Chinese domestic company or Chinese citizen, the same rules of prohibited and restricted technology would apply. If a technology doesn't belong to prohibited or restricted technology, then this will be considered as free technology and its assignment to an overseas company won't require government review and approval. The Chinese government only requires that such a transaction be recorded. Additional regulations for specific technologies owned by Chinese companies or Chinese individuals may need the approval of the Ministry of Science and Technology. Determining whether you will encounter any problems transferring your technology into or out of China therefore depends on the type of technology it is. In nearly all cases, there will be no issue in terms of what types of technology you may transfer into or out of the country.

Employees' Claims for Inventorship Rights

It is clear that technologies developed by the foreign-invested R&D center belong to the center, but what about when a member of your research staff leaves your company and files a patent application based on the work he or she originally started while working for you? As discussed in Chapter 6, protecting your technology and your IP in China must include strategies not just for third-party infringement or misappropriation, but also for infringement or misappropriation from within your own organization. Inventions made by employees during the course of their work are called "service inventions." In accordance with article 11 of the Patent Law Implementing Regulations, a service invention is any invention made by a person:

1. in the course of performing his own duty;

2. in execution of any task other than his duty, which was entrusted to him by the entity to which he belongs; or

3. within one year from his resignation, retirement or change of work, where the invention-creation relates to his own duty or the other task entrusted to him by the entity to which he previously belonged.

Service inventions are further clarified under article 326 of the PRC Contract Law, which states that "a service technological achievement refers to a technological achievement accomplished in the process of carrying out the task of the legal entity or other organization, or mainly accomplished through using the material and technological means of the legal entity or other organization." This notion of "carrying out the task of the legal entity or other organization" was clarified by the Supreme People's Court Interpretation Regarding Technology Contract Dispute Cases of June 15, 2001, as being when:

(i) a member of staff performs his own duty or is in execution of any task other than his duty, which was entrusted to him by the legal entity or other organization to which he belongs; or

(ii) within one year from his resignation, retirement or change of work, where the technological achievement relates to the scientific research and development relevant to his own duty or the other task entrusted to him by the legal entity or other organization to which he previously belonged.

This one-year "claw-back" right which a former employer has over employees who leave and then try to patent service inventions that were developed at the former job can be used to control inventorship rights. This is very useful to companies who have seen employees defect to competitors, reduce the former employer's data or information to some patentable invention, and then file a patent application for it in their or their new employer's name.

It is quite clear from the law that the previous employer has the right to claim ownership of the patent once it is granted. This law is very favorable to the employer, and no written agreement is necessary to assign the ownership of the patentable inventions to the employer. However, the provisions cover only patents or the right to apply for patents. If the employer decides not to apply for a patent, the law is unclear as to ownership of the information. If the invention could be applied for as a patent, it will arguably be owned by the employer. However, if the employer decides to maintain the information as a trade secret rather than to patent it and it needs to enforce these rights later, it is advisable to have agreement on the employer's ownership of all inventions, whether patentable or patented or not.

However, a more strategic approach to this issue, and one that saves the time and expense of litigating the issue or cancelling the patent, is to put the new employer on notice of your former employee's tasks, duties, and work while under your employ and to draw their attention to your claw-back rights. Also, during the course of the employee's exit interview, we advise going over the continuing obligations of confidentiality and other restrictive covenants in the employment agreement described in Chapter 6 and having the employee confirm this again in writing.

Potential lingering employee inventorship rights can threaten future plans for inventions that the FIE has worked hard to develop. We also advise keeping a periodic check on Patent Office patent applications made in the names of former key technical staff or their new employers, at least for the first year after their departure and periodically thereafter. Even if the one-year claw-back period has lapsed, you may be able to defeat their patent applications by other means such as prior art or lack of novelty. If their patent application makes use of your confidential information or trade secrets, and if other means to defeat the patent application cannot be achieved, then you can consider a civil suit for trade secret infringement or breach of an ongoing confidentiality obligation.

On the issue of improvements, the right to apply for a patent belongs to the party that completes or jointly contributes to the improvements. Here, "contribute" doesn't mean providing work conditions/tools, or financial or management support. Rather, it means contributing to the creation of a substantial part of the patentable technology. Therefore, if you only provide the original manufacturing information and work with the Chinese partner, it would be unlikely that you can acquire the ownership of improvements unless the parties agree otherwise under fair and reasonable conditions.

We also recommend that you incentivize employees to disclose all inventions to the employer to ensure that you are able to make decisions about the commercialization options and the best methods of protecting inventions as early as possible in the process. There is also a legal requirement to reward inventors.

Rewarding Inventors

According to article 16 of the Patent Law, the entity that is granted a patent on a "service invention" must reward the inventor or creator once the patent is commercialized. This means that FIEs must compensate Chinese employee inventors for patented technologies they have helped to develop. This reward should be of a reasonable amount based on the patent's commercial profitability. Articles 74–76 of the Patent Law Implementing Regulations require a minimum of 2% of after-tax profits to be given to the inventor. However, this calculation is usually argued as being relevant only to state-owned enterprises (SOEs) and not to foreign-invested enterprises. Article 77 clarifies that these may be referred to by non-SOEs, thereby adding further weight to the position that FIEs are not subject to articles 74–76.

Local regulations may also be relevant and, in some cases, may award the inventor a much higher award. While there is a strong argument that national law (that is, the Patent Law Implementing Regulations) shouldn't apply to FIEs, there is uncertainty in regard to local regulations on employee rewards. For example, Shanghai encourages innovation by allowing some inventors to obtain at least 30% of the rewards obtained from exploitation of a patent. In order to strengthen enterprises' ability to innovate and encourage inventors, Shanghai stipulates that after the patent owner assigns or licenses its rights to another, it should pay no less than 30% of the profits obtained thereby (after tax) as a reward to the inventor. For patents arising from universities and scientific research institutes, the inventor may receive no less than 50% of the profits obtained thereby or may contribute that technology as a form of investment in the industrialization of the patented technology and obtain profits accordingly. Both are potentially substantial numbers!

For foreign-invested labs that are beginning to realize patentable technologies, article 16 rewards seem daunting—especially when the calculation seems to be based on commercial profitability of the technology. While it is clear that article 16 includes foreign-invested R&D centers, it is unlikely that the amount of the reward will be calculated along the same lines as for SOEs.

The reasons are practical, rather than legal. First, most high-tech companies already have some employee reward policy in place and have extended that to their Chinese centers. Second, these same centers pay higher salaries to their R&D staff than would be paid to them at a comparable state-owned research institute, thereby forgoing the purpose of the law to compensate individuals and encourage innovation. Lastly, there are normally additional employee benefits that are negotiated with the inventor and agreed in their employment contract, which can be considered valuable compensation for their work. These additional benefits may include overseas training, stock options, or merit-based promotion. All these benefits combined are usually considered to meet the underlying requirement of "reasonable" reward. We advise that if these or other factors will be used to form the basis of your Chinese employee inventor reward policy, then this be considered by local counsel in light of both national and local labor regulations. The policy then should be clearly introduced to both existing key technical personnel and new hires for their agreement.

4. SUCCESS OF FOREIGN-INVESTED R&D CENTERS IN CHINA

It is difficult to gauge how successful or profitable foreign-invested R&D centers are in China. First, it is simply too soon to determine how well many of them are faring since most have been established only recently, and corporate executives are understandably cautious about discussing publicly any problems their centers might be having. Second, unlike manufacturing ventures, R&D centers may or may not produce anything tangible or quantifiable, especially in the first few years. In most cases, in fact, the results achieved through research—particularly in the computer software industry—are simply forwarded (or e-mailed) to the company headquarters or to a manufacturing plant somewhere else to be integrated into the global product line. For instance, the contribution made by the Microsoft Research Lab in Beijing to Microsoft's new Tablet PC technology was apparent to the public mainly through international press releases and interviews conducted by the lab's deservedly proud director, rather than on the streets of Beijing.

In addition, while some products are emerging from these centers, it isn't clear whether they are entirely new innovations or, more likely, existing products newly adapted to better fit local market conditions—an activity sometimes referred to as "glocalization." The IBM Research Lab, for instance, boasts the "Chinese Workpad," a new-generation personal digital assistant (PDA) device that is loaded with Chinese-language software. Many of the products advertised by R&D centers in China are software upgrades or systems integration solutions. Also, given the size of China's wireless market (currently number one in the world), many of the results are geared toward wireless applications, whether for mobile phones, PDAs, or e-commerce programs (which, in China, are conducted mainly by mobile phone using cash on delivery for payment). Also of note is that much government funding is earmarked for "close to market" technologies that are thought to be commercially viable within three to five years (coincidentally, about the average length of time officials making that investment decision will stay in that particular job). Can this be considered technology or innovation?

As for patents, some R&D centers have applied for patents in the PRC, although most appear to file in their home countries as well, and some do so exclusively. Any new technologies stemming from wholly foreign-owned R&D centers in China—which isn't the preferred type of venture for foreign high-tech investments—are considered to be the intellectual property of the parent company. These patents, therefore, are filed initially (and in some cases exclusively) in the parent home country, since there are no current penalties for breach of China's first filing rule. As such, it is difficult to distinguish patents resulting from R&D centers in China from other corporate R&D efforts around the world. This may change, however, if amendments to the Patent Law setting out penalties for failing to file first in China are adopted by the State Council.

Thus, at this stage, it isn't clear whether foreign-invested R&D centers in China are producing their intended results. There are few indicators of progress available, and collection of much more detailed data is needed to make an accurate assessment. At present, financial and other inputs into foreign-owned R&D centers seem high compared to observable, innovative output. This, plus the fact that management training remains a clear priority and area of concern for foreign R&D managers, suggests foreign investors are encountering some difficulties in conducting innovative research in China, or that producing truly innovative results will take some time. Yet, many of these centers have been established only recently, and more time and data are needed to determine whether they will succeed in the long run.

CHECKLIST

- •. When planning the establishment of your China R&D center, do you understand China's current and future technology needs and encouraged sectors?

- • Do you understand the risks that R&D center approval authorities may encourage you to add to your overall establishment project?

- • If you have an existing corporate policy on rewarding employees for inventions, have you checked its applicability and effectiveness in China against both national legislation and local regulations?

- • Have you communicated your employee reward for inventions policy to relevant key personnel, and have they accepted this in their employment agreement or employee handbook?

- • Have you reminded outgoing employees of their ongoing obligations of confidentiality and restrictive covenants when they leave your employ?

- • Have you considered writing to former employees' new employers to put them on notice that their new employee used to work for you?

- • Have you sought advice from your China IP counsel on the status of current proposed amendments to the Patent Law, especially requirements for filing patents first in China for inventions developed in China?

- • Have you tracked the patent filing behavior of former key personnel closely for the first year after their employment, and periodically thereafter, including searches for patent applications made in the names of their new employers?

APPENDIX: EXAMPLES OF PROHIBITED AND RE-STRICTED TECHNOLOGIES

Prohibited Exports

Traditional Chinese medicine/medicine processing	The key acupoints of the acupuncture anaesthesia craniotomy
	The Chinese medicine crop resources and rare animals or plants breeding technologies or those in imminent danger
	Processing technique and habitat preparation of toxicological Chinese medicine
Agriculture technique	Gun-powder tea, flat tea formation technique and equipment design and manufacture
Pasturage and veterinary	Total step artificial propagation of eel:
	1. incubating technique of parent fish
	2. induced mature and spawning technique
	3. medicine varieties, dosage, and frequency of use
	4. artificial fertilization technique
Engineering material manufacture technique	Certain lower-dimensional inorganic non-metal materials manufacture techniques
Electronic technology	Integrated circuit manufacturing technique (anti-irradiation technique and art)
Automation technology	Manufacturing technique of robots (remote-controlled coring scout robots)
Textile technology	Spinning natural fiber and manufacturing technique (manufacturing technique of fine count of sheer spinning cashmere with fan-number between 30 and 80)
Space technology	Test control techniques of spacecraft (radio telemetric encryption techniques of satellites)

Prohibited Imports

Ferrous metallurgy technology	Cupola furnace steeling process
	Hot iron ore sintering process
Non-ferrous metallurgy technology	Certain technologies
Chemical technology	Ammonia-soda soda manufacturing techniques
Petroleum refining technology	Viscosity-reducing technology
Electro technology	Nickel-cadmium battery production techniques
Technology of light industry	Tin welding techniques in can-making industry
Printing technology	Letterpresses process
Technology of medicine and pharmacology	Horizontal sheet process for plate glass

Restricted Exports

Medicine production technology	Production technology of bio-technological pharmaceuticals with control factors:
	1. Achromycin production technology with fermentation unit with certain yields
	2. Gentamycin production technology with fermentation unit with certain yields
	3. Strains of terramycin with defoaming agent proof and fermentation unit of certain yields
	4. Production technique of terramycin with certain yields
	5. Production technique of penicillin with high-yield strains of penicillin and fermentation unit of certain yields

6. Streptomycin production technology with:
   (1) filtering, centrifuging, segregating, and refining techniques
   (2) streptomycin production technology with fermentation unit with certain yields

7. Bioengineering strain, cell strain acquired through genetic engineering and breeding techniques of:
   (1) recombinant strains of egg cells of hepatitis B—China shrewmouse used for the production of hepatitis B vaccine
   (2) recombinant toxin spawns of hepatitis B—smallpox vaccine used for the production of hepatitis B vaccine

Mining engineering technology	Mine construction technology control factors:

1. Coal mine construction technology:
   (1) freezing construction technique of the inclined well
   (2) freezing sinking technique of the thick surface soil layer [thickness 300mm]
   (3) well-digging technique, shaft lining structure, cutter material and slurry technique of the major diameter shaft drilling method [diameter >6m, well total depth >300m]
   (4) mechanized high-geared operation technique and equipment of the inclined well
   (5) post slip-casting technique of the sand aquifer borehole wall

Mechanical engineering technology	Casting techniques with control factors:
	
	1. Formula of the additive to the pre-coated high-temperature resistant sand
	2. Electroslag casting technique of the large and medium-sized thin wall variable camber casting with:
	   (1) definition of the various temperature fields in transient state
	   (2) software package of construction of the thin wall variable camber casting

Apparatus and instrumental techniques	Manufacturing technique of the bi-vortex shedding flowmeter with certain indices: 1. pipeline diameters 2. survey precision 3. velocity of flow 4. with water or vapor of certain temperatures as the pipeline medium
Civil explosive technology	Industrial explosive and the manufacturing technique: 1. Modification processing, technique, and dedicated equipment of ammonium nitrate 2. Formula, processing technique, and dedicated equipment of modified ammonium nitrate
Food processing technology	Comprehensive utilization technology of the rice husk Processing technique of the oryzanol, sterol, and inositol meat-packing technology (manufacturing technique of Jin Hua ham) Processing technology of drinks (Coco-branded natural coconut milk, Tianfu cola, Maotai liquor, Oolong and Pu'er tea, and others)

Building material production technology	Production technology of non-metal building materials:
	
	1. Production technology of structural glass and products
	   (1) production technology and equipment of China loyang float glass
	
	2. Production technology of architectural ceramics and products
	   (1) formula of the color glaze for structural sanitary ceramics
	   (2) material constituent, formula, and process of vanadium-titanium black ceramic tile

Railway transportation technology	Engine technology: 1. Computer software for the simulation maneuver of the engine driver 2. Constant speed-measuring transducer with certain engine speeds, timing technique of the engine operating control 3. Formula and production technique of the lubricating grease for electric-powered and diesel locomotive 4. Designing technique of the antifriction of the locomotive wheel rim
Waterways transport technology	Production technique of the harbor facilities: 1. Production technique of the nonmotile, self-balancing, and no-break working equipment 2. Design technique of the block single cable polyp-type grab bucket exclusively used for wood and scrap steel, design technique of the asynchronous dispel obstruction grab bucket for scrap steel lump material 3. Engineering data of the catenart chain ore-boat unloader

Space technology	Spacecraft test control technology:
	1. The following technologies of satellite and carry open remote measuring system: (1) concurrent real time processing system software (2) user-oriented system software in the remote measuring system (3) digital receiver
	2. Framework and posture test method of the satellite carry multi-objective measuring technique

Restricted Imports

Biotechnology	Transgenic techniques
Coinage technology	Specific anti-counterfeiting techniques/processes in coinage (*Renminbi* Yuan)
Petroleum refining technology	Kit techniques of catalytic cracking
	Normal depressurization kit engineering techniques
Biochemical technology	Fermentation technology for producing long-chain dicarboxylic acid

Source: A selection from the Catalogue of Export-Prohibited and Export-Restricted Technology and the Catalogue of Import-Prohibited and Import-Restricted Technology promulgated by MOFTEC and the Ministry of Science and Technology on January 1, 2002.

Sports and IP in China:
The Olympic influence

1. SETTING THE SCENE

Sports-mad China

From VW® and Snickers® chocolate sponsoring the Beijing Olympics, to Royal & Sun Alliance sponsoring fun runs, to ANZ sponsoring the Cricket Sixes in Shanghai, many international companies have already taken the plunge into sports marketing in China. Among the numerous success stories are some who have learned some hard lessons. Siemens AG, which sponsors the Chinese National Football Team, extended its sponsorship to the China Football Association's Super League in 2004. However, when the season ended in a near boycott by sports clubs after widespread allegations of corruption and match fixing, Siemens terminated the relationship in early 2005 so as not to have its brand associated with the scandal.

There is also increasing interest from international sports clubs wanting to engage in sports-related activities in China. The National Basketball Association (NBA) in the United States has sent teams to play friendly matches in China. (Yao Ming, the popular Houston Rockets player, was born in China.) Chelsea Football Club, in the United Kingdom, aware of the potential for seeking players from China in the future, has recently announced an agreement with the China Football Association to conduct grassroots training activities for soccer in China and to run a Chinese-language version of its Web site. The Yankees have also announced similar arrangements with the China Baseball Association. Manchester United has conducted tours of China playing friendlies, which it has combined with an anti-counterfeiting awareness campaign to encourage fans to buy genuine merchandise rather than counterfeit products.

Given the growing popularity of sports among Chinese consumers and China's hosting of a number of international sporting events, not least the 2008 Beijing Olympics which will put China center stage on the sports front, it is little wonder that brand owners are seeking sports marketing opportunities in China. But companies must take note of the risks, particularly concerning IP and brand management. Indeed, China's sports marketing environment is relatively new, and many players are inexperienced in the complexities of sponsorship arrangements. Combine this with China's complex regulatory and IP environment, and only companies that manage risks carefully will be able to protect their brands and get the most from their sponsorship marketing dollars. In addition to following the guidelines set out elsewhere in this book about getting the right IP protection, partners, and enforcement strategies, there are some additional unique elements associated with the sports industry that need to be kept in mind.

An Olympic Legacy: A Stronger IP Protection Regime in China?

If there is one consistency in China's IP regime, it is the presence of change. It is a very underdeveloped system that has existed in its current form for only about 25 years. As it struggles to catch up with the more sophisticated IP systems of the world's leading economies, as well as with the complexities that technology and the Internet have thrown at the global IP systems, China's government has searched for a stage through which it can prove its progress to the world. The 2008 Beijing Olympics have been described as "China's coming-out party"—her entry on to the world's stage. The Beijing Organizing Committee for the Games of the XXIX Olympiad (BOCOG) is eager to leave an "IP Legacy" from the Olympics in which China is stronger in its intellectual property awareness, protection, and enforcement. BOCOG plans to deliver this legacy by:

- investing in registration of the Olympic trademarks (by late 2007, it had registered over 69 trademarks in China);

- introducing stronger penalties for infringement of the Olympics name and logos, as well as the Olympic mascots, through specific regulations;

- conducting education campaigns on the protection of IP in the Olympic brand, including copyright lectures and other IP awareness campaigns, as well as a contest to promote Olympic IP awareness;

- encouraging consumers' support in reporting infringements of Olympic IP, including setting up a hotline for reporting infringements and introducing a rewards campaign for strong leads. (This approach has been working well, with consumers reporting sightings of counterfeit Olympic mascots. In return, BOCOG has been quick to respond. For example, Meng Niu, a well-known dairy company in China, was warned in late 2006 by BOCOG not to use an image similar to the five Olympic rings logo for a promotion. According to the Beijing AIC, by the end of 2006 authorities in Beijing had investigated 89 cases of infringement of the Olympic symbols and confiscated 3,225 pieces of infringing goods);

- setting up a joint committee with the relevant enforcement authorities in Beijing to monitor the market, take enforcement action, and conduct education campaigns with the public;

- working closely with the Customs authorities to minimize the import/export of products that infringe the Olympic IP, including putting a fast reporting mechanism in place, handling cases in a more structured way, and conducting education of Customs officials; and

- using anti-counterfeit technologies in all official Olympic merchandise to minimize copying.

All these steps are sound ones that should be taken by any IP rights owner in China. However, BOCOG has one major thing working for it—and one working against it:

- *FOR:* The Olympic spirit has taken a firm hold in China, where consumers are keen to support officials' efforts to protect the Olympic IP. This emotional connection drives consumers' loyalty, which manifests in their buying genuine products and reporting infringements.

- *AGAINST:* The sheer hype of the Olympics, and the desire of many Chinese to purchase the mascots and other merchandise, means there will be a huge demand for counterfeit product from those who either don't have access to or cannot afford the genuine goods. A global event that captures people's hearts and souls is a ripe market for IP infringements, and when you place that in one of the most complex IP markets in the world, it will be interesting to see the results.

Although sightings do exist (we have already been offered "our new national mascots—cheaper for you, I designed them myself" by enthusiastic street sellers in Shanghai), at this stage there is far less infringement of Olympic IP in the market than one might expect. This may be due to respect for the Olympics, as some claim. Others, somewhat skeptically, commend the government for doing a more effective job of stopping these infringements than they do of most brands. Some companies have found a way to work this to their advantage. Many were struggling to convince the authorities to take action against infringements of their products, as the value per piece was so low. However, on discovering through further investigations that the infringer was also offering infringing products in the shape of the Olympic mascots, they had stronger negotiating power with the authorities, who suddenly decided a raid was warranted. Either way, we watch eagerly to see whether BOCOG is able to achieve its goal and leave China a more IP-aware country after the hype of the Olympics moves on.

2. KEY RISK AREAS

Who Are You Negotiating With?

Negotiating sponsorship with either a sporting team or individual athletes in China raises a unique challenge. The state has the right to manage athletes' commercial rights, because most athletes in China are supported by state-run sports organizations. Tian Liang, the 2000 and 2004 Olympic diving champion, and a Hong Kong entertainment group learned this lesson the hard way. After entering into a sponsorship arrangement with the Emperor Entertainment Group without state approval in early 2005, Tian was expelled from the Chinese National Diving Team and placed on a provincial squad. Not only were Tian's hopes of future Olympic glory shattered, but the sponsor lost its sponsorship and the money it had already paid under its agreement with the athlete.

Sponsors need to confirm that the relevant national or local authority, which is determined by the player's team, has approved the sponsorship arrangement, and that the athlete has given his or her approval for use of their image. Companies should expect sports sponsorship agreements to involve the sponsor, the athlete, *and* the state.

Ensure the Sports Rights Holder Has Protected the IP in the Event

To protect the value of their investment, sports sponsors need to ensure that the owner of the rights in the sporting event, athlete, or team (known as "rights holders") have taken steps to protect the relevant IP.

Trademarks

The rights holder should register relevant trademarks in China. In addition to registering more typical items, such as event names, team logos, and event logos, it is possible to trademark some less common items in China for greater protection. For example, for the Athens 2004 Olympics the underwear company Beijing Dani'aier Clothing Co. Ltd. registered the competitor number of a famous Chinese hurdler, Liu Xiang, "1363." Also, China allows registration of athletes' names as trademarks, which is not possible in many countries. Some requirements for this right were established when the grandson of the famous early 20th-century Chinese author Lu Xun tried, but failed, to register his name as a trademark covering wine.

The initial requirements to register a person's name as a trademark in China are basic: the person must give his or her consent, and the name must be distinctive as a trademark. But in the past (such as in the 2001 *Lu Xun* case), the State Trademark Office has also tried to keep the names of famous individuals available for public use; the government evidently believes that when a person is held in high moral, historical, or cultural esteem, his or her name is owned by society and should be available for public use. However, applications to register the names of less well-known athletes are currently being accepted; for example, Lin Dan, China's world top-ranking badminton player, found that his name was already registered for health products when he tried recently to register it as a trademark. A Chinese entrepreneur also tried recently to register Yao Ming's name as a trademark covering sanitary pads!

Portrait Rights Protect the Value of an Image

Internationally known Chinese athletes are quickly becoming the new pop stars of China. In 2005, the Laureus World Sports

Awards named Liu Xiang its "Newcomer of the Year," an award fellow compatriot Yao Ming won in 2003.

Unlike in other jurisdictions, such as the US, Chinese law provides for a portrait right rather than a separate right of publicity; use of a citizen's portrait in China for profit without consent is prohibited. In Australia, celebrities have to rely on passing off or actions under the Trade Practices Act to protect their image. Chinese athletes are increasingly aware of the value of their portrait rights, and several athletes have recently sought to protect their commercial value.

Yao Ming, a household name in China and the United States, has had an impressive career playing basketball in the Chinese Basketball Association (CBA) and for the Houston Rockets in the NBA. In 2003, Yao filed suit against the Coca-Cola Co. in China for using his portrait, which was displayed together with the portraits of two other CBA players on commemorative cans. Coca-Cola argued that it had an agreement with the agent of the national men's basketball team, Chinese Sports Management Co., for sponsorship of the national team to which Yao belonged and therefore had the right to use Yao's image as part of the team. The case, which caused much debate among legal professionals, was settled prior to a court decision. Coca-Cola agreed in the settlement to apologize publicly to Yao.

This case demonstrates that if you are sponsoring a sporting event, team, or player, you must confirm the rights you are paying for and that the sports organizations with which you are negotiating have the relevant rights regarding the athletes. In the future, sponsorship of individual athletes may well conflict with team sponsorship. When sponsoring a team, companies should ensure that their agreement restricts individual athletes from entering into conflicting agreements with the sponsors' competitors.

There is one qualification to the portrait right: it is not absolute. The Haidian District People's Court in Beijing considered its limitations in a recent case involving an image of Liu Xiang winning his gold medal at the Athens Olympics. The photo was placed on the front page of a newspaper above an advertisement for a local department store. Liu believed that the image's placement implied that he had endorsed the department store and therefore infringed his rights. The court divided portraits into two categories: a portrait that is independent of any special significant public event; and a portrait that is associated with a special significant public event. It decided that the portrait right for the former is absolute and the portrait right for the latter is subject to limitations. The court held that Liu's right of portrait, when associated with a major public event such as the Olympics, was subject to a fair use exception. In that case, the photo was used as the cover image for a newspaper article on major events in 2004, and the newspaper had obtained a license from Getty Images, Inc. to reprint the image for news reporting purposes. The court thus ruled in the newspaper's favor.

Although this case was overruled on appeal (on interpretation of the use of the article, rather than the law), it was significant for a number of reasons. First, it underlines athletes' expanding awareness of their portrait rights and the commercial value associated with them for sponsorship opportunities. Second, it shows the court's awareness of the importance of this issue. It seems likely that the district court sought input from the Supreme People's Court, as the judgment was thorough and well argued, and carefully established the reasoning for the decision and the boundaries of the portrait right. The district court likely realized that, in the lead-up to the 2008 Beijing Olympics, more athlete sponsorship arrangements will be negotiated, and more companies will seek to benefit from athletes' fame. A small restaurant owner recently sought legal advice following the judgment, for example, because he wanted to celebrate Liu Xiang's latest hurdling win with a special offer to his customers. He wanted to promote the special offer with a banner and a photo of the famous hurdler. He was told that, although he could use Liu's name in a promotion in celebration of his win, he couldn't use the image as it would infringe Liu's portrait rights.

Domain Names: The Often Forgotten Rights

It is absolutely critical to register all appropriate domain names as soon as possible once sponsorship has been agreed. Domain names are quick and easy to register, and so can often fall prey to cyber squatters who get in first. The domain name "liuxiangvisa.net" was registered by a cyber squatter following the announcement of Visa's sponsorship of the famous athlete. The name was then auctioned and sold for over RMB190,000 (over US$25,000). Although it is possible to recover the domain names in some cases if bad faith can be proved (such as by auctioning the domain name), it is advisable to register all combinations of words in a domain name before the announcement of a sponsorship.

Event Naming Rights

Increasingly, sponsors pay for naming rights to an event—that is, for the right to name an event after their brand—for example, the Royal & Sun Alliance Fun Run in Shanghai. Technically, the regulations require state AIC approval for a brand-named event; however, in practice, there are two levels of approval required, neither of which is at state level:

- *Geography:* Approval from the relevant local AIC—for example, the Shanghai AIC or the Guangzhou AIC; and

- *Sport:* Approval from the relevant sporting authority—for example, the Rugby Union Commission.

One other thing to keep in mind when paying for naming rights: many Chinese broadcasters don't support the commercializing of sporting events and so, despite the fact that all the branding at the event may include the official event title, in broadcasts the naming sponsor is often not mentioned in the commentary, programming, and so on. This can be managed partly through the contract, but will also require education of the broadcasters involved to try to ensure that sponsors get the full value of their sponsorship.

Ambush Marketing

Ambush marketing—where competitors of official sponsors associate their brand with the event without authorization—is a key risk of sports sponsorship worldwide. Examples of clever ambush marketing can be found in many past sporting events. For example, for the 2000 Sydney Olympics, which were officially sponsored by the now-defunct Ansett Australia, Qantas Airways Ltd. launched an intensive advertising campaign that featured a number of Olympic athletes. And adidas-Salomon AG's official sponsorship of the 2002 World Cup was ambushed by Nike Corp.'s sponsorship of the Brazilian team, whose members all wore Nike uniforms. In China, Coca-Cola faced ambush during its sponsorship of the first Formula 1 race in Shanghai by Pepsi. Coca-Cola was the official sponsor within the racetrack grounds. However, a Kentucky Fried Chicken outlet just across the boundary sold Pepsi, and a lot of the competing cola made it over the fence into the grounds. The next year, to avoid a repeat issue, a five-kilometer radius from the venue was included in the sponsorship agreement.

Ambush marketing creates an increased risk, particularly by Chinese companies that use their relationships with authorities to target foreign brand owners' sponsorship of events. To minimize this risk, it is important to ensure that the sponsor addresses all appropriate rights and confirms in the agreement that the rights holder is obligated to prevent ambush marketing.

BOCOG has taken steps to protect the Olympic sponsors' valuable sponsorship rights against ambush marketing, including requiring all athletes to agree only to promote official Olympic sponsors' products. They have also contractually prohibited manufacturers of Olympic uniforms from using their association with the Olympics for promotional purposes.

3.   THE SOLUTION

The Sponsorship Agreement: A Critical Tool

The sponsorship agreement is important for any sports sponsorship arrangement to succeed. In China, however, the role of the agreement is even more crucial. As sports marketing and event management are relatively new concepts in China, it is necessary to have a clear and detailed contract that specifies the parties' rights and obligations. Chinese authorities are often unaccustomed to the types of rights and support that international sponsors expect (for example, where logos should be placed at an event, how the "bundle of rights" is divided among sponsors, and how rights holders should promote official sponsors). Many of the sponsorship strategies and agreements that are tried and tested overseas will require tweaking for successful use in China. While each sponsorship will vary, there are a few key issues sponsors should check, as discussed below.

Confirm the Scope of Your Rights as a Sponsor

Modern sports sponsorships are complex, as companies fight for the sponsorships and rights holders divide them into smaller and smaller pieces. Sponsors also try to squeeze as much value as possible from their sponsorship dollar through innovative logo placements. Problems with, for example, logo placement and co-marketing are likely to arise, particularly with venue operators and broadcasters. It is important, therefore, for sponsors to include these issues in the agreement in order to strengthen their future bargaining position. Companies shouldn't assume that sports sponsorship in China will be as sophisticated as sponsorship overseas. In some countries with more developed sports sponsorship markets, vague language—such as "right to logo placement at the event"—can work to a sponsor's advantage, by bargaining for greater coverage. In China, however, it is more likely to lead to frustration, as the expectation gap between the sponsor and the rights holder will often be wide.

Keep Your Sponsorship Rights Exclusive

The core value of a sponsorship is derived from the extent of its exclusivity. This needs to be carefully negotiated; companies should ensure their sponsorship agreement contains no "gaps" that could allow competitors to reduce the value of the sponsorship through ambush marketing. One of the best ways to prevent ambush marketing is through a strong sponsorship agreement that expressly covers the company's expectations of the rights holder and addresses all the appropriate sponsorship rights. Sponsors must not leave a form of media out of their agreement—such as the Internet, which is commonly forgotten—and risk finding their competitor sponsoring the official Web site.

Compared with their Chinese counterparts, many international sponsors have a distinct advantage: they understand how to get the most out of their sports sponsorships. For example, they don't merely slap a logo on a uniform, but create noise around their brands through associated events and marketing campaigns. On the other hand, Chinese companies' marketing strategies are becoming increasingly sophisticated, and more domestic companies are sponsoring overseas teams and athletes. Sports sponsorships are a strong platform for domestic companies to launch their brands on the international stage. For example, Haier Group Co. sponsored the Australian professional basketball team in 2004, and many high-profile Chinese firms, such as Lenovo Group Ltd. and Haier, will sponsor the 2008 Olympics. Li Ning, a local Chinese brand of sports shoe, has invested heavily in sponsorship to compete with the global giants, Nike and adidas, and it has had to get creative to do so. It has sponsored the Spanish and Argentinean basketball teams, both of which have done very well. Although these sponsorships won't drive sales in the major markets, they give Li Ning great credibility in its local Chinese market as an international company.

Confirm that the Rights Holder Will Also Protect IP

Unfortunately, a boost in a sponsor brand's global exposure and growth in China's sporting industry make infringement of related IP rights ever more likely. Brand owners must take steps to protect their own brands, and must expressly place an obligation on the rights holder to protect the value of the IP in which the brand owner is investing. The sports rights holder should also assist and control infringements in a fast, effective manner (for example, by providing evidence of their rights to Chinese authorities). The sponsorship agreement should expressly cover these expectations.

Learn the Risks, Aim for the Rewards

As the disposable income of China's burgeoning middle class rises, so does the power of sports in China. Recent years have seen a significant shift in the sophistication and prestige of China's sporting events. Shanghai first hosted the Formula 1 Grand Prix in 2004, and the event has continued to grow every year since. In 2005, the same Shanghai track hosted the Moto GP World Championship and the V8 Supercars from Australia. The Tennis Masters Cup, featuring the world's top eight male tennis players, was hosted in Shanghai in 2002, and for the last

CASE STUDY: ELEMENT FRESH

The Tennis Masters Cup was first held in Shanghai in 2002, and has been held there continually since 2005. One of the sponsors is Element Fresh, a chain of stores in Shanghai specializing in fresh salads, sandwiches, and smoothies. Element Fresh has done a superb job of activating its sponsorship. The usual promotional materials—banners in the streets around its stores in Shanghai, point-of-sale materials in its stores, and ticket giveaways offered to customers—helped it connect to its consumers and to capitalize on its association with the hype created around the huge promotional efforts engaged in by the event organizers. However, it was at the stadium during the event that it showed its true flair as a sponsor by offering its trademark fresh food items and salads in a very well-branded environment complete with fast and friendly service. At sporting events, people often expect to be overcharged for average fast food. But Element Fresh changed this perception for the Tennis Masters Cup, gaining it a reputation that fed back through to its popular stores in Shanghai. This is a great example of a small company really finding a sponsorship that fits with its core values and activating it very well to create a real connection for its consumers.

three years, and will continue to be played there in 2008. Shanghai also played host to the Volkswagen 48th World Table Tennis Championships in May 2005.

The opportunities are undeniable, but sports sponsors should be careful as they enter the Chinese market. Event management is still in its early stages in China, and local sports marketing skills are still thin on the ground. It is important for companies to plan carefully and to ensure that the investment they are making is protected, particularly from an IP perspective. Sports marketing is, after all, about the power of brands—the combined power of the sponsor's brand and the rights holder's brand to deliver value to both sides of the table.

4. CONCLUSION

China is a fast-paced, rapidly changing economy whose IP protection regime is struggling to catch up with its developing needs. But the IP laws on paper have come a long way in the past 10 or so years, and the practical implementation continues to develop. With the hope that the 2008 Olympic Games in Beijing will leave a positive legacy of greater IP awareness, and with the current Five-Year Plan's focus on research and development and a movement from China as the world's factory to an innovator in its own right, there is no reason to doubt that things will continue at the same speed. In the meantime, companies can still enjoy the opportunities China provides by taking responsibility for protecting their own IP.

A strong IP strategy for China will involve:

- finding the best partners and working closely with them to develop a level of trust and understanding of the importance of respecting IP;

- identifying and protecting a company's total intellectual assets, and recognizing that this can be more than just the traditional patent, trademark, and copyright, and can include any and all knowledge that a business considers proprietary and advantageous. This may, in some cases, result in IP being kept offshore to ensure its safety;

- considering a lobbying strategy to contribute to the development of China's IP regime as it grows;

- ensuring internally that companies have their own houses in order through management of employees and their supply chains to minimize the risks of IP leakage;
- successfully marrying the company's business plan and commercial strategy with its IP enforcement strategy;
- making appropriate use of all available tools in the IP enforcement toolbox to best deal with any IP infringements faced;
- getting good local advice on the ground in China from experienced counsel who are up to date on the latest law and practice of the courts and enforcement agencies; and
- having an open mind, and displaying persistence in endeavoring to achieve the desired outcomes.

CHECKPOINT

- Have you identified the correct government department to be a party to sports sponsorship agreements?
- Have you obtained the correct approvals from the authorities? Has the athlete obtained the correct approvals?
- Have you expressly set out the sponsorship rights in the agreement—that is, what are you getting for your sponsorship fee?
- Have you taken steps to avoid ambush marketing?
- Have you taken steps to ensure that the IP associated with the event, team, or athlete has been protected?

RESOURCES

- www.bocog.org.cn: Beijing Organizing Committee for the Olympic Games
- www.s2mgroup.com.cn: S2M Group is a sports marketing company in China with substantial experience in navigating the challenges of the Chinese sports market.

Index